Regional Cooperation and its Enemies in Northeast Asia

Northeast Asia is a region of both extraordinary economic growth and dangerous tensions which could explode in war. This book examines how domestic politics in all the countries of the region – China, Japan, Russia, Taiwan, North Korea and South Korea and, of course, the USA – intensifies the forces of both mutually beneficial prosperity and also war-prone tensions. It goes on to provide policy suggestions for making the better prospects more likely and the worse outcomes less likely. The book, highlighting how domestic imperatives shape foreign policies, will be an important contribution to the literature on Northeast Asian regionalism and the prospects for its future development.

Edward Friedman is Professor in the Department of Political Science at the University of Wisconsin-Madison. He is the co-author of *Chinese Village Socialist State*, and *Revolution, Resistance and Reform in Village China*; editor of *China's Rise, Taiwan's Dilemmas and International Peace*; and co-editor of *Asia's Giants: Comparing India and China*.

Sung Chull Kim is Associate Professor at Hiroshima Peace Institute, Hiroshima City University. He is the author of *North Korea under Kim Jong Il: From Consolidation to Systemic Dissonance*. He has also contributed a number of articles on political theory and North Korea in journals including *Systems Research and Behavioural Science* and *Communist Studies and Transition Politics*.

Routledge Security in Asia Pacific Series
Series editors:
Leszek Buszynski
International University of Japan
and William Tow
Australian National University

Security issues have become more prominent in the Asia Pacific region because of the presence of global players, rising great powers, and confident middle powers, which intersect in complicated ways. This series puts forward important new work on key security issues in the region. It embraces the roles of the major actors, their defense policies and postures and their security interaction over the key issues of the region. It includes coverage of the United States, China, Japan, Russia, the Koreas, as well as the middle powers of ASEAN and South Asia. It also covers issues relating to environmental and economic security as well as transnational actors and regional groupings.

1 **Bush and Asia**
America's evolving relations with East Asia
Edited by Mark Beeson

2 **Japan, Australia and Asia–Pacific Security**
Edited by Brad Williams and Andrew Newman

3 **Regional Cooperation and its Enemies in Northeast Asia**
The impact of domestic forces
Edited by Edward Friedman and Sung Chull Kim

Regional Cooperation and its Enemies in Northeast Asia

The impact of domestic forces

Edited by Edward Friedman and Sung Chull Kim

Routledge
Taylor & Francis Group

LONDON AND NEW YORK

First published 2006 by Routledge
2 Park Square, Milton Park, Abingdon, Oxon OX14 4RN

Simultaneously published in the USA and Canada
by Routledge
711 Third Ave, New York, NY 10017

First issued in paperback 2012
Routledge is an imprint of the Taylor & Francis Group, an informa business

Typeset in Times New Roman by Keyword Group Ltd

British Library Cataloguing in Publication Data
A catalogue record for this book is available from the British Library

Library of Congress Cataloging in Publication Data
A catalogue record for this book has been requested

ISBN13: 978-0-415-65140-0 (pbk)
ISBN13: 978-0-415-39922-7 (hbk)
ISBN13: 978-0-203-96870-3 (ebk)

Contents

About the editors and contributors   vii
Acknowledgements   ix
List of acronyms   xi

Introduction: multilayered domestic-regional linkages   1
Sung Chull Kim

PART I
Contextualizing the Northeast Asian region   15

1 Domestic politics and regional cooperation in Southeast
  and Northeast Asia   17
  Etel Solingen

2 Envisioning a Northeast Asian community: regional
  and domestic factors to consider   38
  Haruki Wada

PART II
Domestic dimension of regional interaction   59

3 Washington's policies toward North Korea and the
  Taiwan Strait: the role of US domestic politics   61
  Tun-jen Cheng

4 The two Koreas in Northeast Asia: linkages between
  domestic, inter-Korean, and regional politics   85
  Yong-Pyo Hong

5 The transformation of Chinese foreign policy   101
  Lowell Dittmer

6 The fragility of China's regional cooperation   125
Edward Friedman

7 State consolidation and foreign policy in Russia   143
Leszek Buszynski

8 Mediating geopolitics, markets and regionalism:
domestic politics in Japan's post-Cold War
relations with China   165
Peng Er Lam

PART III
Non-governmental sources of regional cooperation   183

9 Transnational cooperation among NGOs in
Northeast Asia: from re-thinking development
towards re-thinking security   185
Daehoon Lee

Conclusion   205
Edward Friedman and Sung Chull Kim

Index   214

About the editors and contributors

Leszek Buszynski is Professor in the Graduate School of International Relations at the International University of Japan. He was previously Dean of the Graduate School of International Relations and Director of the IUJ Research Institute. He authored *Asia Pacific Security: Values and Identity* (RoutledgeCurzon, 2004), *Russian Foreign Policy after the Cold War* (Praeger, 1996), and *Gorbachev and Southeast Asia* (Routledge, 1992).

Tun-jen Cheng is Class of 1935 Professor in the Department of Government at the College of William and Mary. His primary interests are in comparative political economy and East Asian development. He has published numerous journal articles and book chapters and coauthored and coedited many volumes including *Religious Organizations and Democracy in Contemporary Asia* (M. E. Sharpe, 2006) and *China Under Hu Jintao* (World Scientific Co., 2006).

Lowell Dittmer is Professor in the Department of Political Science at the University of California, Berkeley, and the editor of *Asian Survey*. His published books include *South Asia's Nuclear Security Dilemma* (M. E. Sharpe, 2005, edited), *Informal Politics in East Asia* (Cambridge University Press, 2000, coedited with Haruhiro Fukui and Peter N. S. Lee), *Liu Shaoqi and the Chinese Cultural Revolution* (M. E. Sharpe, 1998), and *China Under Reform* (Westview Press, 1994).

Edward Friedman is Professor in the Department of Political Science at the University of Wisconsin-Madison. He is coauthor of *Chinese Village Socialist State* (New Haven: Yale University Press, 1993). In 2005 he published three books: *Revolution, Resistance and Reform in Village China* (Yale); *China's Rise, Taiwan's Dilemmas, and International Peace* (Routledge); *Asia's Giants: Comparing India and China* (Palgrave).

Yong-Pyo Hong is Associate Professor in the Department of Political Science at Hanyang University, Seoul. He is the author of *State Security and Regime Security: President Syngman Rhee and the Insecurity Dilemma in South Korea* (Macmillan, 2000) and *Kim Jung Il's Security Dilemma and Policies towards the US and South Korea* (KINU, 1997 in Korean).

Sung Chull Kim is Associate Professor at the Hiroshima Peace Institute, Hiroshima City University. He is the author of *North Korea Under Kim Jong Il: From Consolidation to Systemic Dissonance* (SUNY Press, 2006). He has also contributed a number of articles on political theory and North Korea in scholarly journals, including *Systems Research and Behavioral Science* and *Communist Studies and Transition Politics*.

Peng Er Lam is Senior Research Fellow at the East Asian Institute, National University of Singapore. Lam has published many articles on Japanese domestic politics and foreign affairs in scholarly journals including *Pacific Affairs, Asian Survey, Japan Forum* and *Asian Affairs*. His books include: *Green Politics in Japan* (Routledge, 1999) and *Japan's Relations with China: Facing a Rising Power* (Routledge, 2006, edited).

Daehoon Lee is Lecturer in peace studies at Songkonghoe University, Seoul, and the deputy secretary of a non-governmental organization, People's Solidarity for Participatory Democracy. He is the author of *Global Issues of the 21st Century* (1999, in Korean), and has contributed articles to human rights journals in Korea and to *Inter-Asia Cultural Studies* and *Searching for Peace in Asia Pacific*.

Etel Solingen is Professor in the Department of Political Science at the University of California, Irvine, and also serves as Chair of the Steering Committee of the University of California's system-wide Institute on Global Conflict and Cooperation. She authored *Regional Orders at Century's Dawn: Global and Domestic Influences on Grand Strategy* (Princeton University Press, 1998), *Industrial Policy, Technology, and International Bargaining* (Stanford University Press, 1996), and numerous articles on international relations.

Haruki Wada is Professor Emeritus of the University of Tokyo and also a Fellow at the Center for Northeast Asian Studies, Tohoku University. As an expert on Russian and Korean history, he authored a number of books in Japanese, including *Terror and Reform* (2005), *History of the Korean War* (2002), *The Common House of Northeast Asia* (2003), *Russian Revolution, 1991* (1998), and *North Korea: The Present of Guerrilla State* (1998).

Acknowledgements

This book is the culmination of a project conducted under the auspices of the Hiroshima Peace Institute. We, editors of this volume, with deep gratitude acknowledge the funding from the public and the City of Hiroshima to host the two conferences on November 12–13, 2004 and May 26–28, 2005. We are grateful to all contributors for their conscientious and insightful discussions and suggestions and for their full cooperation in revising the papers. We are also thankful to resident scholars in Hiroshima, such as Naoki Kamimura, Tetsuro Saito, Omar Farouk, Richard Parker, Narayanan Ganesan, and Kazumi Mizumoto, for their participation in the discussions. Finally, we would like to acknowledge Michiko Yoshimoto's excellent administrative assistance before, during and after the conferences.

List of acronyms

A

ADB	Asian Development Bank
AFTA	ASEAN Free Trade Agreement
AMF	Asian Monetary Fund
ANEAN	Association of Northeast Asian Nations
APEC	Asia-Pacific Economic Cooperation
APT	ASEAN Plus Three
ARENA	Asia Regional Exchange for New Alternatives
ARF	ASEAN Regional Forum
ASC	ASEAN Security Community
ASEAN	Association of Southeast Asian Nations
ASEM	Asia-Europe Meetings
ASPC	ARF Security Policy Conference

B

BMD	Ballistic Missile Defence

C

CC	Central Committee
CCP	Chinese Communist Party
CEAC	Council on East Asian Community
CICIR	Chinese Institute for Contemporary International Relations
CIS	Commonwealth of Independent States
CMC	Central Military Commission
CNP	Comprehensive National Power
CNPC	China National Petroleum Corporation
CPPCC	Chinese People's Political Consultative Conference
CPU	Central Processing Unit
CSCSP	Council for Security Cooperation in the Asia Pacific
CTBT	Comprehensive Test Ban Treaty

D

DPJ	Democratic Party of Japan

| DPP | Democratic Progressive Party |
| DPPK | Democratic People's Republic of Korea |

E

EAC	East Asian Community
EAEC	East Asian Economic Caucus
EASG	East Asia Study Group
EAVG	East Asia Vision Group
ECCP	European Centre for Conflict Prevention
EEZ	Exclusive Economic Zone
ERINA	Economic Research Institute of Northeast Asia

F

FDI	foreign direct investment
FSS	Federal Security Service
FTA	Free Trade Agreement

G

GATT	General Agreement on Tariffs and Trade
GEN	Green Earth Network
GHQ	General Headquarters of the Allied Forces
GONGOs	government-organized non-governmental organizations
GPPAC	Global Partnership for the Prevention of Armed Conflict

H

| HIV/AIDS | Human Immunodeficiency Virus/ Acquired Immunodeficiency Syndrome |

I

IAEA	International Atomic Energy Agency
IFRC	International Federation of Red Cross and Red Crescent Societies
IGO	Intergovernmental Organization
ILD	International Liaison Department
ILO	International Labour Organization
IMF	International Monetary Fund
INGOs	international non-governmental organizations

J

| JFIR | Japan Forum on International Relations |

K

| KMT | Kuomintang |
| KWAU | Korea Women's Associations United |

L

LDP	Liberal Democratic Party
LSG	Leading Small Group
LWRs	light water reactors

M

MFN	Most Favoured Nation
MOFA	Ministry of Foreign Affairs
MOFTEC	Ministry of Foreign Trade and Economic Cooperation
MOFERT	Ministry of Foreign Economic Relations and Trade
MSS	Ministry of State Security
MTCR	Missile Technology Control Regime

N

NAFTA	North American Free Trade Agreement
NDPG	National Defense Program Guideline
NEACD	Northeast Asia Cooperation Dialogue
NEASPEC	Northeast Asian Subregional Programme on Environmental Cooperation
NEAT	Network of East Asian Think Tanks
NGOs	non-governmental organizations
NIEs	newly industrializing economies
NSCC	National Security Council of China
NPC	National People's Congress
NPR	Nuclear Posture Review
NPT	Non-Proliferation Treaty

O

ODA	Official Development Assistance
OECD	Organization for Economic Cooperation and Development
OSCE	Organization for Security Cooperation in Europe

P

PARC	Public Affairs Research Council
PBSC	Politburo Standing Committee
PKO	Peacekeeping Operations
PLA	People's Liberation Army
PNTR	permanent normal trade relationship
PP21	People's Plan 21
PRC	People's Republic of China

S

SARS	Severe Acute Respiratory Syndrome
SCO	Shanghai Cooperation Organization

SDF	Self Defense Forces
SDPJ	Social Democratic Party of Japan
SEATO	Southeast Asia Treaty Organization

T

TAC	Treaty of Amity and Cooperation in Southeast Asia
TEMM	Tripartite Environment Ministers Meetings
TRA	Taiwan Relations Act
TSEA	Taiwan Security Enhancement Act

U

UEP	uranium enrichment program
UNCTAD	United Nations Conference on Trade and Development
UNDP	United Nations Development Program
UNESCAP	United Nations Economic and Social Commission for Asia and the Pacific
UNESCO	United Nations Educational, Scientific and Cultural Organization
UNIC	United Nations Information Center
UNICEF	United Nations Children's Fund
UNSC	United Nations Security Council

W

WFP	World Food Program
WHO	World Health Organization
WTO	World Trade Organization

Z

ZOPFAN	Zone of Peace, Freedom and Neutrality (declaration)

Introduction: multilayered domestic-regional linkages

Sung Chull Kim

Northeast Asia, covering China, North and South Koreas, Japan, Russia, and the US, is a region of opportunities and challenges. On the one hand, after the financial crisis in East Asia in 1997, the building of an East Asian community, centered on ASEAN Plus Three (APT), became an important agenda item among political leaders and in scholarly circles. The Association of Southeast Asian Nations (ASEAN) has played an important role as a nodal point to facilitate economic cooperation between ASEAN and the three countries—China, South Korea, and Japan. In other words, the three countries have apparently taken advantage of the bandwagon of an established multilateral cooperative institution, ASEAN. On the other hand, contentious security issues in Northeast Asia lie before such a bright vision of regional integration. North Korea's nuclear development and the unstable situation in the Taiwan Strait are facets of the security problem that interferes with the building of a regional community. Also, that the US, which maintains a great deal of influence on regional security affairs, adheres to bilateral security alliances is a serious challenge to the movement toward the ideal of regional community.

For overcoming the challenges and facilitating the opportunities, it is necessary to identify sources of regional cooperation and contention from a multilayered perspective, which examines domestic politics and transnational non-governmental alliances as well as interstate relations. In general, the structure of interstate relations is a composite of long-term national interests and strategies of individual countries prioritizing their own state sovereignty. For this reason, it has been conceived that the structure is not an easily changeable matter by itself. This is especially true in security affairs, because the latter is monopolized by the top political leaders of each country. However, this conception about the structure centered on interstate relations should not interfere with this volume's interests in an examination of diversifying sources of contention and cooperation in Northeast Asia. Indeed, objectives of this volume regarding the domestic dimension include not only elite shifts and political realignments and the following foreign policy changes, but also non-governmental organizations' (NGOs) involvement in interstate fora and transnational interactions. This volume is also concerned with any domestic political event in one country that soon affects neighboring countries.

The purpose of this volume lies in examination of how the domestic dimension either interferes with or contributes to regional cooperation in Northeast Asia. It examines the domestic impact on regional dynamics, ultimately searching for an alternative way of diffusing tensions and contentions and of promoting regional cooperation. The study of domestic dimensions is not really foreign to students of international relations. The significance of domestic politics for foreign policy was first explored by James N. Rosenau four decades ago.[1] Since then, the situation has significantly undergone a change in terms of actors, agendas, and modes of interactions, shedding new light on the notion. Despite the strong tendency of state-centeredness in Northeast Asia, there are some evidences of cutting through the hard shell of state boundaries, either good or bad, which was inconceivable in the Cold War era.

In examining the domestic dimension, most authors in this volume are not really obsessed by the notion of regionalism or regional community of Northeast Asia alone, despite taking into account its categorical value, either in geographical, or psychological, or economic terms. There are a couple of reasons that this volume is interested in the notion of regional cooperation rather than regionalism or regional community. One is that China, South Korea, and Japan have engaged in the more comprehensive regional institution, APT, and the East Asian summit than the scope of Northeast Asia alone. The other is that in order for Northeast Asia to be called a regional community, there should be significant progress both in the free trade agreement (FTA) negotiations and in the substantial security cooperation among six countries, including Russia and the US. The present situation does not nullify the significance of Northeast Asia as a region, but it seems immature to trumpet the notion of Northeast Asian regionalism or regional community.

To capture the diversifying influence of domestic dimensions on regional dynamics and to search for potential ways of cooperation among the Northeast Asian countries requires an examination of definitional and historical matters as follows.

Trials of regional economic cooperation

In the age of regionalism trailing globalization after the end of the Cold War, the centrality of regional cooperation has lain in the deepening of economic integration, in view of the developmental process of the European Union, North American Free Trade Agreement and ASEAN Free Trade Agreement. There is general acknowledgement of the previous existence of trials in economic cooperation in Northeast Asia. After the disintegration of the Soviet Union, the Northeast Asian region, geographically extending its link with the Pacific region, had some experience in regional economic cooperation. In the early 1990s, Russian Far East (Vladivostok, Khabarovsk, and Nakhodka), Northeastern China (Heilongjiang, Jilin, and Hunchun), North Korea (Najin-Sonbong), Japanese coastal area facing the continent (Niigata, Shimane, and Hokkaido), and South Korea were serious aspirants for regionalization. The regional interactions showed some unprecedented features that had not been observed in the Cold War era. Bilateral projects and collective projects, represented by the United Nations Development Program-supported Tumen River Area Development Project, attracted the interests of the countries belonging to the region. More importantly, bilateral economic transactions by business adventurers enlarged along the borders, a situation that was called "border fever."[2]

As a consequence, the increasing trend of interactions featured new trends of ethnic diasporas and population mobility. Of many examples, distinctive trends were the advancement of Chinese into the Russian Far East, the influx of North Koreans into the northeastern part of China, and labor movement of Korean-Chinese into South Korea. It is also worth noting that local governments, either with support of central governments or independent endeavors, became prime actors of the regional interactions. In this respect, the regional interactions seemed to be in line with the general tendency of the spread of the ideal of regionalism, congruent with the decentralizing forces within the nation-state.

However, the initial interests in regional cooperation in the early 1990s, centered on the border fever, have not brought tangible consequences. All countries with strong state-centered propensity—China, Russia, Japan, and North and South Koreas—have retained unyielding national interests, which have seemingly discouraged the border fever led by local actors. Boris Yeltsin's pro-Western diplomacy replaced Mikhail Gorbachev's Asia-Pacific ideal, so that the domestic backing for the eastern booming started to fade away after reaching a peak in 1994. In the same context, the absence of progress in the Japanese-Russo territorial issue on the four islands discouraged the coastal area's dream of "Japan Sea rim age."[3] Furthermore, the rising tensions in the Korean peninsula, especially caused by the nuclear crisis in 1993–1994, not only evidenced the remaining vestiges of the Cold War in the peninsula but also impeded the progress of the Tumen River Area Development Project, benefits of whose success might be shared by localities of China, Russia, and the two Koreas. Also, the escalating tension in the Taiwan Strait, centered on mainland China's "One China" principle and the missile launch in 1995 and 1996, has invited a new tide of American influence and, in turn, has consolidated the Japan–US alliance since the second half of the 1990s. Given this situation, the central government's support for regional cooperation at the local level might be considered luxurious.

More importantly, individual countries' domestic politics in the post-Cold War period was not prepared to prioritize regional cooperation in projecting their own foreign policies. After the Tiananmen Incident in 1989, the Chinese Community Party made a great deal of effort for political integration by emphasizing patriotism in ideological affairs, while encouraging adventurous reform processes. Russia's plunging economy in the process of reform was conducive to the loss of interests in the development of Russian Far East and the deepening of regional cooperation in Northeast Asia. Under the new leadership of Vladimir Putin since 2000, Russia has strengthened state power and pursued corresponding international status and, furthermore, it has attempted to undertake an independent foreign policy for the balance of power in the Asia-Pacific region, as Buszynski noted in this volume. In other words, Putin came to pay attention to the Asia-Pacific, just as Gorbachev did, but the objective has been different: Gorbachev for economic prosperity and Putin for security. For Japan, the burst of the bubble economy resulted in the decline of a leading role of "flying geese,"[4] which is a paradigm that the lead economy reduces risks and errors on the economies behind it and the second-tier economies do the same for the third-tier of economies.[5] Because of the economic decline, Tokyo's assistance for local aspiration of regionalization was apparently discouraged. Moreover, the economic decline has been accompanied by a political realignment to disfavor leftists in the general elections in 1993 and 1996 and, in turn, this situation has resulted in a proactive foreign policy, strengthening the security alliance with the US. In this context, the trial of regional cooperation, initiated by local governments and businesses, could not evolve into an institutionalized one but faded at the embryonic stage.

Old theory unfit for reality

The old interstate-centered theory is no longer able to account for the present situation of diversified layers of interactions. During the Cold War, the realist tradition prevailed in the study of international relations. Within the influence of realist tradition, Rosenau and others in the late 1960s and 1970s attempted to illustrate interactions between domestic and international dimensions by examining either domestic sources of foreign policy, frequently called "linkage politics," or international sources of domestic politics, called "the second image reversed."[6] However, their voice was overwhelmed by neorealism, mentored by Kenneth N. Waltz, who depicted international relations as an anarchy in which survival is the most important motivation of states.[7] Neorealism holds the view that the unit of analysis is the state, which is to say, the sovereign entity that, located at the top of the hierarchy, comprehends domestic politics. Neorealism posits that the state summarizes different interests and diverse processes into a single policy output in foreign affairs. On this assumption, actors such as groups and organizations, as well as domestic political processes, have been considered subordinate to the state in its pursuit of survival.[8] It was not until the late 1980s that Robert Putnam attracted new attention to domestic politics by theorizing negotiator's behavior between international relations and domestic politics into the notion of "two-level games."[9] Scholars have started to investigate pluralistic dispersion of power and its effect on foreign policy and international relations. Furthermore, they have asserted that in contrast to neorealism, decision-making processes are not directly related to survival of the state but to actors' preferences, institutional arrangements, and coalitions.[10]

Such a theoretical revisit to domestic considerations of regional dynamics, which may be called domestic-regional linkages, is applicable to the Northeast Asian case. That is, recent interactions between countries in Northeast Asia cannot be explained simply by realist interpretations of the world. First of all, transitions in domestic politics matter in the regional dimension, as seen in the impact of an electoral realignment on the national strategy in foreign affairs. For instance, in Japan, the Social Democratic Party of Japan (SDPJ)'s Tomiichi Murayama's assumption of the position of Prime Minister in 1994 had two different impacts. Socialists for the first time took offices in the SDPJ-LDP coalitional government. At the same time, it has resulted in a continuous decline of public support for the socialists because of their contradictory stance in foreign policy as well as of the North Korean effect (nuclear development and abduction issues). The strengthening of the security alliance with the US belied socialists' previous commitment to peace-prone policy orientation. Coupled with the negative effect on the socialists owing to the adoption of a single-seat electoral system in 1996, Murayama's self-contradictory foreign policy brought about the consequence that the socialists could never restore their previous degree of public support and that the decline of the socialist camp has led Japanese politics to move in a conservative direction.

Second, domestic actors have engaged in various ways to expand institutionalization of fora between top political leaders in the region. In the late 1990s, Chinese, South Korean, and Japanese leaders have met state heads of ten ASEAN members and finally institutionalized the East Asian summit. At the Kyoto meeting in May 2005, foreign ministers of APT agreed that the East Asian summit would extend to include the leaders of Australia, New Zealand, and India, now totaling 16 country leaders.[11] The first East Asian summit was held in accordance with the agreement in Kuala Lumpar in December of the year. It is notable that along this governmental line, the Track 2 interactions for regional cooperation have been diversified. Examples of Track 2 are the Council for Security Cooperation in the Asia Pacific, the Northeast Asia Cooperation Dialogue, the East Asia Vision Group (EAVG), and the East Asia Study Group (EASG). Above all, Track 2 interactions mitigate bilateral bias and build habits of dialogue, opening backdoor lines of communication.[12] Their contribution is distinctive in the case of APT. In particular, EAVG, established by the suggestion of South Korean president Kim Dae-Jung at the Hanoi APT meeting in 1998, started to envision the East Asian community for regional peace, prosperity, and progress. This task was undertaken by EASG that submitted the final report to the APT summit, held in Phnom Penh in November 2002, on how to facilitate in detail the process of East Asian integration.

Multilayered domestic—regional linkages

The domestic–regional linkages, which is a handy notion to illuminate the ways in which domestic dimension matters for regional dynamics, are multilayer in nature, as seen in Figure 1. As T. J. Pempel argues, interactions in a certain region are multiple, so that to exclusively rely on one aspect is to miss the greater complex of relations.[13] Indeed, the interactions relevant to regional dynamics in Northeast Asia take place in more than one layer, that is, interstate level. Each country has a unique vertical mode of interactions between the society and the state, interactions which are marked domestic politics in the figure. The interaction is not strictly confined to the domestic level but open to external interactions, either interstate relations, or business relations, or activities of NGOs.

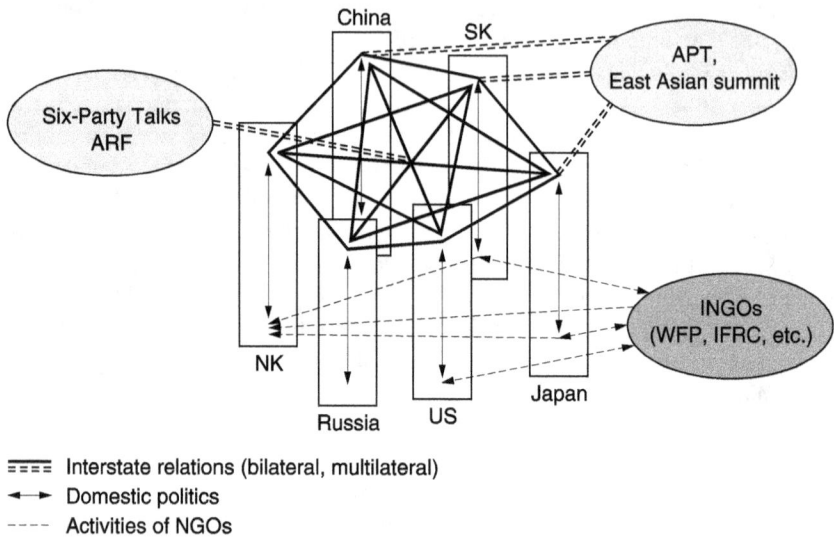

```
China          SK              APT,
                               East Asian summit
Six-Party Talks
ARF

                                               INGOs
                                               (WFP, IFRC, etc.)
      NK
                           Japan
      Russia   US
```

===== Interstate relations (bilateral, multilateral)
◄──► Domestic politics
---- Activities of NGOs

Figure 1 Multilayered domestic–regional linkages.

At the top, the interstate relations among Northeast Asian countries, which may be called the "first layer," are built on APT and the East Asian summit, which are supported by individual countries' study groups for agenda-setting functions. The three countries—China, South Korea, and Japan—have been enjoying an effect of the bandwagon of ASEAN, but the relationship between them is not solid enough yet for becoming a pillar to sustain the integration of Northeast Asia and Southeast Asia together. For security purposes, the interstate relations have taken place at the ASEAN Regional Forum (ARF) and Six-Party Talks. ARF is a multilateral forum for security dialogue, whose membership is indeed not limited to ASEAN countries but regionally open to all Asia–Pacific countries. The Six-Party Talks is the unique dialogue channel that includes six Northeast Asia countries exclusively for the particular purpose of resolving the North Korean nuclear crisis.

In domestic politics, the "second layer," the perception on neighbors as well as political realignment has mattered for the regional dimension. This is particularly true in the "three countries," which are still not free of the lingering historical memory of victimizer–victim relations. Regarding Japan's past acts, negative bilateral images are frequently stimulated at the public level, a situation that impedes cooperation between Japan on the one hand and China and the two Koreas on the other. Furthermore, there is a possibility that historical issues may be manipulated, either for the demonstration of politicians' compassion or for the justification of the national strategy—for example, Japanese Prime Minister Koizumi's visit to Yasukuni Shrine for showing his determined patriotism and the Chinese leaders' *de facto* authorization of mass demonstrations against Japanese efforts for obtaining a permanent seat in the United Nations Security Council.

More often than not, the strategic consideration—related to broader national interests such as expansion of exports and economic growth—usually prevails over the perception and its related historical issues in bilateral relations. If the political leaders' strategic consideration and profit-seeking motivation of business corporations are combined together, they will suppress the domestic backlash perception and sentiment in order to mitigate interstate tensions and eventually contribute to regional cooperation. This proved true even in the tense situation in the interstate relationship between Beijing and Tokyo in 2005. In spring 2005, leaders in both China and Japan showed their restraint to stop escalation of the tension from a common recognition that economic decline of either one of the two sides would hamper their own economy. Japan stopped demanding an apology from the Chinese government of the negligence of anti-Japanese demonstrators' violence on two Japanese students and the facilities of Japanese Consulate-General in Shanghai, whereas China rejected an apology on that matter but paid compensation to redeem the damage. More importantly, Beijing stopped authorizing anti-Japanese demonstrations on the logic that they would harm national interests and social order.

In this respect, a strong coalition between a ruling political circle and business corporations is an important factor for more open markets and investments and for the continuation of cooperative policy direction, discouraging elevation of conflicts and contention in the region. As Solingen suggests in this volume, ruling coalitions in ASEAN countries for internationalization of markets and investments has brought about prosperity of the member countries and solidification of the consensus model of security cooperation. But the Northeast Asian countries are more diverse in power, size, and regime than ASEAN countries; furthermore, despite the increasing economic interdependence, ruling coalitions of Northeast Asian countries are to a certain extent preoccupied by confrontational perceptions.

At the bottom, most NGOs in Northeast Asian countries have had a relatively weak international orientation until now; however, some of them now extend the scope of vision and the domain of activities by working together with INGOs. NGOs may press their political leaders to accept the policies with universal values, even though opposite values also exist in reality. The expansion of cooperation among NGOs at the transnational level is the "third layer" of domestic–regional linkages. The third layer, in an analytical sense, is an addition to the "first layer" of interstate relations and to the "second layer" of domestic pressure. Insofar as its role is concerned, the third layer has a great potential for forging regional cooperation in coming years. In particular, information technology has in a remarkable way opened a new era in the sharing of information, one of the most essential elements for cooperation among NGOs. The significance of information for the third layer lies in its contribution to the disseminating of alternative sources that are frequently unavailable in the mass media and in the official propaganda of each country.[14] For example, the Peace Depot is a Japanese peace NGO that, owing to the information revolution, can provide web searchers with magazine articles and newspaper reports on the region and in three languages: Japanese, Korean, and English.[15]

As far as effectiveness of the third layer is concerned, the types of issues that they deal with matter. In general, the issues related to human security, rather than arms control issues, tend to promote effectiveness in political influence. Humanitarian aid and human rights issues tend to positively influence the state. This is so because these issues involve safety concerns of specific people or groups and because objectives and consequences of the engagement with these issues are visible and concrete. Furthermore, the universal characteristics of norms and values related to human security resonate powerfully in the minds of the general public, and thus the state cannot completely ignore this appeal. The empirical fact that INGOs are more involved in human rights issues than in other issues partly evidences the effectiveness of the human security-related NGOs activities.[16] In the northeastern part of China and North Korea, there are ample cases of NGOs' engagement in human security problems of North Koreans, like famine and refugee issues. World Food Program, World Vision, Médecins Sans Frontières (Doctors Without Borders), Hong Kong Caritas, International Federation of Red Cross and Red Crescent Societies, and religious NGOs in South Korea—Protestant, Catholic, and Buddhist—are handy examples with more or less successful outcomes of humanitarian engagements.

In contrast, the effectiveness of the third layer is relatively low in the security and arms control issues. Speaking in general, development, deployment, and sales of arms are confidentially dealt with by a handful of political leaders, who monopolize power and technical knowledge on such matters. Indeed, NGOs in Northeast Asia have failed to form effective transnational alliances on arms control for attracting significant public attention and for influencing decision-making processes. Therefore, it is fair to say that NGOs' activities and transnational alliances on the issues of security and arms control, despite their salience and urgency, lag behind the cases of human security issues. In this region, some exceptions may be seen in Japan Council against A & H Bombs (Gensuikyo) and Japan Congress against A & H Bombs (Gensuikin) for exercising an influence on the government's non-nuclear policy and in the Hong Kong-based Asia Regional Exchange for New Alternatives for disseminating the ideal of demilitarization of the society, as shall be discussed by Lee in this volume.

Relationship between security and economic affairs

The Northeast Asian region includes China, Russia, North and South Koreas, Japan, and the US (Haruki Wada in this volume adds Mongolia and Taiwan to this criterion). Then, why is Northeast Asia, instead of East Asia, a special concern in this volume? Can Northeast Asia alone become an object of regionalism? These questions involve the rationale how to define the Northeast Asian region. It is notable that the Northeast Asia region is not mature enough to be considered a regional bloc, which requires both strong demand for economic interdependence and the absence of a divisive situation in security affairs (or existence of outside threat for regional cooperation). Compared to existing examples of the regional bloc in other parts of the world, Northeast Asia meets the economic requirement to some extent but not the security requirement. Along with a relatively high speed of integration into the global economy,[17] there is a growing momentum of the "three countries" for FTAs with ASEAN and a growing trend of economic interdependence in Northeast Asia, especially between China and Japan. In contrast, North Korea's nuclear weapon development impedes such positive development. Furthermore, the security competition between the Japan–US alliance and China has continued to produce tensions in this region. At the Security Consultative Committee (2+2) meeting held in Washington, DC in February 2005, the allies explicitly defined the Taiwan Strait issue and China's military build-up as common security concerns.[18] Therefore, it is fair to say that Northeast Asia as a region has potential for the furthering of economic cooperation, while revealing vulnerability in security affairs.

The attempts for building a multilateral institution, especially in trade affairs, cannot prevail over the looming security threats in Northeast Asia: the North Korea's nuclear weapons development, the Taiwan Strait tension, the two-against-one relationship between US and Japan on the one hand and China on the other. APT has been considered a promising institutional trial for economic cooperation encompassing East Asia. In 1998, South Korea, with a leadership shift to Kim Dae-Jung, envisioned the idea of regional community in East Asia. The envisioning of the East Asian community was a revival of Malaysian Prime Minister Mahathir bin Mohamad's proposal of an East Asian Economic Grouping in late 1990. In spite of its own merit and prospect of APT, the lack of security cooperation between the three—China, South Korea, and Japan—would leave ASEAN a simple nodal point to separately link the three economies. Without security cooperation, particularly between China on the one hand and US and Japan on the other, it would be difficult or would delay the time to achieve free trade among them. In fact, Japan and South Korea have continued the FTA negotiation since late 2003, but China and Japan simply agreed in October 2004 to start a preliminary study of examining the FTA's impact on their economy. Furthermore, the security contention between China and Japan leads them to compete with each other, with different strategies, for more privileged trade access to ASEAN. China has forged the negotiation for FTA with ASEAN as a collectivity, whereas Japan has focused on bilateral FTAs with the member countries of ASEAN, based on the long history of engagement through official development assistance since the early 1960s.

It is noteworthy that the US has resisted the emergence of an ideal of community building in Northeast Asia in particular and East Asia in general.[19] The US has been interested in comprehending Asia *and* Pacific for economic collaboration and security talks, adhering to Asia-Pacific Economic Cooperation (APEC) and the bilateral alliances with South Korea and Japan. The American opposition to the regional community in East Asia may be best exemplified by its resistance to the Japanese proposal of the establishment of a regional financial institution, Asian Monetary Fund (AMF), amid the financial crisis in 1997. For Japan, the initiation of AMF might be the last chance of exercising a leadership role in Asia's economy, given the situation of the decline of its leading role in the flying geese model. For the US, the opposition was a clear sign of its determination not to relinquish its national power via the International Monetary Fund.[20] Furthermore, the deep involvement of the US in security affairs in Northeast Asia renders the US displeased with the building of an East Asian community. The bilateral alliances between the US, on the one hand, and Japan and South Korea on the other, have been essential elements of the US security engagement in Northeast Asia. The bilateral security commitment in Northeast Asia is the legacy of the San Francisco system, which has constituted the American-led Asia-Pacific order since its birth in 1952.[21] And yet, in the post-Cold War period, the Japan–US alliance has expanded Japanese security commitment from self-defense to proactive engagement in global security. Based on the Nye Report in 1995, Tokyo drafted the New Guideline in 1997 and, in turn, the Guideline has facilitated the Guideline of Defense Planning in late 2004, which stipulated Japan's extended commitment to the so-called Arch of Instability that ranges from the Korean peninsula to the Middle East.[22] Given this situation, the US has never shown interest not only in economic integration in East Asia but also in the institutionalization of multilateral security cooperation in Northeast Asia, as seen in the case of the Organization for Security Cooperation in Europe.

On the other hand, it is noteworthy that lack of security cooperation does not deny the *urgency* of regional cooperation. The opposite is true. The "three countries," which are in a desperate need of energy (oil and natural gas), have to cooperate for obtaining the resources. The rapidly rising demand of oil and gas in the region should not end up with "energy nationalism."[23] Here lies the logic of interconnectedness between security and economics. For instance, any practice of security cooperation between China and Japan will slow down the competition for connecting the Eastern Pipeline in Russia to their own countries. Likewise, any cooperation between Japan and Russia in the territorial dispute on the four disputed islands will not render Russian President Putin sensitive in weighing the destination point of the pipeline. Also, if either coexistence between the two Koreas or peaceful solution of North Korea's nuclear issue is achieved, the energy competition between China and Japan will be dissipated to a certain extent and, finally the connection between the Trans-Siberian and Trans-Korean railroads will meet energy demands of China, the two Koreas, and Japan. Furthermore, the Russian Far East will benefit from the revitalization of economic cooperation in the Tumen River area.

Considering the uniqueness of the Northeast Asian region as discussed above, the seeming trajectory of the European experience—the military conflict, the economic prosperity, and the hyper- or supra-nationalism—is unlikely to be repeated in this region.[24] Because of the discordance between the demand for regional economic cooperation and the existing security contention, it is not an easy or optimistic task to envision regionalism in Northeast Asia. This fact shows that Northeast Asia is the region where opportunities and challenges are mixed. It is also notable that the ideal of East Asian community is by and large constrained by the security contention in Northeast Asia. Rivalry between China and Japan, in particular, seems to reproduce the perception of zero-sum game and rationalize backlash elements, such as patriotism in China and institutionalizing nationalism in Japan. Furthermore, the six countries in Northeast Asia have been involved in the multilateral talks for solving the nuclear development in North Korea, which is the last remaining zone of the Cold War. Their involvement provides a challenge and an opportunity at the same time. A successful solution may contribute to institutionalization of regional security cooperation. In case of failure, the existing rivalry between China on the one hand and Japan and the US on the other hand may invite a divisive situation of security in the region, a situation in which nationalists may logroll—to use Jack Snyder's term[25]—the public for the unfolding of backlash, confrontational policies towards the other side.

Tour of the book

In examining regional dynamics in Northeast Asia, this volume intends to overcome the limitation of the state-centered concept of international relations, a concept that has been dominant not only in academia but also in political circles. The two chapters in Part I discuss how to locate Northeast Asia in the context of East Asia. Solingen compares Northeast Asia with Southeast Asia, highlighting the latter's domestic ruling coalitions for a successful model of regionalization. Wada envisions the emergence of a Northeast Asian community and discusses domestic requisites for it, especially in Japan and the two Koreas.

The six chapters in Part II elaborate the role of domestic factors of each country for regional contention or cooperation. Cheng explores institutional relations between the presidency and Congress in the US regarding foreign policies towards the North Korean nuclear crisis and the Taiwan Strait tension, and then he illustrates the North Korean case's heavy reliance on presidential judgment, a situation that hinders its solution. Hong analyzes how South Korea's policy towards the North is besieged by domestic politics and circumvented by regional politics. Dittmer and Friedman's chapters are complementary. Dittmer investigates the evolution of Chinese foreign policy pursuing a national security state in the context of multilateral approaches, whereas Friedman examines the ways whereby party and military leaders in Beijing justify and maintain the authoritarian government, projecting antagonism against Taiwan and the West. Buszynski shows that the centralization of power by President Putin has contributed to the enhancement of Russia's leverage role in regional politics. Lam maintains that rising interdependency and forging regional FTAs are no guarantee that Sino-Japanese relations will remain cordial or sound.

Lee's chapter in Part III examines the non-governmental role for regional cooperation. Lee presents emerging transnational alliances in Northeast Asia for desecuritization and demilitarization, alliances which attempt to melt down security-oriented mentality at the grass-roots level. Friedman and Kim in the concluding chapter pay a particular attention to looming dangers of domestic politics for regional contention centered on newly sensitized issues in the post-Cold War period, such as history, territories, and energy.

Notes

1 James N. Rosenau, "Pre-Theories and Theories of Foreign Policy," in R. Barry Farrell (ed.) *Approaches to Comparative and International Politics*, Evanston: Northwestern University Press, 1966, pp. 27–92.
2 Gilbert Rozman, *Northeast Asia's Stunted Regionalism: Bilateral Distrust in the Shadow of Globalization*, Cambridge: Cambridge University Press, 2004, pp. 72–73.
3 Ibid., p. 107.
4 Andrew Macintyre and Barry Naughton, "The Decline of a Japan-Led Model of the East Asian Economy," in T. J. Pempel (ed.) *Remapping East Asia: The Construction of a Region*, Ithaca: Cornell University Press, 2005, pp. 90–91.
5 William W. Grimes, "Japan's International Relations: The Economic Dimension," in Samuel S. Kim (ed.) *The International Relations of Northeast Asia*, Lanham, MD: Rowman & Littlefield, 2004, p. 180.
6 See Graham Allison, *The Essence of Decision: Explaining the Cuban Missile Crisis*, Boston: Little, Brown, 1971; Alexander L. George, "The Case for Multiple Advocacy in Making Foreign Policy," *American Political Science Review*, Vol. 56, 1972, pp. 751–785; and Peter Gourevitch, "The Second Image Reversed: The International Sources of Domestic Politics," *International Organization*, Vol. 32, No. 4, Autumn 1978, pp. 881–912.
7 On the state's motive, see chapter 5 of Kenneth N. Waltz, *Theory of International Politics*, Reading: Addison-Wesley, 1979.
8 It is ironic that neorealism has extensively utilized the term *system*. This term depicts a set of international relations among states as being an international system from which state behavior and state interests are deduced. The logic inherent in neorealism is that the relationship between the parts and the whole is uni-directional, which is to say, neither interactive nor mutually causal. However, this logic is not in accordance with the ideas presented by the interdisciplinary tradition of systems sciences, such as interconnectedness, indeterminacy, complexity, and the macro-micro link. Recently, Robert Jervis, within the paradigm of neorealism, made an attempt to incorporate the propositions of systems sciences into the study of international relations. See his work, *System Effects*, Princeton: Princeton University Press, 1997.
9 Robert D. Putnam, "Diplomacy and Domestic Politics: The Logic of Two-Level Games," *International Organization*, Vol. 2, No. 3, Summer 1988, pp. 427–60.
10 On the extending discussions of interactions between the domestic and the international, see Jack Snyder, *Myths of Empire: Domestic Politics and International Ambition*, Ithaca: Cornell University Press, 1991; Bruce Russett, *Grasping the Democratic Peace: Principles for a Post-Cold War World*, Princeton: Princeton University Press, 1993; Robert O. Keohane and Helen V. Milner (eds), *Internationalization and Domestic Politics*, Cambridge: Cambridge University Press, 1996; James N. Rosenau, *Along the Domestic-Foreign Frontier: Exploring Governance in a Turbulent World*, Cambridge: Cambridge University Press, 1997; Helen V. Milner, *Interests, Institutions, and Information: Domestic Politics and International Relations*, Princeton: Princeton University Press, 1997; and Etel Solingen, *Regional Orders at Century's Dawn: Global and Domestic Influences on Grand Strategy*, Princeton: Princeton University Press, 1998.
11 *Asahi Shimbun*, 7 May 2005.
12 Brian L. Job, "Track 2 Diplomacy: Ideational Contribution to the Evolving Asia Security Order," in Muthiah Alagappa (ed.) *Asian Security Order: Instrumental and Normative Features*, Stanford: Stanford University Press, 2003, p. 271.
13 T. J. Pempel, "Introduction: Emerging Webs of Regional Connectedness," in Pempel, *Remapping East Asia*, p. 6.
14 Margaret E. Keck and Kathryn Sikkink, *Activists beyond Borders: Advocacy Networks in International Politics*, Ithaca: Cornell University Press, 1998, p. 19.

15 See Peace Depot. Online. Available HTTP: <http://www.peacedepot.org/> (accessed 27 July 2005).
16 Proportionally speaking, human rights organizations account for roughly a quarter of INGOs. See Keck and Sikkink, *Activists beyond Borders*, p. 11.
17 Samuel S. Kim, "Northeast Asia in the Local-Regional-Global Nexus: Multiple Challenges and Contending Explanations," in Samuel S. Kim, *International Relations of Northeast Asia*, p. 35.
18 Joint Statement of US–Japan Security Consultative Committee, Washington, DC, 19 February 2005.
19 For instance, the former Deputy Secretary of the State, Richard Armitage, opposed the idea of East Asian community, stressing significance of the Japan–US alliance in coping with the rise of Chinese influence. See *Asahi Shimbun*, 1 May 2005.
20 Saori N. Katada, "Determining Factors in Japan's Cooperation and Non-Cooperation with the United States: The Case of Asian Financial Crisis Management, 1997–1999," in Akitoshi Miyashita and Yoichiro Sato (eds) *Japanese Foreign Policy in Asian and the Pacific: Domestic Interests, American Pressure, and Regional Integration*, New York: Palgrave, 2001, p. 163.
21 Kent E. Calder, "Pacific Co-Prosperity? The San Francisco System and Its Implications in Comparative Perspective," in David I. Steinberg (ed.) *Korean Attitudes toward the United States: Changing Dynamics*, Armonk, NY: M.E. Sharpe, 2005, pp. 22–23.
22 Tetsuro Maeda, Sigeru Handa, and Akira Kawasaki, "Anzenhosyoseisaku no daitenkanga hajimatta" (A great transformation started in the security policy), *Sekai*, December 2004, pp. 77–86.
23 Mikkal E. Herberg, "Asia's Energy Insecurity: Markets or Mercantilism," presented at the conference on Remaking Economic Strengths in East Asia: Dealing with the Repercussions of Increased Interdependence, held at the Institute of East Asian Studies, the University of California, Berkeley, 8–9 April 2005.
24 Peter J. Katzenstein and Rudra Sil, "Rethinking Asian Security: A Case for Analytical Eclecticism," in J. J. Suh, Peter J. Katzenstein, and Allen Carlson (eds) *Rethinking Security in East Asia: Identity, Power, and Efficiency*, Stanford: Stanford University Press, 2004, pp. 16–20.
25 Snyder, *Myths of Empire*, pp. 97–108 and 142–150.

Part I

Contextualizing Northeast Asian region

1 Domestic politics and regional cooperation in Southeast and Northeast Asia

Etel Solingen

This chapter addresses the domestic foundations of regional cooperation in East Asia. I begin with an overview of the domestic politics drivers of regional cooperation in Southeast Asia. Section 2 provides an analysis of the main domestic issues promoting and discouraging regional cooperation in Northeast Asia. The first two sections thus address both inside-out effects (from the domestic arena to the international one) as well as outside-in effects (from the regional arena to the domestic one). Section 3 examines the role of Japan and China as important economic links between the Southeast and Northeast Asian complexes. Section 4 analyzes the role of the ASEAN Regional Forum (ARF) as the main political-institutional bond between the two sub-regions as well as various alternative fora. The concluding section distils some general implications.

The domestic foundations of regional cooperation in Southeast Asia

Despite significant national, ethnic, religious, and linguistic heterogeneity, wide diversity in power attributes and socio-economic development, a severe economic and political crisis in the late 1990s, and lingering territorial/maritime disputes within the region, Southeast Asian states have moved from an era of conflict into an era of cooperation. In the early 1960s president Sukarno engaged Indonesia in a military *konfrontasi* against Malaysia. Malaysia itself expelled Singapore from the Federation of Malaysia in 1965. All of Southeast Asia was engulfed by ideological internal struggles and interstate wars, largely related to the Cold War, which explains its characterization at the time as "the Balkans of the East." Among the many bilateral territorial disputes that afflicted the region, in some cases to this day, were the cases of Malaysia and the Philippines over Sabah, Malaysia and Brunei over Limbang (in Sarawak), Malaysia and Singapore over the island of Pedra Branca, Malaysia and Thailand over border-crossing issues, Malaysia and Indonesia over Sipadan, Sebatik, and Ligatan, Indonesia and Vietnam over Natuna, and others.[1]

Notwithstanding significant outstanding disputes Southeast Asia progressively developed into a highly cooperative regional framework. In 1967 Thailand, Singapore, Indonesia, Malaysia, and the Philippines signed the ASEAN Declaration (Bangkok Declaration).[2] In 1971 they followed up with a Zone of

Peace, Freedom and Neutrality Declaration and a commitment to develop collective strength and solidarity. In 1976 the first ASEAN summit of heads of state convened in Bali and adopted the Declaration of ASEAN Concord and the Treaty of Amity and Cooperation. These emphasized "perpetual peace, everlasting amity, and cooperation," guided by three principles: respect for state sovereignty, non-intervention, and renunciation of the threat or use of force in resolving disputes. By 1982, Singapore's foreign minister described intra-ASEAN disputes as irrelevant or considerably muted. Several informal mechanisms—known as the "ASEAN way"—emphasized consultation (*musjawarah*), consensual decision-making (*mufakat*), accommodation among members, informal diplomacy, reciprocity, and confidence-building. In time Brunei, Vietnam, Laos, Myanmar, and Cambodia joined what by the late 1990s had become known as the "the ASEAN 10." In 1997 the Southeast Asia Nuclear Weapon-Free Zone Treaty (Treaty of Bangkok) entered into force, committing signatories not to acquire nuclear weapons and restricting nuclear weapon states from outside the region from using or threatening to use nuclear arms anywhere within the zone. Southeast Asia had evolved from a cauldron of war into a cooperating region, avoiding armed conflict for over three decades now.

Notably, much of the literature on the emergence and evolution of ASEAN cooperation has focused on classical security considerations—from bilateral alliances to geostrategic predicaments—as well as on ideational processes.[3] On the one hand, external threats were certainly important but cannot explain the texture of Southeast Asia's regional order. As Foot argued, most ASEAN states were concerned with internal insurgency but disagreed over the nature of external threats.[4] On the other hand, ASEAN has certainly been an agent of norm socialization, but some consider its enormous political, cultural, and normative diversity to be a continuous challenge to deeper cooperation.[5] As Ganesan notes, these two approaches overlook the role of policy élites as agents of regional policy.[6] Politicians and state bureaucracies filter external threats and adopt and adapt norms in a way that makes them compatible with the requirements of their respective domestic political landscapes.

Domestic politics thus provides an important perspective on regional cooperation, what ASEAN is about, and what makes it tick. The domestic foundations of this transformation are in a slow, initially very tentative, process that began in the late 1960s, when domestic coalitions ruling some key Southeast Asian states began forging a new model of political control.[7] The model, designed to curtail external and internal communist advances in the region, was pivoted on export-led industrialization that would enhance economic growth and improve living standards at a time when serious armed insurgencies threatened from within. Indeed, the 1967 ASEAN Declaration listed as its first purpose the acceleration of economic growth, social progress, and cultural development. Most ASEAN declarations since then, including those in response to the 1997 crisis, maintained that focus on economic viability. ASEAN's ruling coalitions, mostly authoritarian, privileged domestic political stability and global access to capital, investment, technology, and markets. These required a political-economy model sensitive to synergies across the domestic, regional, and international spheres, where stability and a peaceful regional environment could yield foreign investment, financial resources, and access to international markets. As stipulated in Article 1 of the Concord Declaration: "The stability of each member state and of the ASEAN region is an essential contribution to international peace and security. Each member state resolves to eliminate threats posed by subversion to its stability, thus strengthening national and ASEAN resilience."[8] As Malaysia's Foreign Minister argued: "The concept of free enterprise ... is the philosophical basis of ASEAN";[9] global markets are the engine. Although an absolute increase in regional trade and investment resulted, regional integration per se was not necessary for the cooperative logic to be sustained.

Summarizing the links between global, regional, and domestic imperatives, Singapore's Lee Kuan Yew proclaimed: "The most enduring lesson of history is that ambitious growing countries can expand either by grabbing territory, people and resources, or by trading with other countries. The alternative to free trade is not just poverty, it is war".[10] Kishore Mahbubani described how ASEAN ruling coalitions closely watched their ranking in the World Economic Forum's competitiveness tables, and how they understood that "those engaged in civil war and conflict" could not compete well internationally. Poverty levels in all of East Asia declined by two-thirds between 1975 and 1995, the fastest rate of poverty reduction in the industrializing world. A significant middle class emerged and internationalizing constituencies favoring foreign direct investment, as well as natural resource and manufacturing exports, grew stronger. Ruling coalitions retained compensating mechanisms for adversely affected (including protected) constituencies and for political allies. Relative to the rising level of resources military expenditures were restrained despite some modernization efforts. ASEAN's average military expenditures relative to GDP were slightly above 5 per cent at their height in the late 1970s-early 1980s, but declined significantly to 2.8 per cent of GDP in 1990.[11] From a high of 5.4 per cent of GDP in the early 1960s (under Sukarno) Indonesia's declined to 1.2 per cent by the 1980s, Thailand's from 5 to 2.5 per cent, Malaysia's from 5.6 to 3.9 per cent, Singapore's and Brunei's from 6.7 to 4.8, and Vietnam's from 19.4 to 4.7 per cent with the adoption of ASEAN's model. ASEAN's military expenditures were lower than the 5 per cent average for industrializing regions in the 1980s and many concurred that there had been "no highly focused competitive arms accumulations" or arms races in Southeast Asia.[12]

The 1997 Asian crisis unleashed great concern with the viability of this model and its vulnerability to international capital flows.[13] Both IMF-style reforms and lingering cronyism aggravated the effects of the crisis. Yet, despite the most dramatic economic, political, and social shock to the model since its inception, fresh capital inflows, positive current accounts, stronger currencies, and improved foreign reserves had returned to the region by 2000 (except in Indonesia). The crisis adversely affected some business, popular sectors, and military budgets quite dramatically but also enhanced political reforms and deepened internationalization. Yet pressures for new social pacts to safeguard against future crises have not yet

congealed into formal safety-net mechanisms. Many feared that the 1997 debacle—domestic crisis, social disarray, and increased nationalism—might unravel
cooperative regional patterns. Indeed, uncertainties and tensions at first aggravated some bilateral frictions, particularly among Singapore, Malaysia, and
Indonesia, including Mahathir Mohamad's currency curbs and forceful repatria-
tion of Indonesian foreign workers. However, despite the rise of some nationalist
rhetoric, ruling coalitions reasserted common, cooperative internationalizing
commitments. The Manila Framework Agreement created an innovative "surveil-
lance mechanism" and reaffirmed a commitment to resist protectionism. The
Kuala Lumpur summit adopted the Vision 2020 plan calling for "a concert of
Southeast Asian nations, outward-looking, living in peace, stability and prosperity, bonded together in partnership in dynamic development and in a community
of caring societies," emphasizing sustainable and equitable growth and regional
resilience.[14] The Hanoi Plan of Action stressed the need to restore confidence,
foreign direct investment (FDI), economic growth, and financial stability. AFTA
entered into effect in 2003.

Indonesia, Malaysia and Singapore also established joint patrols over the
Malacca Strait against terrorism and piracy. Domestic repression by Burma's
military junta created pressures for ASEAN's intervention but these were largely
resisted, as was ASEAN's intervention in East Timor and Aceh. Terrorism and
extremist Islamist activities threatened some ASEAN states in the aftermath of
9/11, leading to cooperative arrangements, a Southeast Asian Antiterrorism
Centre in Kuala Lumpur, and the creation of an ASEAN Security Community
(ASC) that would combat terrorism among other objectives.[15] The 2003 Bali
Concord 2 establishing the ASC, an Economic Community, and a Socio–cultural
Community was among the most significant developments since 1997. The
Concord reaffirmed converging internationalizing strategies, common commit-
ments to enhance "economic linkages with the world economy," a competitive
investment environment, adherence to the Treaty of Amity and Cooperation in
Southeast Asia, and "the need for a secure political environment based on a strong
foundation of mutual interests generated by economic cooperation."[16]

In sum, ASEAN as an institution reflects the priorities of its domestic ruling
coalitions. It is *market-friendly, sovereignty-sensitive,* and *consensus-oriented,*
weakly institutionalized in formal terms, and far from a collective security
arrangement.[17] There have been no wars in recent decades although many doubt
this amounts to a security community. Indeed, ASEAN cannot be imputed with
improving bilateral relations between Vietnam and Indonesia, Thailand and
Malaysia, and Malaysia and Singapore. The most effective cooperation on
counter-terrorism has been bilateral, trilateral, or in coordination with extra-
regional actors. ASEAN's institutional effects should thus not be over-estimated.
Nor should the domestic incentives of ruling coalitions seeking a stable region,
growth-oriented economies, and foreign investment be under-estimated. These
commitments have survived the dramatic test of the 1997 crisis and appear
stronger with China's regional emergence. Some construe ASEAN's expansion as
a response to China's ascendancy but it can also be interpreted as an effort to

incorporate transitional states in continental Southeast Asia into the region's favored domestic model.

Domestic barriers and incentives for regional cooperation in Northeast Asia

The Northeast Asian regional landscape differs from the Southeast Asian one just described, with large states with great power attributes that have historically vied for power and dominance. At the same time, strong bilateral US alliances with Japan and South Korea are said to provide a stabilizing influence.[18] Furthermore, the Northeast Asian complex has the advantage of linking relatively advanced industrialized states such as Japan, South Korea, Taiwan—which are also democracies—and a modernizing China. Instead, Southeast Asia includes both highly industrialized states such as Singapore and relatively poor ones in continental Southeast Asia, with several in-between. Some are democracies but others are not. Despite these differences, Northeast Asia shares some of the attributes characterizing ruling coalitions in Southeast Asia. Indeed, Japan, and later South Korea and Taiwan, pioneered the model of export-led orientation to the global economy, later emulated by others in the region, including Southeast Asia and China. North Korea remains the outlier in Northeast Asia. How has this model influenced the relationship between domestic and regional politics in the Northeast Asian complex?

Japan

Japan's post-war domestic political economy was pivoted on LDP-led ruling coalitions of big business, farming interests, and small business under the umbrella of rapid growth, exports, and economic protectionism.[19] The iron triangle (stone-scissors-paper) included a powerful bureaucracy. Japan's model differed from its subsequent imitations throughout the region, on the role of state entrepreneurship, the military, the availability of natural resources, and openness to foreign direct investment, among others. At the same time, the consolidation of a ruling coalition progressively integrating the domestic with the global economy and seeking to shape a cooperative peaceful environment supportive of domestic growth remained a common trait. Japan's GNP grew at 11 per cent on average between 1952 and 1973, quadrupling its share of global trade during that period. The development of an educated middle class and a more egalitarian income distribution pattern than most other regions was also a shared objective.[20]

Japan's regional and international policies since 1945 relied primarily on economic rather than on military means. A constitution prohibiting both war and conventional military forces became law in 1947. Since the 1950s the Yoshida doctrine ("economy first") underpinned Japan's relations with the rest of the world. In the early 1950s Japan joined the IMF, GATT, the UN, and in the 1960s the OECD. In 1967 Prime Minister Sato announced Japan's three non-nuclear principles: not to possess, not to manufacture, and not to introduce nuclear weapons into Japan. In February 1970 Japan signed the Non-Proliferation Treaty (NPT) and in 1976 ratified it. By the early 1970s Japan also normalized relations with China. In the 1980s, partly but not uniquely as a consequence of US pressure (*gaiatsu*), Japan began liberalizing some of its domestic protectionism. The 1980s also witnessed the regionalization of Japan's political economy, particularly in the form of a dramatic expansion of investments into Southeast Asia, a development that I address in the next section. Prime Minister Nakasone Yasuhiro crafted a more proactive Japanese policy in alliance with the US.

The tension between internationally-oriented domestic interests and more inward-looking ones continued in Japan to this day. However, Japan's domestic political economy has evolved significantly in recent decades, with deepening internal divisions within business, the LDP, and the bureaucracy. Some big business began pressing for greater domestic deregulation, particularly following its regional expansion. The role of the media, academia, and perhaps to a lesser extent labor, expanded in tandem with corruption scandals in the bureaucracy, the LDP, and the business sector. Changes in the electoral and party-system, and decreased bureaucratic independence, made the formulation of clear-cut domestic and foreign policy more difficult. Although most politicians are parochially oriented, domestic politics (as reflected in Diet debates, bureaucratic politics, and the media) have strongly shaped Japan's foreign policy, particularly towards China and North Korea.[21] Pekkanen and Krauss trace post-2000 changes in Japan's security policies to shifts in the party system after a major electoral reform and to a stronger prime minister role.[22] Conversely, the progressive internationalization of Japan's economy and politics has made US–Japan relations, policy toward the Korean peninsula, and agricultural liberalization more central to domestic debates. As Fukai argues, international events have provided necessary but not sufficient conditions for the split of the LDP, the formation of the LDP–SDPJ coalition government, and the reversal of the SDPJ's policies on the Self Defense Forces, the US alliance, and nuclear power, in the direction of greater harmony with the LDP.[23]

Both Japan's earlier pattern of reacting rather than initiating policy and Japan's new assertiveness in political and military terms are traced to domestic constraints.[24] Politicians such as Ozawa warned that Japan's foreign policy must cease to be captive to domestic interests, including big business, and must respond according to "national interests."[25] His concept of Japan becoming a "normal" nation implied placing its own welfare and interests above others. Even this more proactive and assertive policy, however, retained the basic premise that only international peace and stability and free trade can help maintain Japan's affluence and stability. At the same time, several domestic developments signal a potential departure of Japan's foreign policy from the one it followed between the 1950s and the 1980s.

To begin with, Japanese nationalism has risen as an electoral consideration. Ishihara Shintaro was once a rather isolated figure, supported by a few former military officers and some small industries and labor in declining sectors, but his appeal has broadened, as has that of other nationalist politicians. North Korea's abduction of Japanese citizens during the Cold War became a dramatically important domestic concern in Japan, mobilizing support for a tougher position on North Korea. Prime Minister Koizumi Junichiro continued his annual visits to the Yasukuni Shrine to maintain support among nationalist constituencies. In addition, there has been increased pressure for diluting Japan's human rights violations in Asia prior to and during World War Two in school textbooks. Finally, moves to change the Constitution's Article IX, expanding overseas operations by the Self-Defense Forces (Afghanistan, Iraq), expanded military budgets and commitments to deploy missile defense systems provided by the US, were also regarded as instances of Japan's evolution towards "normal" status. Japan already has the most technologically sophisticated military force in the Asia Pacific after the US, although its military expenditures have rarely risen above one per cent of its GDP.

These changes in Japan's policies have resulted in increased tensions with Japan's neighbors, particularly China and South Korea. In April 2005 these tensions reached record heights when China coordinated nationalist responses to Japan's policies, as I discuss below, in the largest anti-Japanese demonstrations in China since diplomatic relations were restored in 1972. At the same time, China has become central to Japan's economic revival, highlighting the stakes for Japan's politicians, industrial interests, and bureaucratic agents responsible for restoring Japan's export-led model back to health. Nationalist upheaval in China was immediately reflected in declining stock indexes in Japan and downgraded growth estimates for Japan by the International Monetary Fund. In 2004 Japan's FDI in China surpassed FDI from North America. China (including Hong Kong) accounted for over 20 per cent of Japan's total trade (exports plus imports) in 2004, or $215 billion. Kakutaru Kitashiro, chairman of the Japan Association of Corporate Executives and of I.B.M. Japan acknowledged that "if the situation caused the Chinese economy to slow, it would affect not only Japan but the whole Asian economy."[26] Against this background, Koizumi addressed an Asia—Africa summit in Jakarta on April 22, 2005 as follows: "Japan squarely faces these facts of history in a spirit of humility. And with feelings of deep remorse and heartfelt apology always engraved in mind, Japan has resolutely maintained, consistently since the end of World War Two, never turning into a military power but an economic power."

South Korea

Following the demise of Rhee Syngman's corrupt regime based on import-substitution and hostility towards North Korea, Park Chung Hee purged the bureaucracy, the political leadership, and the military itself, while introducing his own model of political survival pivoted on export-led economic growth in 1963. The new regime's motto became: "Nation Building through Exports," and "Think Export First!"[27] Park's "sword-*won*" coalition included military and technocratic administrators and big enterprises *(chaebol)*. The shift into an export-led model trebled the share of exports to GDP between 1966 and 1973 while manufactured goods grew from 17 per cent of exports in the early 1960s to 83 per cent a decade later.[28] As US aid declined in the 1960s efforts to attract Japanese capital and technology intensified. Reliance on IMF funds grew from virtually nil in the early 1970s to about 300 per cent of its quota a decade later. A large middle class had emerged by the 1970s, followed by financial liberalization and lower tariffs in the 1980s, when South Korea repaid all its debts.[29] Park resisted military expenditures that could impair his model, restricting them to 4 per cent of GDP on average before 1975 and 6 per cent with declining US aid. They declined to 5 per cent by 1985 and about 3.6 per cent by the 1990s, close to the average for the industrializing world but lower than other high-conflict regions such as the Middle East.[30] Whereas South Korea's GDP grew by 10 per cent on average between 1965 and 1989, military expenditures remained lower than GDP growth. A growing economy still enabled higher military expenditures in real terms.

These policies required Park to advance "the compass of peace," abandoning old "Let us march North" slogans, declaring the need to "avoid another conflict at all cost," and proclaiming that "only through peaceful means could the goal of unification coincide with the nation's objective of bringing about development and prosperity."[31] The drive to broaden international access to markets, capital, and technology led to an Open Door Policy of global access through economic and political relations with all states. Despite nationalist opposition, Park ratified the 1965 treaty normalizing relations with Japan that provided South Korea with $800 million in grants, loans, and credit. Park signed and ratified the NPT. Roh Tae-woo launched Nordpolitik in 1988 to initiate dialogue with North Korea and normalized relations with the Soviet Union and China in 1990 and 1992, respectively. The transition to democracy did not alter the export-led strategy and its regional corollaries, although some defiance of the model remained, largely confined to some small and medium-sized businesses, agricultural interests, and the student-worker movement.[32] Kim Young-sam helped ensure a peaceful outcome to the 1993 nuclear crisis, so vital to the continuity of the South's model. Kim Dae-Jung, elected with strong support from labor and inward-looking economic nationalists, nonetheless pledged support for free markets, safe foreign investment, and tight IMF conditions in response to the 1997 crisis. "We are," he said "living in a globalized economy."[33] Accordingly, he tightened relations with the US and Japan while coordinating the first inter-Korean summit in 2000. Officials acknowledged that promoting *chaebol* activities in the North was "an inexpensive insurance policy to calm investors, contributing to the $50 billion that has flowed into South Korea since 1997."[34] Roh Moo-hyun maintained support for "the peace and prosperity policy." Precursors and successors of the Sunshine policy were all efforts to placate North Korea's leadership while offering *chaebols* low cost labor from North Korea. Although South Korea has not been immune to the rise of nationalism primarily against Japan but also against the US, even Roh Moo-hyun has maintained the broad economic and security parameters of the prevailing model.

Taiwan–China relations

Taiwan resembles many of the characteristics of South Korea's model. Chiang Kai-shek's early years of heavy state intervention and import-substitution led in the late 1950s to reforms of monetary, fiscal, trade, taxation, and foreign investment policies, including the liquidation of state enterprises. By the early 1960s an export orientation was in place even as state enterprises, banks, and some party ideologues resisted it.[35] In time, small and medium-sized firms flourished, with extensive FDI flowing to smaller component manufacturers, preventing the emergence of big monopolies such as South Korea's *chaebol*.[36] Kuomintang's (KMT) openness to FDI also helped Taiwan break through its international isolation. Its growth strategy was pivoted on price stability, an egalitarian income distribution, and decentralized (small-medium) entrepreneurship, having learned important lessons from its defeat by China. The bureaucracy was infused with highly-educated professionals and technicians that had fled the mainland and, progressively, with more native Taiwanese. The KMT kept private business at arms' length while creating conditions for expansion through global integration, price and political stability.

Tight fiscal and monetary policy, high real interest rates, low money supply and stable foreign exchange rates were core instruments even during economic crises in the 1970s. Exports as a share of GDP doubled between 1966 and 1973, from 21.3 per cent to 46.7 per cent. The overall rate of effective protection by the 1970s was 5 per cent. Foreign trade amounted to about 85 per cent of Taiwan's GNP by 1985.[37]

This model had also forced the monitoring of military expenses, resented by a military fearing that an export-led strategy might impair economic sufficiency and war preparedness. However, the KMT's overriding concern with economic stability diluted pressures for expanding the military industrial complex. The model's very success infused the ruling coalition with "an evermore absorbing interest in economic growth."[38] Despite its fragility vis-à-vis China, Taiwan allocated on average about 8 per cent of its GNP for defense between 1961 and 1987, with rates declining by the 1970s as the export-led model took root. Defense expenditures thus played a minor and indirect role on GNP growth, export expansion, and improving income equality. The KMT was always reluctant to finance expensive indigenous arms industries, as was the US, which sought to downplay incentives to challenge the mainland.[39] Thus, the initial phase of statism, militarization, and aggressive foreign policies towards China gave way to less confrontational postures, even while facing Mao's adversarial policies. Following US–Chinese normalization and the abrogation of the Washington–Taipei Mutual Security Treaty, Taiwan's leadership perceived US commitment to its security to have eroded dangerously.[40] Yet in the 1970s it renounced an expensive nuclear competition in response to both US pressure and domestic considerations. Taiwan also joined the non-proliferation regime, although in the 1980s there appears to have been another effort in the direction of a nuclear weapons program.

The next logical evolution of Taiwan's model was developing closer economic relations and enhanced investment in China. Indeed, private Taiwanese entrepreneurship became central to the economic transformation of its reputed arch enemy. By the turn of the century over 70 per cent of Taiwan's foreign investment was flowing into China and over one million Taiwanese entrepreneurs were working in the mainland. At the same time, with the inception of democracy in the 1990s, Taiwan's independence movement grew stronger. China's test-firing of missiles in Taiwan's direction in 1995 and Lee Teng-hui's formulation of a "two states" principle fuelled nationalistic positions on both sides. The pro-independence Democratic Progressive Party led by Chen Shui-bian assumed power in 2000 and has retained it ever since.

Across the Straits, China's emergence from domestic turmoil and widespread hunger into a budding superpower had changed the nature of its interaction with Taiwan. On the ashes of an autarkic Maoist model Deng Xiaoping developed a coalition of light industry, agricultural producers, and consumers (particularly in the coastal provinces), which eventually led China into WTO membership. The internationalization of China's economy also involved transfers from the military-industrial to the civilian sector, a 40 per cent reduction in the People's Liberation Army (PLA)'s size and an eventual decline of its relative power within the party leadership.[41] The post-1979 model required a new matrix of regional relations that, in time, led to the so-called "charm offensive" vis-à-vis ASEAN and a set of more mature economic and political relations with North East Asian neighbors, including Japan. In the 1990s leaders favoring internationalization became more open to multilateral regional institutions despite China's previous aversion to anything but bilateralism.[42] China's ambiguous hot-and-cold tactics regarding the Spratly Islands, Taiwan, and Japan, revealed a protracted domestic contest between internationalizing and inward-looking camps, the latter grouping some elements of the People's Liberation Army, state enterprises, agriculture, and local governments resisting economic openness.[43] Military modernization efforts geared to satisfy the PLA were not allowed to derail the outward-oriented model of economic growth and political control, with estimated military expenses kept at about 4 per cent of GDP in the late 1990s.[44] However, a booming economy has turned China into the second largest military spender worldwide according to US government estimates, which have enabled China to upgrade its navy, fuelling concerns in Taiwan, Japan, and the US.

China's internationalizing coalition faces discontent among forces adversely affected by integration in the global economy. Whereas the main beneficiaries in the coastal areas—about 200 million—have now joined the middle class, farmers and rural workers still endure economic hardship and official corruption. State enterprises, banks, and military agencies resist different aspects of domestic and foreign policies. In an effort to deflate domestic opposition to reform and/or to Communist Party rule, some party leaders favored the mobilization of nationalist support as a rallying theme. Skillfully exploiting some of Japan's policies described earlier, nationalist fervor was allowed to reach new heights in April 2005, at least partly as a means to co-opt themes wielded by opponents of China's global integration. Japan's textbooks, Yasukuni visits, efforts to join the UN Security Council, and its March 2005 joint declaration with the US that Taiwan is a common security interest, provided convenient justifications for triggering a wave of sometimes violent nationalist demonstrations. A second track for nationalist manipulation was offered by Chen Shui-bian's proposals for constitutional change and the use of referenda on China's missiles aimed at Taiwan along Fujian province. In response, the National People's Congress approved a law in March 2005 that mandates the use of "non-peaceful" means against Taiwan if it declares independence.

Efforts to placate domestic opposition in China via nationalism backfired, sensitizing the leadership to the possibility that such manipulation can run out of control. Domestic instability and xenophobia could derail both China's rise into an economic powerhouse and the Communist Party's stewardship of that process. As May 4 nationalist protests had a history of deviating into protests against China's own government, nationalist activism was suppressed in April 2005, after weeks of vandalism against Japanese commercial interests and diplomatic delegations. Furthermore, the official press declared that "a positive attitude is needed if a dispute is to be resolved through dialogue and peaceful negotiations."[45] Indeed, the nationalist tool is not favored by all Chinese leaders and Premier Wen Jiabao made several proposals to improve relations with Japan and resolve "issues left over from history."[46] Following the passage of the anti-secession law against Taiwan, Wen warned that, although there was a US precedent for outlawing secession in 1861, this had ended up in a war between North and South. "We do not wish to see that kind of outcome," Wen repeated, contradicting the law's uncompromising commitment to "pay any price" to maintain unity.[47] Pointedly, Wen's last statement was omitted from China's official transcripts, controlled by the Propaganda Department (which, in turn, is in the hands of inward-looking forces), suggesting internal divisiveness on this issue within the Chinese leadership. China's Ministry of Commerce declared that boycotts of Japanese goods would harm the economic interests of both Japan and China. Qin Yaqing, deputy president of Beijing's Foreign Affairs College and an influential scholar of China's international relations, had stated that China should restrain itself from using force against Taiwan.[48]

Chen Shui-bian's response to these developments was a planned "million people" protest march in Taipei (that never reached that size), joined by some supporters of the opposition Nationalist Party. The latter's leader Lien Chan followed with a meeting with President Hu Jintao in China. The popularity of this step with Taiwanese constituencies searching for compromise with China forced Chen Shui-bian into compromising steps of his own. Chen's own party and the small People First Party have a limited alliance despite holding dramatically opposed views on cross-Straits relations. Chen's need to increase support within the legislature, among other domestic considerations, limits his willingness to sacrifice Taiwan's economic relations with China on the altar of "independence now!"

North Korea

Kim Il Sung forged a state characterized as "ideologically paternalistic, economically collectivist, ethnically racist, diplomatically isolationist, and culturally nationalist."[49] *Juche*, "the material basis of *chajusong*" (all-round independence in international relations), was a cornerstone of the "hermit kingdom" and an important tool for Kim's own mythification, leading to one of the lowest levels of foreign trade worldwide (about 13 per cent of its GNP).[50] North Korea bartered military exports, including missiles and non-conventional technology to the Middle East for oil and eventually discontinued paying its foreign debts, further limiting its access to additional capital. The armed forces controlled economic fiefdoms and Soviet assistance helped build an extensive military-industrial complex. Army personnel grew to over 600,000 million by 1958, and the air force to an estimated 900 planes, one of the largest armed forces in the industrializing world. The "four great military policy-lines" involved arming the entire people, fortifying the entire country, cadetifying and modernizing the entire army.[51] As the backbone of Kim Il Sung's dominance, the military received one-third of the budget and one fourth of GNP.

North Korean leaders depicted the South as *sadaejuui* (mercenary, flunkey, "puppet") of imperialist USA, launching terrorist attacks in the 1970s, assassinating South Korean ministers in Rangoon in 1983, and destroying a South Korean civilian aircraft in 1987. China's opening had a very limited impact on North Korea, leading to extremely slow and piecemeal economic reform. The contrast with the rest of Northeast Asia could not be sharper. A 1984 Joint Venture Law — spearheaded by Kim Jong Il — sought to attract Western and Japanese capital and technology into special export zones. The collapse of the Soviet Union dealt a heavy blow to *juche*, requiring payments to Russia in convertible currency. North Korea's trade plummeted from $4.6 billion in 1990 to $2.6 billion in 1991.[52] Military budgets in the late 1980s remained as high as 20 to 25 per cent of GDP. The Party and the military-industrial complex revealed remarkable staying power in the midst of a rapidly changing East Asian region. The People's Army was 1.1 million strong by 1994. Yet Kim Il Sung sought improved relations with the West and normalization with Japan. In a dramatic reversal, he accepted separate UN membership for North and South in 1991 and signed an "Agreement on Reconciliation, Nonaggression, and Exchanges and Cooperation," and a "Joint Declaration for the Denuclearization of the Korean Peninsula" with the South. Some efforts to expand special export zones and attract foreign capital and technology followed.

Kim Jong Il became supreme leader in 1994, upon his father's death, presiding over a political dance pitting upholders of the *ancien regime* against proponents of a soft-landing à-la-China. External signs of a domestic cleavage were evident in contradictory foreign policy actions, intermittently cooperative and aggressive. Kim Jong Il straddled this domestic divide to maintain his rule, spearheading the 1993 withdrawal from the NPT but also supporting promoters of special economic zones and hushed advocates of joining the global economy.[53] Yet economic reform and foreign investment is still embryonic, despite recent changes and the rise of informal markets. Meager exports still involve mostly weapons, missiles, and drug trafficking. North Korea clearly remains an outlier in a region where integration with the global economy has been the modal strategy. Its regional relations, including its race toward nuclear weapons, reflect these differences. Continued closure burdens the ability to trace the precise dynamics of domestic political competition but its very exit from the NPT in 2003 appears nested in a domestic tug of war between an apparently weak reformist camp and the old guard.

Japan–ASEAN–China relations: connecting Southeast and Northeast Asia

Close economic relations between ASEAN and Japan have provided an important link between Northeast and Southeast Asia.[54] Southeast Asian countries began emulating Japan's model in the 1960s and 1970s. By the 1980s, particularly following the currency realignments of 1985 Plaza Accord, Japan had become the leading regional economic player in Southeast Asia, heading the "flying geese."[55] Japan paid war reparations, promoted official aid to Southeast Asian countries, and became the largest foreign investor in Indonesia, Malaysia, and Thailand, and second largest in the Philippines and Singapore. Japanese investments and transborder production networks helped catalyze the region's economic integration. However, by the 1990s Japan's role diminished as a result of its own domestic debacle or "lost decade."

Prime Minister Koizumi has sought to revive Japan's presence in Southeast Asia for political, economic, and strategic reasons. Singapore offered him a golden opportunity by proposing what became Japan's first comprehensive free-trade-area (FTA). The Japan–Singapore Economic Partnership Agreement of 2002 aimed at liberalizing and facilitating trade and investments and promoting bilateral economic cooperation in various areas. China's Premier Zhu Ronji proposed a China–ASEAN FTA and a framework agreement was signed in 2002 to establish an FTA by 2012, with the potential for creating the world's largest trading zone (1.8 billion people). China has become far more attractive to FDI than ASEAN in recent years, receiving 9 per cent of all global foreign investment in 2001, as opposed to ASEAN's 1.7 per cent. This development raised no less concern among some ASEAN states than the 1997 crisis did.

The Japan–Singapore Partnership Agreement was conceived of as a prelude to a potential Japan-ASEAN FTA. Koizumi proposed a "Japan–ASEAN Comprehensive Economic Cooperation Plan" as a major new policy initiative to cement relations with ASEAN countries and Japan launched a special "ASEAN–Japan Exchange Year" in 2003, culminating in the signing of a Framework Agreement for a Japan–ASEAN FTA. The China–ASEAN free trade zone, which some key ASEAN states find quite attractive, loomed large in Japan's initiatives, catalyzing similar negotiations between Japan on the one hand, and Malaysia, the Philippines, Thailand, and Indonesia on the other. Protectionist interests in Japan, including agricultural and service-oriented sectors (in nursing, for instance) actively intervened to slow this process down but have, on the whole, been overpowered by domestic interests who stand to benefit from this process and by state agencies promoting it.[56]

Economic Partnership Agreements between Japan, China, and South Korea are even further into the future, as Japan walks ever more cautiously on the path to agreements with larger powers, stronger competitors, and more burdened security implications. These economic processes of creating FTAs within East Asia and beyond are quite new to Japan and other East Asian partners. The trend has many sources, including stalled global negotiations toward liberalization in the WTO up until 2004 as well as responses to economic integration in other regions, such as the EU. However, these processes could have hardly come about without the maturation of domestic political constituencies, both in the private sector and in state structures that seek to enhance a market-oriented evolution in a context of domestic and regional stability. These constituencies will be driving the expansion of bilateral and sub-regional FTAs into a future East Asia FTA.

The ASEAN Regional Forum: the only game in town?

The economic dynamics outlined in the previous section seem to have overtaken developments in the area of security cooperation across the Southeast Asia-Northeast Asia complexes. The ARF, with 22 participants, emerged in 1994 as Asia-Pacific's only all-inclusive security forum. The ARF commits studies to the Council for Security Cooperation in the Asia Pacific established in 1993 as a non-official network linking security NGOs throughout the region. Fears of China's ascendancy and assertiveness over the Spratly Islands are said to have played a role in its creation. ASEAN's 1992 decision to include security in Post-Ministerial Conferences and Japan's Nakayama proposal played catalytic roles in launching the ARF.[57]

The logic of East Asia's domestic political models explains the ARF's rationale well. The fastest growing region in the world requires political stability, continued investments, and global access to markets and technology. Institutions that help maintain the underlying conditions for economic growth and political stability while containing militarization can advance the respective and collective interests of ruling coalitions throughout the region. Shirk and Johnston acknowledged the ARF's relevance to minimizing uncertainty (particularly vis-à-vis China) but also to shared interests in economic prosperity and to avoiding costly arms races.[58] Furthermore, an informal, consensus-based institution accommodates variation in domestic arrangements, which differ across the region given different levels of economic development, different rates of economic liberalization, and different political systems. Thus, an informal institution such as the ARF can buttress the synergies between domestic and regional stability without imposing strains. The ARF is supposed to provide domestic ruling coalitions with the regional conditions that their domestic policies require. The ARF's 1998 communiqué noted the financial crisis' repercussions for peace and security. The 2000 meeting reaffirmed the links between globalization and regional peace and stability, revealing a common understanding that the ARF's future is inextricably linked to the domestic coalitional foundation that has underpinned the region's evolution. For instance, Kim Dae-Jung has sought to activate the ARF in support of his "Sunshine Policy" of accommodation with North Korea, in an effort to tame belligerent factions in the North.

Initially the PLA resisted the ARF as threatening its institutional interests in the Spratly Islands and advocated balance of power and bilateralism instead. Subsequently, supporters of China's internationalizing model in the Foreign Ministry prevailed against PLA efforts to block the ARF.[59] China may have a preference for bilateralism but variation across regional institutions suggests that different domestic configurations may weigh differently on each. Where internationalizing agencies and constituencies were more salient (APEC) there was lower resistance to multilateralism than was initially the case for the ARF, where PLA interests were more directly challenged.[60] Informal multilateral forms have not only assuaged at least some of China's domestic concerns but have also enabled North Korea's inclusion in the ARF process. The ARF advanced confidence-building including "White Papers" on defense policy and exchanges between military academies, encouraged participation in the UN Register of Conventional Weapons, and approved a "Concept paper" identifying a three-step evolutionary approach from confidence building to preventive diplomacy and conflict-resolution.

However, the ARF has some built-in limitations. ASEAN insists in retaining a controlling role in the ARF, despite its inherent weaknesses and the skepticism on the part of some of its more powerful neighbors in East Asia.[61] At the same time, ASEAN's ability to steer the ARF stems precisely from its ability to reassure those same powerful neighbors. Japan can cooperate with ASEAN in promoting certain issues on the security agenda while maintaining its reserved *modus operandi*. Similarly, China can dispel concerns with renewed regional hegemony by working through ASEAN's institutional framework as part of its "charm offensive." The ARF's 11th ministerial meeting in Jakarta (2004) approved a Chinese proposal to establish a new security forum—the ARF Security Policy Conference (ASPC)—with the participation of defense officials. China hosted the 1st ASPC meeting in late 2004. The Jakarta meeting also approved a special statement on preventing the proliferation of weapons of mass destruction, including black-market transactions of nuclear materials, and another on fighting piracy and terror on the Strait of Malacca. In the end, however, the ARF has failed to progress beyond declared objectives in preventive diplomacy, chiefly due to China opposition (China also resists Taiwan's inclusion). The ARF's consensus rule is strong and resilient. Its thin institutional structure lacks even a secretariat to provide coordination between meetings. Some limited coordination on terrorism, piracy, and other non-traditional security issues has been achieved. However, the ARF's limited contribution to the resolution of core outstanding conflicts has enabled APEC, the ASEAN Plus Three (APT), and other fora and "coalitions of the willing" to seize some initiative in security matters.

Among them is the Six Party Talks, hosted by China, which enjoys a closer relationship with North Korea than most other participants (Japan, South Korea, the US, and Russia). China has shielded North Korea from the possibility of discussing its nuclear activities at the UN Security Council and has refused to join the Proliferation Security Initiative launched by the US with the objective of interdicting illegal traffic involving weapons of mass destruction. Japan has publicly supported some US positions but has also tried to soften them, withholding the normalization of diplomatic and economic relations to North Korea (discussed at a September 2002 summit between Koizumi and Kim Jong Il) until the abductees issue and North Korea's nuclear activities are settled. South Korea's role in the Six Party Talks has remained an extension of its Sunshine Policy. So has Russia's position reflected a general low profile in East Asian politics, combined with a gentle nudging of North Korea to abandon its nuclear ambitions.

The APT process evolved from the first East Asian Summit in 1997 and now involves annual meetings of heads of state and regularized meetings of foreign and finance ministers. The "Chiang Mai Initiative" in 2000 launched a currency swap system to increase hard currency reserves and defend economies against liquidity crises. In 2005 South Korea's central bank signed currency-swap agreements with its counterparts in China and Japan, supplementing previous commitments. The 1998 APT meeting established an East Asian Vision Group that introduced the concept of an East Asian community. This began with an economic emphasis on what president Roh Moo-hyun labeled "a community of prosperity."[62] A Network of East Asian Think Tanks came into being in 2003, coordinated by China. The East Asian community concept gained growing support among Japanese research, business, intellectual, some Foreign Ministry circles, and from Koizumi himself.[63] A task force headed by Professor Tanaka Akihiko studied Japan's Strategy toward the East Asian Community. Although a work in progress, the seeds of a stronger cooperative future in Northeast Asia are in place, underpinned by rapidly expanding economic networks promoted by internationalizing coalitions throughout the region.

Conclusions

Both Northeast Asia and Southeast Asia share common domestic foundations of regional cooperation, rooted in the adoption of export-led models of political control. These models required domestic and regional political and economic stability, and East Asia has, for the most part, created such conditions in recent decades. China's economic opening to the world has enabled the consolidation of this strategy within a pivotal regional state. However, this model is not universally strong. It is practically non-existent in North Korea, quite feeble in some continental Southeast Asian states, and continuously vulnerable to a potentially sharp economic decline. The robustness of these conditions should not be taken-for-granted.

Furthermore, as the introductory chapter by Sung Chull Kim stipulates, an intense focus on history significantly distinguishes Northeast from Southeast Asia. The political-economy models put in place in recent decades are not immune to the nationalist virus. Some leaders throughout the region have sought to muster domestic support for the model by rallying around nationalist themes.

Domestic issues—from visits to the Yasukuni Shrine to school textbooks, from Shimane prefecture's declaration of Takeshima Day as a gesture to its fishermen to identity politics in Taiwan—have joined lingering territorial and boundary conflicts as arguably useful themes for mobilizing relevant domestic constituencies. At the same time, the confrontational heights reached in 2005 have also sensitized leaders in the region to the potentially uncontrollable nature of the nationalist weapon. For China, the lessons seem to be that nationalist fervor cannot be fine-tuned to aim at external targets alone. The potential for mass mobilization to turn against the Communist Party itself makes this a risky strategy. The coming years will tell whether or not there is still time to reverse the nationalist tide, and whether or not the beneficiaries of East Asia's political economy model have become strong enough to prevent its demise.

Notes

* The author would like to acknowledge the Social Science Research Council-Japan Foundation Abe Fellowship and the helpful comments of T. J. Cheng, Lowell Dittmer, N. Ganesan, Sung Chull Kim, and all other participants at the Hiroshima conferences in 2004 and 2005.

1 For a survey of outstanding bilateral conflicts in Southeast Asia, see N. Ganesan, *Bilateral tensions in post-cold war ASEAN*, Singapore: Regional Strategic and Political Studies Programme, Institute of Southeast Asian Studies, 1999.
2 For all documents on ASEAN, see "The Official Website of the Association of Southeast Asian Nations Homepage," *ASEAN Secretariat*, 2003. Online. Available HTTP: <http://www.aseansec.org> (accessed 27 July 2005).
3 For an overview, see Sorpong Peou, "Withering realism? A Review of Recent Security Studies on the Asia-Pacific Region," *Pacific Affairs*, Vol. 75, No. 4, Winter 2002, pp. 575-86.
4 Rosemary Foot, "Pacific Asia: The Development of Regional Dialogue," in Louise Fawcett and Andrew Hurrell (eds) *Regionalism in World Politics*, New York: Oxford University Press, p. 234.
5 View propounded by Surapong Jayanama, director general of Thailand's Foreign Ministry's East Asia department.
6 N. Ganesan, "Mirror, Mirror, on the Wall: Misplaced Polarities in the Study of Southeast Asian Security," *International Relations of the Asia–Pacific*, Vol. 3, No. 2, 2003, pp. 221–40.
7 For more comprehensive overviews of coalitional interpretations of ASEAN prior to, and after the 1997 crisis, see Etel Solingen, "ASEAN Cooperation: The Legacy of the Economic Crisis," *International Relations of the Asia-Pacific*, Vol. 5, No.1, 2005; and Solingen, "ASEAN, Quo Vadis? Domestic Coalitions and Regional Cooperation," *Contemporary Southeast Asia*, Vol. 21, No.1, 1999, pp. 30–53.
8 On the synergy between national and regional resilience, see Donald K. Emerson, "Indonesia, Malaysia, Singapore: A Regional Security Core?" in Richard J. Ellings and Sheldon W. Simon (eds) *Southeast Asian Security in the New Millennium*, Armonk: M.E. Sharpe, 1996, pp. 62–3.
9 Amitav Acharya, "Culture, Security, Multilateralism: The 'ASEAN Way' and Regional Order," in Keith R. Krause, *Culture and Security: Multilateralism, Arms Control, and Security Building*, London: Frank Cass, 1999, pp. 55–84.
10 Lee Kuan Yew, "Survey: Asia. A Billion Consumers," *The Economist*, 30 October 1993.

11 Stockholm International Peace Research Institute. *Yearbook 2003: Armaments, Disarmament and International Security*, Oxford University Press, 2003; International Institute of Strategic Studies, *The Military Balance 1995–6*, 1995, pp. 266–7; International Institute of Strategic Studies, *The Military Balance 1997–8*, 1997, p. 295; Desmond Ball, "Arms and Affluence: Military Acquisitions in the Asia Pacific Region," *International Security*, Vol. 18, No. 3, Winter 1993, pp. 78–112.

12 Barry Buzan and Gerald Segal, "Rethinking East Asia Security," *Survival*, Vol. 36, No. 2, Summer 1994, pp. 3–21; Ball, *"Arms and Affluence;"* Desmond Ball, "A New Era in Confidence Building: The Second-Track Process in the Asia/Pacific Region," *Security Dialogue*, Vol. 25, 1994, pp. 157–76.; Pauline Kerr, Andrew Mack and David Evans, "The Evolving Security Discourse in Asia-Pacific" in Andrew Mack and John Ravenhill (eds), *Pacific Cooperation: Building Economic and Security Regimes in the Asia Pacific Region* , Sydney: Allen & Unwin, 1994; Acharya, *Culture, Security*, p. 73; and, dissenting, Tim Huxley and Susan Willett, *Arming East Asia*, New York: Oxford University Press, 1999. For cross-regional comparisons, see "Mapping Internationalization: Domestic and Regional impacts," *International Studies Quarterly*, Vol. 45, No. 4, 2001, pp. 517–56.

13 World Bank, "Poverty in East Asia" in *Social Policy and Governance in the East Asia and Pacific Region,* 1999a. Online. Available HTTP: <http://www.worldbank.org/eapsocial/sector/poverty/povcwp2.htm> (accessed on 8 September 2005) and World Bank, "What is the Social Crisis in East Asia?" in *Social Policy and Governance in the East Asia and Pacific Region*, 1999b. Online. Available HTTP: <http://www.worldbank.org/eapsocial/whatis.htm> (accessed on 9 September 2005). On the effects of the crisis on ruling coalitions, see Etel Solingen, "Southeast Asia in a New Era: Domestic Coalitions from Crisis to Recovery," *Asian Survey*, Vol. 44, No. 2, March/April 2004a, pp. 189–212.

14 "ASEAN Summits", *ASEAN Secretariat*, 2003. Online. Available HTTP: <www.aseansec.org/summit/vision97/htm> (accessed on 27 July 2005).

15 Zachary Abuza, "Funding Terrorism in Southeast Asia: The Financial Network of Al Qaeda and Jemaah Islamyia," *Contemporary Southeast Asia*, Vol. 25, No. 2, August 2003, pp. 169–199; David Leheny, *Terrorism, Social Movements, and International Security: How Al Qaeda Affects Southeast Asia*, Ms. Department of Political Science, University of Wisconsin-Madison, 30 June 2003.

16 "Press Statement by the Chairperson of the 9th ASEAN summit and the 7th ASEAN + 3 Summit," *ASEAN Secretariat*, 7 October 2003. Online. Available HTTP: <http://www.aseansec.org/15259.htm> (accessed on 27 July 2005).

17 For a more complete analysis of East Asian regional institutions, see Etel Solingen, "East Asian Regional Institutions: Characteristics, Sources, Distinctiveness," in T. J. Pempel (ed.) *Remapping Asia: Competing Patterns of Regional Integration*, Ithaca: Cornell University Press, 2005, pp. 31–53.

18 Takashi Inoguchi, "Possibilities and Limits of Regional Cooperation in Northeast Asia," *Perspectives Asiatique*, Nos. 9–10, January 2001, pp. 24–32; Masashi Nishihara, "New Frameworks for Northeast Asian Security: Bilateral Alliances and Multilateral Unofficial Talks," *Japan Center for International Exchange*. Online. Available HTTP: <http://www.jcie.or.jp/thinknet/insights/nishihara.html> (accessed on 12 May 2005). For an application of ASEAN's framework to Northeast Asia, see Mary Byrne McDonnell, "Towards a Multilateral Security Framework for Northeast Asia," Paper prepared for presentation at the 14th Hokkaido Conference on North Pacific Issues, 2002.

19 T. J. Pempel, *Regime Shift: Comparative Dynamics of the Japanese Political Economy*, Ithaca: Cornell University Press, 1998; Shigeko N. Fukai, "The Impact of Changes in the International System on Domestic Politics: Japan in the 1990s," in Yoshinobu Yamamoto (ed.) *Globalism, Regionalism, and Nationalism: Asia in Search of Its Role in the Twenty-first Century*, Oxford: Blackwell, 1999, pp. 199–225.

20 T. J. Pempel, *The Politics of the Asian Economic Crisis*, Ithaca: Cornell University Press, 1999.
21 Akihiko Tanaka, "Domestic Politics and Foreign Policy," in Inoguchi Takashi and Pumendra Jain, *Japanese Foreign Policy Today*, New York: Palgrave, 2000, pp. 3–17.
22 Robert Pekkanen and Ellis S. Krauss, "Japan's 'Coalition of the Willing' on Security Policies," *Orbis*, Summer 2005.
23 Fukai, "The Impact of Changes in the International System on Domestic Politics," in Yoshinobu Yamamoto, *Globalism, Regionalism, and Nationalism*, pp. 199–225.
24 Akihiko Tanaka, "Domestic Politics and Foreign Policy," in Takashi and Jain, *Japanese Foreign Policy Today*, pp. 3–17.
25 Ichiro Ozawa, *Blueprint for a New Japan: The Rethinking of a Nation*, Louisa Rubinfien (trans.) and Eric Gower (ed), New York: Kodansha International, 1994.
26 Howard W. French, "By Playing at 'Rage' China Dramatizes Its Rise," *New York Times*, 21 April 2005, sec. A4. About 28,000 Japanese companies employ more than 1 million people in China.
27 Stephan Haggard, Richard N. Cooper, and Chung-in Moon, in Robert Bates and Anne O. Krueger (eds), *The Politics of Economic Policy Reform*, Oxford: Basil Blackwell, 1993, pp. 294–6; Chung Hee Park, *To Build a Nation*, Washington: Acropolis Books, 1971; Chung Hee Park, *Toward Peaceful Unification: Selected Speeches*, Seoul: Kwangmyong Publishing, 1976; Chung Hee Park, *Korea Reborn: A Model for Development*, Englewood Cliffs, NJ: Prentice-Hall, 1979; Alice H. Amsden, *Asia's Next Giant: South Korea and Late Industrialization*, New York: Oxford University Press 1989. Tun-jen Cheng; Chung-in Moon and Stephen Haggard, "Institutions and Economic Policy: Theory and a Korean Case Study," *World Politics*, Vol. 42, No. 2 (January 1990): 210–38. For a more complete treatment of domestic-external interactions in South and North Korea, see Etel Solingen, *Regional Orders at Century's Dawn: Global and Domestic Influences on Grand Strategy*, Princeton: Princeton University Press, 1998, pp. 62–87.
28 Park, *To Build a Nation*, pp. 172–3.
29 Byung-Sun Choi, *Economic Policymaking in Korea: Institutional analysis of economic policy changes in the 1970s and 1980s*, S.I.: s.n., 1990, pp. 27–9; Byung Chul Koh, "The Foreign Policy Systems of North and South Korea," *Foreign Affairs*, September 1998, p. 215.
30 U.S Arms Control and Disarmament Agency, *ACDA Annual Report*, 1990; International Institute of Strategic Studies, *The Military Balance 1995-6*, p. 266; Byung Chul Koh, "The Foreign Policy Systems of North and South Korea," pp. 210–11; Chung-in Moon, and In Taek Hyun, "Muddling Through Security, Growth and Welfare: The Political Economy of Defense Spending in South Korea," in Steve Chan and Alex Mintz (eds) *Defense, Welfare and Growth*, London: Routledge, 1992, pp. 137–62; Nicole Ball, *Security and Economy in the Third World*, Princeton: Princeton University Press, 1988, p. 54.
31 Park, *To Build a Nation*, p. 99; and Park, *Korea Reborn*, pp. 50–6, 90, 120–4.
32 Jang Jip Choi, "Political Cleavages in South Korea," in Hagen Koo (ed.) *State and Society in Contemporary Korea*, Ithaca, Cornell University Press, 1993, pp. 29–32, 44–6.
33 Bernard Kirshner, "Kim Dae Jung: Linking Liberal democracy to Economic Growth in South Korea," *Los Angeles Times*, 11 January 1998, sec. M3.
34 James Brooke, "Tentatively, North Korea Solicits Foreign Investment and Tourism," *New York Times*, 19 February 2002, sec. C1.
35 Tun-jen Cheng, "Institutions and Economic Policy: Theory and a Korean Case Study," p. 154; Bruce Cumings, "The Origins and Development of the Northeast Asian Political Economy: Industrial Sectors, Product Cycles, and Political Consequences," *International Organization*, Vol. 38, No. 1, Winter, 1984, pp. 1–40.

36 Cheng, "Institutions and Economic Policy: Theory and a Korean Case Study," p. 158; Jei Guk Jeon, "Exploring the Three Varieties of East Asia's State-Guided Development Model: Korea, Singapore, and Taiwan," *Studies in Comparative International Development*, Vol. 30, No. 3, Fall 1995, pp. 70–88.

37 Stephan Haggard, *Developing Nations and the Politics of Global Integration*, Washington D.C.: Brookings Institution, 1995, p. 129; Steve Chan, "Defense Burden and Economic Growth: Unraveling the Taiwanese Enigma," *American Political Science Review, Vol* 82, 1988, pp. 913–20; Colin I. Bradford, Jr., "Policy Interventions and Markets: Development Strategy Typologies and Policy Options," in Gary Gereffi and Donald L. Wyman, eds. *Manufacturing Miracles – Paths of Industrialization in Latin America and East Asia*, Princeton, N.J.: Princeton University Press, 1990, p. 38.

38 See Amsden, *Asia's Next Giant*; and Cheng, "Institutions and Economic Policy: Theory and a Korean Case Study," p. 155.

39 Cumings, "The Origins and Development of the Northeast Asian Political Economy," p. 26; Steve Chan, "Military burden, economic growth, and income inequality: the Taiwan exception." in Steve Chan and Alex Mintz, eds., *Defense, Welfare, and Growth*, London: Routledge, 1992, p. 167; UNDP-United Nations Development Programme, *Human development Report 1994*, New York: Oxford University Press, 1994, p.170 and International Institute of Strategic Studies, *The Military Balance 1995–6*, 1995, pp. 266-7.

40 Lewis A. Dunn, *Controlling the Bomb*, New Haven: Yale University Press, 1982, pp. 56–7.

41 Dittmer, "The Transformation of Chinese Foreign Policy," (in this volume); Geoffrey Lamb and Valeriana Kallab (eds), *Military Expenditure and Economic Development: A symposium on research issues*, Washington D.C.: World Bank, 1992, p. 70.

42 Interviews by Author, Beijing, 11–14 December 2003, 9–11 August 2004.

43 Thomas J. Christensen, "Posing Problems without Catching Up: China's Rise and Challenges for U.S. Security," *International Security*, Vol. 25, No. 4, Spring 2001, pp. 5-40; Sheldon Simon, "Southeast Asia" in Richard Ellings and Aaron Friedberg, eds., *Strategic Asia: Power and Purpose, 2001–2002*, Seattle: The National Bureau of Asian Research, 2001, p. 284. On pressure on Jiang Zemin as "soft" on Taiwan by retired generals, see Friedman, "The Fragility of China's Regional Cooperation" (in this volume).

44 IISS (International Institute of Strategic Studies), *The Military Balance 2003–04*, 2003. As Henry Kissinger recognized, China's military expenditures were neglected during the first phase of its economic reform but are now ahead of Japan's. See Henry Kissinger, "Containment Won't Work," *Washington Post*, 13 June 2005. Online. Available HTTP: <http://www.washingtonpost.com/wp-dyn/content/article/2005/06/12/AR2005061201533.html> (accessed 14 June 2005).

45 Jim Yardley, "Chinese Police Head off Anti-Japan protests," *New York Times*, 5 May 2005, sec. A8.

46 "China passes Taiwan law," *Daily Yomiuri*, 15 March 2005, sec. 1.

47 Joseph Kahn, "China Propaganda Office May be Censoring the Premier," *New York Times*, 16 March 2005, sec. A3.

48 Howard W. French, "China Opens a Window on the Really Big Ideas," *New York Times*, 2 June 2004, sec. A4.

49 Han S. Park (ed.) *North Korea: Ideology, politics, economy*, Englewood Cliffs, NJ: Prentice Hall, 1996, p. 2; Bruce Cumings, "The Corporate State in North Korea" in Hagen Koo (ed.) *State and Society in Contemporary Korea*, Ithaca, Cornell University Press, 1993, pp. 197–230., 204–7, 214–15, 223–4.

50 Andrew Pollack, "Nuclear Fears? Noodle Sales Say No," *The New York Times*, 9 May 1994, p.A3; Hazel Smith, "The Democratic People's Republic of North Korea and Its Foreign Policy in the 1990s," in Chan and Williams, eds., *Renegade States: The evolution of revolutionary foreign policy,* Manchester and New York: Manchester

University Press, 1994, p.10; Vasily Mikheev, "Politics and Ideology in the Post Cold War Era" in Han S. Park, ed., *North Korea: Ideology, Politics, Economics,* Englewood Cliffs, NJ: Prentice Hall, 1996, p. 92.

51 Jong-Chun Baek, *Probe for Korean Reunification*, Korea: Research Center for Peace and Unification of Korea, 1988, p. 169. On military expenditures, see International Institute of Strategic Studies, *The Military Balance 1995–6*, p. 266; Kiwon Chung, "The North Korean People's Army and the Party," *The China Quarterly*, No. 14, April 1963, pp. 119–20; Iuli Banchev, "Prerogatives of the New Foreign Economic Policy Making," in Han S. Park, ed., *North Korea: Ideology, Politics, Economics,* Englewood Cliffs, NJ: Prentice Hall, 1996, pp. 195, 226.

52 Exports reached about $2 billion at the end of the 1980s down to $1 billion by the mid-1990s.

53 Mikheev, "Politics and Ideology," op.cit.; Byung-joon Ahn, "The man who would be Kim: The future of North Korea under Kim Jong Il, son of the late Korean leader Kim Il Sung," *Foreign Affairs*, Vol. 73, No. 6, November–December 1994, pp. 94–109.; Takashi Sakai, "The Power Base of Kim Jong Il: Focusing on Its Formation Process" in Han S. Park, ed., *North Korea: Ideology, Politics, Economics,* Englewood Cliffs, NJ: Prentice Hall, 1996, pp. 106–22; Michael J. Mazarr, *North Korea and the Bomb: A Case Study in Nonproliferation*, Houndmills, Basingstoke, Hampshire and London: Macmillan, 1995, pp. 166–7; Byung-joon Ahn, "Who is Kim Jong Il," *World Press Review*, Vol. 41, No. 9, September 1994, pp. 18–20.

54 See Susumu Yamakage, "Nihon-ASEAN kankei no shinka to henyo" (Deepening and Transforming the Japan-ASEAN relationship), in Susumu Yamakage (ed.) *Higashi Asia Chiikishugi to Nihon Gaigo* (*East Asian Regionalism and Japanese Diplomacy*), Tokyo: Japan Institute for International Affairs, 2003; and Sung Chull Kim, "Introduction: Multilayered Domestic-Regional Linkages" (in this volume).

55 See T. J. Pempel, *Remapping Asia*.

56 Interviews by Author, Tokyo, June 2003, July–August 2004.

57 Interviews by Author, Bangkok and Tokyo, June–July 2003.

58 See Susan Shirk, *How China Opened its Door: The Political Success of the PRC's Foreign Trade and Investment Reforms*, Washington D.C.: Brookings Institution, 1994; and Alastair I. Johnston, "The Myth of the ASEAN Way? Explaining the Evolution of the ASEAN Regional Forum," in Helga Haftendorn, Robert O. Keohane, and Celeste A. Wallander (eds) *Imperfect Unions: Security Institutions over Time and Space*, New York: Oxford University Press, 1999, pp. 287–324.

59 See Shirk, *How China Opened its Door*, 1994; and Alastair I. Johnston, "The Myth of the ASEAN Way? Explaining the Evolution of the ASEAN Regional Forum," in Helga Haftendorn, Robert O. Keohane, and Celeste A. Wallander, eds. *Imperfect Unions: Security Institutions over Time and Space*, New York: Oxford University Press, 1999, pp. 287–324. Simon (2001:284) argues, the PLA has resisted any disclosure by China of its order of battle, future arms acquisition plans, or full participation in the UN Conventional Arms Register or a Regional Arms Register.

60 Thomas J. Christensen, "China, the U.S.-Japan Alliance, and the Security Dilemma in East Asia," *International Security*, Vol. 23, No. 4, Spring 1999, pp. 49–80.

61 Interviews by Author, Singapore, May 2004.

62 Haruki Wada, "Envisioning a Northeast Asian Community: Regional and Domestic Factors to Consider" (in this volume).

63 Interviews by Author, Tokyo, 22 July and 18 August 2004.

2 Envisioning a Northeast Asian community: regional and domestic factors to consider

Haruki Wada

Northeast Asia[1] is a unique place where the notion of regional community-building has been neglected even during the post-Cold War era. There are reasons for the uniqueness. Northeast Asia is a heterogeneous region in terms of culture, history, politics, and social background. Furthermore, the region has been rife with conflicts. Co-existence has not been peaceful in this stretch of land where East Asian, Russo–Eurasian, and Western values come together. Other divisive elements, alongside cultural diversity, have promoted contention in the region. There are the former imperialist aggressors (Russia and Japan) and their victims (China and Korea). There is great distrust among the remaining socialist countries (North Korea and China), former socialist countries (Mongolia and Russia), and capitalist countries (Japan, South Korea, and the United States). There are three longstanding nuclear powers (the United States, Russia, and China) that have experienced bitter rivalries with one another, and a recent nuclear power (North Korea) that contributes to the instability. There are two divided countries (Korea and China). There are three widely known territorial controversies (the northern four islands dispute between Japan and Russia, the Takeshima/Dokdo dispute between Japan and Korea, and the Senkaku/Diaoyu Islands dispute between Japan and China). Moreover, various lingering historical issues continue to divide the peoples of Northeast Asia. Both its pronounced heterogeneity and its embittering contentiousness have discouraged Northeast Asia from any attempt to build a genuine regional community.

The purpose of this chapter is to historically survey discussions on regionalism and regional community-building in Northeast Asia and barriers to development. First, the historical survey starts with Japan's wartime slogan of "Greater East Asia Co-prosperity Sphere," which brought about long-term indifference towards regionalism, not to mention a regional community, in Northeast Asian countries in the postwar period. Second, the analysis focuses on the proposals for a Northeast Asian community, presented by certain political leaders and myself in the post-Cold War era. The proposals not only reflected intellectual efforts for envisioning a regional community in times of transition in international relations but also mirrored changes in domestic politics, for example, democratic consolidation in South Korea. Third, this chapter examines the nature of two outstanding issues awaiting resolution before community building: North Korea's nuclear crisis and Japan's recognition of the past militarism. Finally, it points out logical linkage between building Northeast Asian community and the emerging East Asian community.

Lingering memory of the past

The people in this region have experienced the ill effects of the previously practiced regionalism. Indeed, persistent memories of these effects have hindered discussions about a new regionalism. The memories derive chiefly from Japan's invasion of its neighbors. Expanding the war from Manchuria into the Chinese mainland, Japanese Prime Minister Konoe Fumimaro declared, on 3 November 1938, that the aim of the Japanese war was the "construction of a new order in East Asia in order to secure the eternal stability of the region." According to him, the realization of this goal depended on the cooperation between three countries: Japan, Manchukuo, and China. In that year, Japanese intellectuals began to talk about the "East Asian Community" (Toua Kyodotai). The first leading article on the subject, "A Theory of the East Asian Community," was published in the November issue of *Kaizo* (*Reorganization*) by Royama Masamichi, a professor at Tokyo Imperial University. Criticizing Chinese nationalism, he maintained that the principle intended by Japanese continental expansion was, unlike that of Western imperialism, based on regional defense and development. Royama asserted that the East Asian Community was to include the Japanese Empire and its colonies of Korea and Taiwan, as well as Manchukuo and China.[2] On 1 August 1940, Japanese Foreign Minister Matsuoka Yosuke issued a statement according to which Japan would endeavor to build a "Greater East Asia Co-prosperity Sphere" (Daitoua Kyoeiken), including not only Japan, Manchukuo, and China but also Southeast Asia and India. This slogan became one of the official war aims after the Japanese government's declaration of war against the United States and Great Britain on 12 December 1941.[3]

The two slogans—"East Asian Community" and "Greater East Asia Co-prosperity Sphere"—proved to be nothing but embellishments that camouflaged Japanese aggression against China and the war in Southeast Asia. With Japan's defeat and surrender in August 1945, the two slogans ceased to exist. Japanese people wanted to forget the whole story of their wartime regionalism, and since then they have given regionalism hardly a passing thought. Also, East Asian people not only indignantly rejected these deceptive Japanese slogans but they have also long refused to listen to arguments for a new regionalism. Many East Asians believe that the notion of regionalism *per se* harbors remnants of past militarist regionalism. Even a half century after the end of World War Two, these negative memories of regionalism, and particularly of the Japanese war, foster and preserve among the peoples of East Asian countries a deep resentment toward Japan. In this respect, Japan has never been entitled to take the initiative in proposing, much less in building, a regional community. Only if Japan feels remorse for its past history and sincerely apologizes for past wars and for colonial rule shall it gain the trust of neighboring East Asian peoples and play a role in the development of a regional community.

Even after the defeat of Japanese imperialism, peace did not prevail in Northeast Asia. Communist countries and anti-communist countries waged three wars: the Civil War in China, the Korean War, and the Vietnam War. What is notable is that, waged in Southeast Asia, the Vietnam War nevertheless involved all the powers of Northeast Asia. The anti-communist forces were joined by US and South Korean forces and were assisted by Japan, whereas the communist forces were assisted by the Soviets, the Chinese, and the North Koreans. During the thirty-year stretch of wars, which lasted from 1946 to 1975, the only existing regional cooperation was the anti-communist and anti-Chinese military alliance in which the United States always maintained supremacy. With the birth of the Southeast Asia Treaty Organization in September 1954, the communist countries in the region came to be in trouble.[4] North Korea began to speak out against the United States' preparation for the Northeast Asia Treaty Organization (NEATO) in the early 1960s, when negotiations for normalization between South Korea and Japan proceeded. The view of North Korea was shared by the Japanese Communist Party and propagated widely by the mass campaign against the Japan–South Korea normalization.[5] In this way, for the first time since the end of World War Two, the notion of Northeast Asia (Tohoku Azia) was pierced through with negative connotations, at least in the political context. But once the Japan–South Korea treaty was concluded and mass protests receded, the ghost of NEATO disappeared.

Envisioning regional community

The Common House of Northeast Asia

The thirty consecutive years of war in East Asia showed signs of abatement after President Nixon's visit to Beijing in 1972 and came to an end with the fall of Saigon in 1975. New political circumstances fueled arguments in the 1980s about the necessity of regional cooperation in Northeast Asia. In Japan, several prefectural and municipal authorities endeavored to initiate economic cooperation among prefectures and cities surrounding the Japanese Sea (or the "East Sea," as Koreans would refer to it in English). Matsue City of Shimane Prefecture took the lead in holding the Matsue International Conference for Friendship Surrounding the Japanese Sea (Kannihonkai Matsue kokusaikoryu kaigi) in 1986. Owing to this Conference, the term "Sphere of Economic Cooperation Surrounding the Japanese Sea" (Kannihonkai keizaiken) became popular, although Koreans expressed their displeasure with this term and attempted to replace it with the term "Economic Cooperation of Northeast Asia." It was in 1990 when Niigata City and Niigata Prefecture organized the annual Niigata Economic Conference of Northeast Asia, inviting Russian, Chinese, and both North and South Korean representatives to the event. In 1993, eight other prefectures on the coast of the Japanese Sea joined Niigata Prefecture and Niigata City to establish an institute named the Economic Research Institute of Northeast Asia.

The notion of Northeast Asian economic cooperation spread widely both in the northeast part of China and in South Korea. In 1988, research centers whose main focus would be Northeast Asia were set up in Jilin Province and Jilin University. They began to publish magazines entitled "Study of Northeast Asia" from 1990 and "Northeast Asian Forum" from 1992. Similar research institutes were established in Liaoning Province in 1990 and in Beijing University in 1993. During this initial phase, the main agendas were the economic development in the Tumen River area and the foundation of the Northeast Asia Development Bank. But it is regrettable that such efforts have not yet brought about satisfactory results.[6] A visible success of Northeast Asian cooperation in the initial phase was achieved in environmental cooperation. In 1992, the Northeast Asian Conference on Environmental Cooperation got underway and hosted government representatives of China, South Korea, Japan, Mongolia, and Russia. In 1993, the Northeast Asian Subregional Program on Environmental Cooperation began operating and received assistance from the Economic and Social Commission for Asia and the Pacific, which is a United Nations department. And in 1999, China, South Korea, and Japan agreed to regular annual Tripartite Environment Ministers Meetings.[7]

In scholarly circles, Kim Young-ho, a South Korean scholar, pioneered the idea of such regional conferences. It was in Japan in 1991 that he first voiced his related hopes and concerns, which gained significant public attention when they appeared on the pages of the Japanese journal *Keizai Hyoron* (*Economic Review*).[8] Kim discussed this issue with economists Kenichi Honda and Pak Il, the latter of whom, a Korean–Japanese scholar, paid particular attention to the role of Koreans living in each country of this region.

Since 1990, I have, among others, proposed the organizing of a regional community in Northeast Asia, naming it the "Common House of Northeast Asia." The first occasion on which I spoke about my idea of the Common House was the Japanese–Korean Symposium jointly organized by *Donga Ilbo* and *Asahi Shimbun* in Seoul in 1990. There I proposed the Common House for Mankind in Northeast Asia by suggesting that "a new alliance of the Soviet Union, China, South and North Korea, the United States, and Japan in Northeast Asia can be called a house where peoples of the world live together and where the rapprochement and the merger of South–North Korea, on the basis of democracy, constitute the core of that house." The second occasion on which I proposed my idea of the Common House was at the Symposium of the "Reunification of Korea and the Future of the Twenty-first Century of Korea" organized by the Policy Committee of the Democratic Party, South Korea, on 31 May 1994. In the following year, I published an article entitled "A Common House of Northeast Asia and the Korean Peninsula" in the journal *Changjak kwa Pipyong*.[9] This article contained a systematic description of my idea. The term "Common House" is taken from Mikhail Gorbachev's proposal for European regional cooperation. Borrowing Gorbachev's term, I intended to stress my idea's novelty in contrast to the notorious "Greater East Asia Co-prosperity Sphere."

It is generally thought that the two Koreas, Japan, China, and Russia make up Northeast Asia. However, the United States should be acknowledged as a constituent member of this regional cooperation. One cannot and need not deny the reality of the presence of eighty thousand American soldiers in the region. Also, big islands, such as Taiwan, Okinawa, Sakhalin, the Kuriles, and Hawaii should be included as junior participants. Because of their historical past and the present composition of their inhabitants, these islands should become partners of the regional cooperation. Cheju Island may be supplemented to this list.

In this Common House of Northeast Asia, the Korean peninsula may play a key role. From ancient times, the Korean peninsula has been the bridge between continental China and the Japanese Islands. The Korean peninsula may link the continental countries, Russia and China, with the maritime countries, Japan and the United States. For this reason, the peninsula may become the center of this Common House. On the other hand, just as the Chinese diaspora dispersed in Southeast Asia, so too has the Korean diaspora spread throughout Northeast Asia. The Korean diaspora — some 2.04 million Korean-Chinese, 2.07 million Korean-Americans, 870 thousand Korean–Japanese, and 487 thousand Koreans in the Commonwealth of Independent States — can play a pivotal role for the Common House of Northeast Asia.

Sincerely wishing to gain support for my idea among Koreans, I continued to talk throughout the 1990s to Koreans about the Common House of Northeast Asia. But, at that time, my argument sounded like a pipe dream among both Koreans and Japanese. Also, Michio Morishima, a Japanese economist at the London School of Economics, repeatedly advocated after 1995 the necessity of a regional community that would include Japan, China, the Korean peninsula, and Taiwan. Morishima called it the "Asian Community" in 1995, the "Northeast Asian Community" in 1997, and finally the "East Asian Community" (EAC) in 2001.[10] But Morishima always lamented public indifference, including among Japanese people, to his proposal.

New perspective in the new century

With the beginning of the twenty-first century, regional thinking became a reasonable topic even in political circles. The first remarkable and positive momentum was provided by the Summits of ASEAN Plus Three (APT). ASEAN, which was inaugurated in August 1967, has taken sincere and constructive steps in promoting regional cooperation not only *within* but also *beyond* Southeast Asia. For instance, ASEAN countries became core members of APEC, organized in 1989. ASEAN took the initiative of organizing a forum on security issues affecting the Asia-Pacific region by establishing the ASEAN Regional Forum in 1994.

After such constructive activities, the ASEAN undertook a novel initiative for coping with the monetary and economic crisis in Asia, which struck the region in the summer of 1997. The initiative evolved through the APT, at whose second conference held in Hanoi in December 1998, the newly elected South Korean President Kim Dae-Jung proposed the establishment of the East Asian Vision

Group (EAVG). This group was to hold thorough discussions about how to overcome the economic crisis. The proposal was adopted and the EAVG was set up and was chaired by Han Song-Joo, former Foreign Minister of South Korea. In December 2001, on the occasion of the fifth conference, held in Kuala Lumpur, the EAVG presented its report entitled "Towards an East Asian Community: Region of Peace, Prosperity and Progress." This report begins with the following sentiments: "We, the people of East Asia, aspire to create an East Asian community of peace, prosperity and progress based on the full development of all peoples in the region. Concurrent with this vision is the goal that the future of the East Asian community will make a positive contribution to the rest of the world."[11]

This report presented a number of proposals covering economic, financial, political, environmental, social, cultural, and educational aspects. Among them, it is notable that the EAVG called for "the evolution of the annual summit meetings of the APT into the East Asian Summit."[12] This was a bold recommendation that has brought about the conceivable evolution of a regional community. As the recommendation was welcomed by heads of the APT, the notion of an East Asian Community gained currency in the public sphere and may concretize with economic cooperation among related countries. The EAC comprises ASEAN countries plus China, South Korea, and Japan. Indeed, this proposal has had a great impact on the region's countries.

The next significant event was the Japan–North Korea Summit in Pyongyang. Japan's Prime Minister Junichiro Koizumi and North Korea's National Defense Commission Chairman Kim Jong Il met on September 17, 2002. They concluded the summit by adopting the Pyongyang Declaration, in which the two leaders expressed their determination to take every possible step toward an early normalization between the two countries. This declaration included a paragraph-length pledge to cooperate in regional security affairs:

> Both sides confirmed that they would cooperate with each other in order to maintain and strengthen the peace and stability of North East Asia. Both sides confirmed the importance of establishing cooperative relationships based upon mutual trust among countries concerned in this region, and shared the recognition that it is important to have a framework in place in order for these regional countries to promote confidence-building, as the relationships among these countries are normalized.
>
> (Ministry of Foreign Affairs, Japan)[13]

At the summit, Prime Minister Koizumi said, and Chairman Kim Jong Il agreed, that it was "important for a place to be found where talks could take place between the six parties."[14] The six parties consisted of North Korea, South Korea, the United States, China, Japan, and Russia. The Japan–North Korea Summit and the Pyongyang Declaration were the first occasions on which Japan raised the banner of new regionalism. Until this time, Japan had turned its back to regionalist thinking for almost five decades because of the wartime fiasco of the

"Greater East Asia Co-prosperity Sphere" and because of the postwar US–Japan security alliance. The summit and the declaration were, together, a significant step toward a new regionalism in the sense that Japan dared to shake hands with its longtime adversary North Korea. But after the Summit, a public backlash swept over Japan because of the emergence of two issues: the issue of North Korean agents' abduction of Japanese citizens in the 1970s and the 1980s and the issue of North Korea's nuclear weapons development. Nevertheless, the horizon of new regionalism, once opened up, was not to be sealed off.

Roh Moo-hyun and the age of Northeast Asia

In his inauguration speech delivered on 25 February 2003, the newly elected South Korean president Roh Moo-hyun proposed a new idea for the Northeast Asian community.[15] Roh appeared to be a strong champion of a new regionalism in Northeast Asia and of South Korean initiatives for regional community-building. He stated,

> The Age of Northeast Asia is fast approaching. Northeast Asia, which used to be on the periphery of the modern world, is now emerging as a new source of energy in the global economy.... The Korean Peninsula is located at the heart of the region. It is a big bridge linking China and Japan, the continent and the ocean. Such a geopolitical characteristic often caused pain for us in the past. Today, however, this same feature is offering us an opportunity. Indeed, it demands that we play a pivotal role in the Age of Northeast Asia in the twenty-first century.... Initially, the dawn of the Age of Northeast Asia will come from the economic field. Nations of the region will first form a 'community of prosperity', and through it, contribute to the prosperity of all humanity and, in time, should evolve into a 'community of peace'. For a long time, I had a dream of seeing a regional community of peace and co-prosperity in Northeast Asia like the European Union. The Age of Northeast Asia will then finally come to full fruition. I pledge to devote my whole heart and efforts to bringing about that day at the earliest possible time.
>
> (Roh Moo-hyun, *Press Statement*)

This speech is a clear landmark along the path to community-building in Northeast Asia. What is noteworthy in the speech is not only that the Korean peninsula is located at the core of the community-building but also that for this reason, South Korea should step forward and take the initiative. Considering that in South Korea, which has long remained a middle-state, its president approached his inaugural stage as an advocate of the Northeast Asian community, one can conclude with reason that the nation's history concurrently entered a new phase. It was not until June 2004 that Roh Moo-hyun took concrete measures for the implementation of this idea by establishing the Committee of the

Age of Northeast Asia, headed by Moon Chung-in, a professor at Yonsei University.

A half year later, a conspicuous event occurred in Northeast Asia. The Six-Party Talks were launched in an effort to solve the problem of North Korea's nuclear development. In the midst of the second North Korean nuclear crisis, which erupted in 2002, representatives of the two Koreas, Japan, China, Russia, and the United States gathered in Beijing on August 27, 2003. It makes sense, then, to refer to the Six-Party Talks as the Northeast Asian nuclear talks. It was the first time in history that the six countries met together to discuss a security-related issue. Although the multilateral meeting took place at a precarious moment, its success might develop directly into regional security cooperation. The important task of the Six-Party Talks has been to identify how North Korea can be persuaded to dismantle its nuclear weapons program and, in turn, how to induce the United States government to promise not to attack North Korea. It seems that Northeast Asia now appears to be the forefront of regional security cooperation.

Discussions about East Asian community

Steadfast efforts to establish a viable East Asian community were made in 2003. The establishment of the Network of East Asian Think Tanks (NEAT) in Beijing on September 30, 2003, was based on a proposal of the EAVG, according to which the regional networking of think tanks should "explore long-term policy issues of strategic importance to the region."[16] The Chinese government reissued the adoption of this proposal in the May 2003 meeting of foreign ministers of the APT. Finally, the secretariat of the NEAT was set up in the Social Science Academy of China.[17]

Following this move, the East Asian Forum was established in Seoul on December 16, 2003. This move was based partly on an EAVG proposal, which recommended the inclusion of not only governmental officials but also non-governmental representatives from various sectors, all of whom might contribute to the development of an institutional mechanism for broad-based social exchanges and, ultimately, for regional cooperation.[18] President Roh Moo-hyun, along with former President Kim Dae-Jung, joined each other at the inaugural meeting to display the strong will of the South Korean government to actively participate in this move.[19]

Again in December 2003, the Japan–ASEAN Tokyo Declaration for the Dynamic and Enduring Japan–ASEAN Partnership in the New Millennium was issued. Since that time, the Japanese government has made some effort to play a role in preparations to launch the East Asian community. Meanwhile, the Japanese government has attempted to gauge the Chinese government's attitude toward, and involvement in, the issue of the East Asian community. On December 11 and 12, the government heads of Japan and member countries of the ASEAN gathered in Tokyo for the Japan–ASEAN Commemorative Summit and adopted the Tokyo Declaration. In the Declaration, Japan and the ASEAN countries rec-

ognized that the APT process is an important channel through which these countries can promote cooperation and regional economic integration networks in East
Asia, and perhaps even realize the goals of sustainable development and common
prosperity. Also, the countries' representatives declared that they would seek to
build "an East Asian community which is outward-looking, endowed with the
exuberance of creativity and vitality and with the shared spirit of mutual understanding... upholding Asian traditions and values, while respecting universal
rules and principles."[20]

The Tokyo Declaration was the first official declaration by the Japanese government that, alongside ASEAN countries, it would contribute to the building of
an East Asian community. Because of China's absence from this declaration, the
significance of which was largely symbolic for Japan, Tokyo has been pressed to
go along with China in building the East Asian community. For this reason, the
Council on East Asian Community (CEAC) was established as an organization
that would promote discussions about the East Asian community in Japan. Ito
Kenichi, President of the Japan International Forum, joined the inaugural meeting of NEAT in Beijing, where Chinese eagerness impressed the Japanese representatives. After returning home, Ito attempted to establish a Japanese
organization for the community-building in East Asia. Supported by various people, Ito finally succeeded in establishing the CEAC on May 18, 2004. For its
membership, the CEAC, headed by President Nakasone Yasuhiro (the former
prime minister) and Chairman Ito, gathered 40 intellectuals, together with representatives of 11 Japanese think tanks and 13 successful companies. By the spring
of 2005, the CEAC decided to write the policy-oriented report entitled "East
Asian Community and the State Strategy of Japan." The report's task force has
been led by Professor Tanaka Akihiko.[21]

What is noteworthy is the speech made by the third top official in the Foreign
Ministry, Tanaka Hitoshi, at the first policy meeting of the CEAC held on June
24, 2004 in the Foreign Ministry. On the necessity of the East Asian community,
he mentioned the following three points: (1) the East Asian community is in
Japan's medium- and long-term national interests; (2) it is necessary to create a
system in which Japan cooperates with China; and (3) it is necessary to temper
"nationalism without aims," which is "a very unhealthy nationalism." According
to Tanaka, the East Asian community is a movement that absorbs such nationalisms and that points them toward constructive aims. He argued that concrete
measures for both the mitigation of threats and the expansion of mutual dependency are needed. It seems that Tanaka proposed a combination of functionalist
and systemic approaches that would cultivate a sense of unity; and it seems that
he also pointed out the need to define both the concept of community and membership in the community.[22]

In 2004, the APT discussed the issue of the East Asian Summit and decided to
hold the first summit in Kuala Lumpur in December 2005. In line with this development, the new year editorial of *Asahi Shimbun* mentioned that the year of 2005
will be the first year of the East Asian community. Also, Prime Minister Koizumi
stated in his general policy speech to the House of Representatives on January 20,

2005 that he would play an active role in constructing the East Asian community and that Japan should share common economic prosperity, while fostering diversity.[23] Koizumi's speech has had significant political implications in the sense that it was uttered by the head of the Japanese government sixty years after both the humiliation of military defeat and the collapse of the Greater East Asia Co-prosperity Sphere. But Koizumi's mention of the regional community was totally ignored by the mass media. No newspaper commented on it. This glaring neglect was the result of serious obstacles that I analyze in the following section.

Obstacles to the emergence of regional community

The North Korean crisis

In Northeast Asia, two serious obstacles now hinder the evolution of a regional community: the North Korean crisis and the Japan problem. North Korea poses the greatest difficulties in this region. The North Korean crisis consists of the development of nuclear weapons and the domestic economic distress.

North Korea has regarded the United States as its main enemy—as the chief threat to its security. During the Cold War era, the United States, the ally of South Korea, was a nuclear superpower. Consequently, North Korea felt that its safety could be secured only under the nuclear umbrella of the Soviet Union. But when the Soviet Union expressed its willingness to establish diplomatic relations with South Korea, North Korea feared that the Soviets would no longer provide it with protection from a US-based nuclear attack. On September 2, 1990, the North Korean foreign minister handed to the Soviet foreign minister a memorandum in which North Korea's basic will was expressed as follows: "If the Soviet Union is to start diplomatic relations with South Korea, it will practically annul the Korean–Soviet Mutual Aid and Cooperation Treaty. Then we are obliged to make arrangements to procure some sorts of weapons for which we hitherto depended on our counterpart by this treaty."[24] It is reasonable to think that, since then, North Korea has been obsessed by the idea of possessing nuclear weapons. As the national resources of North Korea deteriorated in the 1990s and the early 2000s, its obsession with nuclear weapons expanded.

The first nuclear crisis of 1993–1994 was resolved owing to former President Carter's visit to Pyongyang. The Agreed Framework was signed between the United States and North Korea in October 1994. The North Korean government hoped to translate this achievement into a higher degree of reconciliation between the two countries in 2000, but these hopes were in vain. With George W. Bush's victory in the 2000 presidential election, the bilateral relations worsened. In a speech made in January 2002, President Bush referred to North Korea as part of the "the axis of evil." In the same year, the United States government began to suspect that North Korea had started a uranium enrichment program. On the occasion of his visit to Pyongyang in October 2002, Assistant Secretary of State James Kelly informed the North Korean government of this suspicion and of his government's related concerns. Kelly later informed the media that Kang Sok-Ju, the

First Deputy Foreign Minister of North Korea, had acknowledged the existence of his country's uranium enrichment program. This was the beginning of the second nuclear crisis of North Korea.

However, North Korea issued its own public statements. On October 25, 2002, the spokesman of the Foreign Ministry denied the existence of the uranium enrichment program and remarked that North Korean negotiators had "made it clear that the DPRK was entitled to possess not only nuclear weapons but any other type of weapon more powerful than those so as to defend its sovereignty and right of existence." [25] As a response, the United States government decided to halt shipments of heavy oil to North Korea, a move that prompted North Korea to withdraw from the Nuclear Non-Proliferation Treaty and to end the freeze on its reactor at Yongbyon. Finally, North Korea admitted that it had nuclear deterrent potential.

The Bush administration has refused to engage in bilateral negotiations with North Korea. The American high-tech military campaign in the Iraq War might have terrified North Korea so that the latter was obliged to accept the Chinese arrangement of tripartite talks in Beijing in April 2003, which were expanded into the Six-Party Talks later. The first Six-Party Talks began in Beijing on August 27, 2003 but failed to bring about any concrete result. The United States demanded a complete, verifiable, irreversible dismantlement of the North Korean nuclear program, whereas North Korea demanded an agreement of step-by-step solutions with the United States. The two adversaries' seemingly incompatible standpoints remained a major obstacle throughout the talks.

At the end of 2003, President Bush won a second presidential term. Bush swore in his inaugural speech that he would fight for the dissemination of freedom with all his might. The newly appointed secretary of state, Condoleeza Rice, identified North Korea as one of the five "outposts of tyranny" in her January speech at Capitol Hill. On February 10, 2005, the North Korean Foreign Ministry issued a statement that it would not participate in the Six-Party Talks, declaring its possession of nuclear weapons. Meanwhile, North Korea demanded that the United States withdraw such wording as "outposts of tyranny." [26] As China persuaded the United States to change its attitude and its policy toward North Korea, the United States government made contacts with North Korean representatives in New York to inform them that it would refer to North Korea as a sovereign state. As a result, in July 2005, North Korea returned to Beijing to join in further Six-Party Talks. Despite honest and sincere discussions between the United States and North Korea, this round of Six-Party Talks made no real progress because, at the final stage, North Korea insisted that it has a right to peaceful use of nuclear energy. The Six-Party Talks were temporarily suspended until the end of August, a situation that raised skepticism as to whether the resumed talks would lead to a breakthrough in the nuclear crisis.

Nevertheless, the North Korean nuclear crisis may pave a way for regional cooperation. If North Korea would abandon its nuclear program following the Joint Statement of the 4th Six-Party talks in September 2005, South Korea and Japan could provide the communist state with substantial economic aid, which is indispensable to the moribund economy. It is worth noting that, in addition to its offering of aid, Japan could establish diplomatic relations with North Korea.

North Korea has been experiencing serious economic distress in the post-Cold War era. The distress is due to the obsolescence of North Korea's current economic system, the abrupt suspension of North Korea's preferential trade status with the now-extinct Soviet Union, and the stoppages of imports of Russian machinery parts and raw materials. On top of the shortage problems, natural disasters in three consecutive years hit cities and villages and brought about a disastrous famine. Many people died out of hunger, and schools, hospitals, and factories stopped functioning. In this dire situation, China came to North Korea's assistance by providing the peninsular neighbor with a large amount of heavy oil and grain products.

On January 1, 2001, North Korea's three leading newspapers published a new year editorial in which a technology-driven reconstruction (*kegon* in Korean, meaning perestroika) of the economy was declared a national task and in which "new thinking" was recommended. The same editorial noted that modern technology can be brought in only from abroad.[27] Indeed, in July 2002, North Korea undertook a series of economic reforms, raising prices and wages radically as a reflection of market circumstances.[28] On the one hand, the successful realization of the radical reform measures requires supplements in the forms of investment by foreigners and expansion of external economic relations—supplements that themselves require improved relations between North Korea and its neighbors. On the other hand, the countries of Northeast Asia should acknowledge and act on their shared obligation to support the North Korean economy's recovery. In sum, if North Korea becomes a nuclear-free and economically developing country, then it qualifies for membership in the Northeast Asian community. In this respect, North Korea should pursue changes in its domestic situation and in its external policies for the sake of its survival and of regional cooperation.

The Japan problem

The second obstacle is the Japan problem. After Prime Minister Koizumi's official statement about the East Asian community in the spring of 2005, fierce anti-Japanese campaigns erupted in China and South Korea. If the Prime Minister had made up his mind to support a regional community, he should have consulted with his people and with neighboring countries. But he could not abandon his obsession with the visit to the Yasukuni Shrine despite persistent criticisms from these neighboring countries. Most Chinese can never reconcile themselves with Koizumi's visit of the Yasukuni Shrine, where A-class war criminals were enshrined. And in South Korea, the Dokdo/Takeshima served to focus intense criticism on Japan. The Shimane prefectural council's passage of an ordinance establishing Takeshima Day (which commemorates Japan's seizure of the island) fueled Koreans' rage because, one hundred years after the fact, Koreans still strongly resent Japan's termination of Korean sovereignty. Furthermore, vehement voices were raised anew in both China and South Korea against new

Japanese history textbooks. In the spring of 2005, this aggravating issue surfaced on the diplomatic front when the Chinese campaigned against Japan's attempt to gain permanent membership on the United Nations Security Council.

After fifteen years of war, Japan's defeat in 1945 ushered in no revolutionary changes on the island-nation. The ancient regime survived under the occupation of the Allied Forces and remodeled itself in the new constitution, which was virtually presented by the GHQ of the Allied Forces. Emperor Hirohito remained on his throne, neither recognizing his own moral responsibility nor abdicating the throne. The three ministers who co-signed the Emperor's declaration of war in December 1941 returned, during the postwar period, to the political scene as Diet members under the constitution, and one of them, Kishi Nobusuke, even became Prime Minister in 1957. Despite its many superficial and substantial changes, postwar Japanese democracy retained many of its war actors and ideas.

In 1952, Japan concluded with Nationalist China the Sino–Japanese Peace Treaty, rejecting completely Nationalist China's demand for war reparations, which was a mere repetition of the corresponding clause of the San Francisco Peace Treaty. In 1965, Japan concluded the Japan–South Korea Treaty, which contained neither apologies nor compensation for Japan's colonization of the peninsula. Prime Minister Sato Eisaku declared in the Diet that the 1910 Annexation Treaty was concluded by parties that stood on equal footing and that acted out of free will. But it was not until 1972 that Japan for the first time expressed deep remorse to the Chinese people in a joint statement: "Japan feels responsible for the enormous damage it has inflicted on the people of China through war in the past, and expresses deep remorse for this." And yet, in return for this apology, China was obliged to abandon all rights to demand war reparations.[29] After the Vietnam War ended in 1975, Asian countries gradually began to reflect on their relations with Japan during the war in the Pacific and, indeed, issued critical statements regarding Japan's role therein. But Japanese prime ministers continued to couch their responses—which indicated a certain amount of remorse—in vague terms. Any radical change in Japanese attitudes toward Asian countries except China did not occur.

It was not until 1993 that a Japanese prime minister, Hosokawa Morihiro, presiding over the first coalitional cabinet that replaced the Liberal Democratic Party's government, mentioned the colonial rule as such, expressed feelings of remorse, and apologized for the damage and the pain inflicted by militarist Japan. In 1995, on the occasion of the fiftieth anniversary of the end of World War Two, the Liberal Democratic Party and the Social Democratic Party, in cooperation with each other, passed on June 9 a Diet resolution of remorse, which covered Japan's past wars and which contained Japan's vaguely worded admission that imperial Japan had brought pain to Asian nations through its colonial rule and its acts of aggression.[30]

On August 15, 1995, Prime Minister Murayama Tomiichi issued an official statement that was based on the cabinet decision and expressed his remorse and his apologies relative to imperial Japan's legacy:

During a certain period in the not too distant past, Japan, following a mis-taken national policy, advanced along the road to war, only to ensnare the Japanese people in a fateful crisis, and, through its colonial rule and aggres-sion, caused tremendous damage and suffering to the people of many countries, particularly to those of Asian nations. In the hope that no such mis-take be made in the future, I regard, in a spirit of humility, these irrefutable facts of history, and express here once again my feelings of deep remorse and state my heartfelt apology.

(Murayama Tomiichi, *Press Statement*)[31]

In addition to this statement, Murayama's government set up the Asian Women's Fund to convey to former wartime comfort women the Prime Minister's apology, Japan's national atonement, and governmental medical-welfare aid.

Following the end of both Japanese wars of aggression and Japanese colonial rule, significant expressions of remorse and apology from the Japanese govern-ment took fifty years to materialize. But these expressions of changed Japanese attitudes could not satisfy the victims abroad and the public at home for different reasons. On the one hand, it was natural that the victims considered this change to be too late and too little. At the same time, the Japanese government, in rela-tion to the issue of the Asian Women's Fund, became the target of harsh criticism from North Koreans, South Koreans, and Taiwanese. The Chinese abroad started to campaign against the Nanking massacre anew. Comparisons of Japan's and Germany's post-war measures became popular topics. There spread a stereotyped image about Japan, according to which Japan never learns from history and never apologizes for the past. On the other hand, a number of intellectuals and social activists at home remained unsympathetic toward the Asian Women's Fund. Moreover, right-wing forces, shocked by the prime minister's statement, began to criticize the apology for Japan's past and defended their interpretation of Japan's wartime objectives. Critics of the prime minister even organized campaigns in an attempt to undermine Japan's new official stance toward the imperial past. In this way, Prime Minister Murayama's statement was ignored at home and abroad.

It is widely understood that nations that have been invaded by and colonized by foreign aggressors suffer grave damage and deep pain, especially when the aggres-sors are neighbors with whom the victims have had long and close relations. Japanese aggression against China and its colonial rule over Korea are disasters that brought just such damage and pain to the two countries. It is perhaps the case that such pains can be neither forgotten nor forgiven. However, it is perhaps equally the case that the painful past can be overcome, or at least mitigated, only insofar as the related parties undertake a common effort to ensure a peaceful and just future. In order to engage in this effort, both the Japanese government and the Japanese people must make three indispensable offerings: an undiluted recogni-tion of the past, a sincere expression of remorse, and an unequivocal apology.

Despite the criticism, Murayama's 1995 statement of remorse and apology had attained such momentum that his position was inherited by succeeding Liberal Democrat Prime Ministers Hashimoto, Obuchi, Mori, and Koizumi as an official policy stand of the Japanese government. The remorse and apology were expressed toward South Korea in the Joint Declaration of President Kim Dae-Jung and Prime Minister Obuchi in December 1998.[32] Moreover, on September 17, 2002, Japan issued an expression of remorse and apology to North Korea in the Pyongyang Declaration of Chairman Kim Jong Il and Prime Minister Koizumi: "The Japanese side regards, in a spirit of humility, the facts of history that Japan caused tremendous damage and suffering to the people of Korea through its colonial rule in the past, and expressed deep remorse and heartfelt apology." [33] According to the declaration, the way in which Japan–North Korea relations would be normalized would differ from the 1965 Japan–South Korea treaty. While rejecting the payment of compensation, Japan declared that it would provide economic support as an expression of sincere remorse and apology for the past.

In Japan, far-right conservatives have forcefully opposed the government policy that intends a breakthrough in diplomatic relations with the neighbors. In 1996, prominent Japanese critics of these recent policies rejected, in particular, the descriptions of comfort women in middle school history textbooks. Among these critics were young nationalist diet members headed by Abe Shinzo; nationalist intellectuals, such as Nishio Kanji, Fujioka Nobukatsu, and Sakamoto Takao; and cartoonist Kobayashi Yoshinori. Later, the conservatives set up an organization for their new nationalist history textbook. In 2000, their new history textbook was presented to the people and generated quite a stir at home and abroad. After fierce competition, Japan widely rejected their textbook for adoption in the nation's schools. In a sense, the Japanese repulsed nationalist counterattacks and, consequently, defended Murayama's statement.

It is noteworthy that Japan's negotiations with, in particular, North Korea provided Japan's conservative nationalists with an important opportunity to denounce Japan's innovative posture toward the past. These nationalists have transformed the sentiment of resistance against the government's posture into public anger over the abduction of Japanese citizens by North Korean secret agents in the 1970s and the 1980s. Indeed, elements of Japan's mass media, like TV programs and weekly magazines, have ignored Japan's traumatic historical relations with the Korean peninsula and have, instead, focused on the sensational abduction cases. In some instances, the argument was advanced that Japanese are victims of North Korean crimes and that Japanese crimes against Koreans have been overblown. This reversing trend has not gone unnoticed in North Korea, in which propaganda machines express resentment at the Japanese public anger.

These developments mentioned above fostered unprecedented diplomatic strains in 2005 between Japan, on the one hand, and South Korea and China, on the other. South Korean President Roh Moo-hyun, who had been critical of the Japanese history issue, publicly sympathized with North Korean resentment. Meanwhile, as Prime Minister, Koizumi insisted on the continuation of his annual visit to Yasukuni Shrine. Particularly for this reason, the Chinese government refrained from hosting Koizumi in Beijing. Furthermore, the Chinese vice prime minister canceled a scheduled meeting with Koizumi and returned to China. The relations between China and Japan entered their worst stage since the establishment of diplomatic relations in 1972. Chinese nationalism and Japanese nationalism now clashed head on.

There is little doubt that if it fails to engage Chinese leaders in open and cooperative relations, the Japanese government cannot play any role in promoting either the East Asian community or community-building in Northeast Asia. The Japanese people should re-examine their history and identify possible paths toward reconciliation and cooperation with the Chinese people. At the public level, the Japanese feel that South Koreans are far friendlier than the Chinese. There are innumerable channels of intellectual and cultural exchange between the two countries. If sincere mutual efforts continue between Japanese and South Koreans, the latter may help the Japanese improve relations with Chinese and North Koreans.

Linkage between Northeast Asian community and East Asian community

Another important factor underlying the possible expansion of regional cooperation in East Asia or Northeast Asia merits our attention. That is the US factor. The United States has long had a vital national interest in Asia. The United States maintains a military presence in this region, allocating eighty thousand forces to the bases in Japan and South Korea. Therefore, the United States cannot be indifferent to any idea of regional cooperation in Asia; and it frowns upon a regional community of East Asian countries that does not include American participation. On the other hand, because of Japan's long reliance on its bilateral alliance with the United States, some Japanese, who have been comforted by the alliance, balk at the idea of joining a regional community in which the United States does not participate. In this vein, Prime Minister Koizumi's proposal for the construction of an East Asian community prompted conservative Japanese to argue that such a proposal would intrigue against the US–Japan alliance.[34] In accordance with this division, the Japanese Foreign Ministry itself shows signs of division over the issue of an East Asian community. Some former US high-ranking officials also began to openly oppose the idea.[35]

Given this situation, the CEAC in Japan, for the time being, has accepted the idea that related discussions should start without the United States. However, under various forms of pressure, a hesitation spread among CEAC members. It might be the reason for the long delay in the publication of the CEAC's policy report. On August 11, 2005, the policy report, entitled "The Present Situation and Background of the Idea of East Asian Community and the State Strategy of Japan," was published at last. But the report left open the question regarding membership in an East Asian community by referring simply to the ASEAN policy of expanding the membership of the East Asian Summit.[36]

Worthy of note in this situation is Francis Fukuyama's position that the ongoing Six-Party Talks develop to the discussion of regional cooperation in Northeast Asia.[37] For him, in this context the United States may become a full member.

Although he did not mention anything about an East Asian community, there is no doubt that he preferred the idea of a Northeast Asian community to an East Asian community.

I believe that today's deadlock—centered on the US membership—can be resolved through a combination of two visions of regional community, a Northeast Asian community and an East Asian community. The two visions are compatible. Because community-building is a multiple process, Northeast Asia and Southeast Asia should come together. The model for the Northeast Asian community may derive from that of ASEAN. ASEAN itself, based on the ASEAN Concord 2 signed in Bali on October 7, 2003, has become a more integrated community, comprising a security community, an economic community, and a socio-cultural community. If only this trend of the integration in ASEAN continues, Northeast Asia will fall substantially behind Southeast Asia, a situation that would bring about an abnormal imbalance between the two regions. In principle, Southeast Asia and Northeast Asia should unite to form a regional community in East Asia as a whole. The point is that, without strengthening Northeast Asian cooperation, an East Asian community cannot possess adequate strength. Northeast Asia should include the Russian Far East and some parts of the United States. And Northeast Asian cooperation should get underway in the Six-Party Talks. The region has already made progress in environmental cooperation. APT now plays a role combining ASEAN and three Northeast Asian countries through the envisioning of economic ties; therefore, the East Asian community that eventually emerges will at first be an economic community.

China has maintained that Northeast Asia should include five countries and six sides. China has not wanted the United States to join the regional community. But in Northeast Asia, the American presence should be accepted. If two regional communities—one in the southeast and one in the northeast—are combined with each other, they may form a regional community in East Asia, that is, a new Greater East Asia community, which can stand in stark contrast to the notorious Greater East Asia Co-prosperity Sphere.

Conclusion

A region itself does not exist a priori but should be defined. The case of Northeast Asia is not an exception. If one wishes peace in the region, Northeast Asia should include the United States and Taiwan. It is well known that China does not want to have the United States as a member of this region. When South Korean President Roh Moo-hyun spoke passionately about Northeast Asia, he was referring chiefly to China, South Korea, and Japan. But the continuation of the Six-Party Talks demonstrates the feasibility that a Northeast Asian community, including the United States and Russia, can emerge and take root. Likewise, cooperation among ASEAN countries has given rise to a new region, that is, APT. Now, with strong support from the ASEAN, an East Asian community is emerging as a model of regional cooperation. Two regional communities—the Northeast Asian community and the East Asian community—should be linked together.

Two obstacles have hindered advances toward a regional community: the North Korean crisis and the Japan problem. The North Korean nuclear and economic crises are so serious that, as long as they remain unresolved, it is impossible to talk about a Northeast Asian community. But long-term solutions to these crises will constitute the first, and perhaps the most significant, step toward region-wide security cooperation in Northeast Asia. In this regard, the crises, themselves, provide us with an opportunity to realize a greater good. Meanwhile, an adequate solution to the Japan problem requires that Japanese continue to reflect on, and to acknowledge, their past and that Chinese and Koreans continue to distinguish the positive aspects of Japanese society from its negative aspects. Here, South Koreans can play an important role in overcoming and tempering narrow nationalisms on both sides.

A satisfactory treatment of the US factor is difficult, but any serious promoter of a regional community in East Asia must draw support from the US. The security dilemma in Northeast Asia cannot be solved without US cooperation, a situation that is an essential condition for the development of an East Asian community.

Notes

1 On the discussion on Northeast Asia as a region, see Wada Haruki, *Tohokuazia Kyodo no Ie* (*A Common House of Northeast Asia*), Tokyo: Heibonsha, 2003; Christopher M. Dent and David W. F. Huang (eds) *Northeast Asian Regionalism: Learning from the European Experience*, New York: RoutledgeCurzon, 2002; and Samuel S. Kim (ed.) *The International Relations of Northeast Asia*, Lanham, MD: Rowman & Littlefield, 2004.

2 See Wada, *Tohokuazia Kyodo no Ie* (*A Common House of Northeast Asia*), chapter 2. On Royama Masamichi's theory, see his collection of eighteen articles, *Toua to Sekai: Shinchitsujo heno Ronsaku* (*East Asia and the World: Proposals for a New Order*), Tokyo: Kaizousha, 1941.

3 The war was declared on 8 December 1941, without mention of "Great East Asia." It was on December 12 that the Japanese government decided to name the war the "Great East Asian War," whose purported aim was the construction of a new order, Greater East Asia. *Asahi Shimbun*, 13 December 1941.

4 See Lee Jongwon, "Higashiazia ni okeru Reisen to Chiikishugi: Amerika no seisaku wo chuushin ni (The Cold War in East Asia and Regionalism: with special reference to the American Policy)," in Kamo Takehiko (ed.) *Seikikan no Sekaiseiji (World Politics between Centuries): Azia no Kokusaichitsujyo*, Tokyo: Nihon Hyoronsha, 1993, Vol. 3, pp. 199–204.

5 For example, see Lee Song-un's and Miyamoto Kenji's addresses of 15 March 1966 at Pyongyang, *Akahata*, 16 March 1966.

6 See Wada, *Tohokuazia Kyodo no Ie* (*A Common House of Northeast Asia*), pp. 66–70.

7 Ibid., pp. 243–9.

8 *Keizai Hyoron (Economic review)*, No. 3 and No. 9, 1991; No. 12, 1992.

9 Wada Haruki, "Tonbuk asea kongdongeui chip kwa hanbando (The Common House in Northeast Asia and the Korean peninsula)," *Changjak kwa Pipyong*, Vol. 87, Spring 1995.

10 Morishima Michio, *Nihon no Sentaku: Atarashii Kunizukuri ni Mukete* (*A Choice for Japan: Toward New State Building*), Tokyo: Iwanami Shoten, 1995; *Naze Nihon wa Botsuraku Suruka* (*Why Is Japan Going to Perish?*), Tokyo: Iwanami Shoten, 1997;

Nihon ni Deriru Koto wa Nanika: Higashi Azia Kyodotai wo Teiansuru (*What Can Japan Accomplish? Proposal for East Asian Community*, Tokyo: Iwanami Shoten, 2001.

11 East Asia Vision Group, *Towards an East Asian Community: Region of Peace, Prosperity and Progress*, p. 5. Online. Available HTTP: <http://www.mofa.go.jp/region/asia-paci/report2001.pdf> (accessed 1 September 2005).

12 Ibid., p. 18.

13 Ministry of Foreign Affairs, Japan. Online. Available HTTP: <http://www.mofa.go.jp/region/asia-paci/n_korea/pmv0209/pyongyang.html> (accessed 1 September 2005).

14 *Asahi Shimbun*, 18 September 2002.

15 For the text of President Roh's speech, see online. Available HTTP: <http://english.president.go.kr/warp/app/en_speeches/view?group_id=en_archive&meta_id=en_speeches&id=e40ed9569d2173bc02d99563&list_op=YTo3OntpOjA7czo1OiJsc3RvcCI7aToxO3M6MTI6ImFyY2hpdmVfbGlzdCI7aToyO2E6Mjp7czo3OiJzcmNoY2F0OIjtzOjA62I7czo3OiJzcmNoY29uIjtzOjA62I7fWk6MztzOjEzOiJyZWdpc3Rlcl9kYXRlIjtpOjQ7aToxO2k6MjA7aToyO2k6MTA7fQ%3D%3D> (accessed 2 September 2005).

16 East Asia Vision Group, *Towards an East Asian Community*, p. 20.

17 *Nihon Kokusai Forum Kaiho*, Winter Issue, 2003.

18 East Asia Vision Group, *Towards an East Asian Community*, p. 27.

19 *Nihon Kokusai Forum Kaiho*, Spring Issue, 2004.

20 Ministry of Foreign Affairs, Japan. Online. Available HTTP: <http://www.mofa.go.jp/region/asia-paci/asean/year2003/summit/tokyo_dec.pdf> (accessed 2 September 2005).

21 CEAC, "Higashi Azia Kyodotai Hyogikai setsuritsusokai: sokkiroku oyobi shiryo" (The Inaugural Meeting of the CEAC: Stenographic Record and Materials).

22 CEAC, "Higashi Azia Kyodotai Hyogikai seisaku honkaigi daiikkaikaigo: sokkiroku" (The First Policy Meeting of the CEAC: Stenographic Record).

23 *Asahi Shimbun*, 21 January 2005.

24 *Asahi Shimbun*, 1 January 1991.

25 *Nodong Sinmun*, 26 October 2002.

26 *Nodong Sinmun*, 11 February 2005.

27 *Nodong Sinmun*, 1 January 2001.

28 See Ijuin Atsushi, *Kim Shonichi Kaikaku no Kyojitsu* (*The Truths and the Lies in Kim Jong Il's Reforms*), Tokyo: Nihon Keizai Shimbunsha, 2002.

29 See Wada Haruki, "Economic co-operation in place of historical remorse: Japanese post-war settlements with China, Russia, and Korea in the context of the Cold War," in Junji Banno (ed.) *The Political Economy of Japanese Society: Internationalization and Domestic Problems*, Oxford: Oxford University Press, 1998.

30 For all the processes, see Haruki Wada and Koji Ishizaka (eds) *Nihon wa Shokuminchishihai wo Dou Kangaetekitaka* (*How Japan thought about the Colonial Rule?*), Tokyo: Nashinokisha, 1996.

31 Murayama Tomiichi, *Press Statement*. Quoted in document online. Available HTTP: <http://www.isop.ucla.edu/eas/documents/jpnregret9495.htm> (accessed 1 September 2005).

32 *Japan Times*, 9 October 1998, p. 4.

33 Ministry of Foreign Affairs, Japan. Online. Available HTTP: <http://www.mofa.go.jp/region/asia-paci/n_korea/pmv0209/pyongyang.html> (accessed 1 September 2005)

34 For an exemplary case, see Kasai Noriyuki, "Kuron 'Higashi Azia Kyodotai': nichibei bundan chugoku no nerai" (Illusive discussion on 'East Asian Community': China aims at dividing Japan and the United States), *Yomiuri Shimbun*, 27 March 2005. The author is President of Japan Railway Tokai.

35 See the interview with Richard Armitage, the former Deputy Secretary of the US State Department, in *Asahi Shimbun*, 1 May 2005.
36 CEAC, "The Present Situation and Background of the Idea of East Asian Community and the State Strategy of Japan," p. 10. According to the Report, in the spring of 2005 the ASEAN countries agreed to invite countries to the Kuala Lumpur Summit so long as there be (1) real relations with the ASEAN, (2) substantive dialogue with the ASEAN, and (3) a signature under the Treaty of Amity and Cooperation in Southeast Asia. Under these conditions, India, New Zealand, and Australia could join the Kuala Lumpur Summit. However, the United States may not be invited to Kuala Lumpur.
37 See Francis Fukuyama, "Re-envisioning Asia," *Foreign Affairs*, January–February 2005.

Part II

Domestic dimension of regional interaction

3 Washington's policies toward North Korea and the Taiwan Strait: the role of US domestic politics

Tun-jen Cheng

Introduction

The Korean Peninsula and the Taiwan Strait are two flash points in post-Cold War East Asia in which the US has long been embroiled. Carrying high stakes, US policies toward North Korea, an anachronistic communist regime believed to be armed with nuclear weapons and a threat to its neighbors, have been heatedly disputed. The debate has focused on the shift or balance between engagement and coercion, carrot and stick, in order to defuse the nuclear crisis on the peninsula. US policies toward Taiwan, a prosperous democracy under the long shadow of authoritarian China, also have been a contentious issue. The controversy centers on the efficacy of the doctrine of strategic ambiguity, or the shape and mode of US commitment to Taiwan's defense. Treating the US as a unitary actor, much of the literature assesses the virtues and vices of competing approaches to managing the situation in the Taiwan Straits and the Korean peninsula.[1] To the extent that the domestic side of the story is examined, the attention is primarily an inter-agency squabble and the analysis typically revolves around the tenet of good old bureaucratic politics model—where you stand depends on where you sit (State, Defense or National Security Council). This paper looks at the role of domestic politics more broadly, considering the possible impacts of not merely bureau-cratic politics, but also public opinion, partisan difference, and executive-legisla-tive nexus on US policy toward North Korea and Taiwan. While most observers would readily agree that domestic politics, especially in a democracy, can con-strain or drive foreign policy, very few have endeavored to specify the conditions under which, and the mechanisms by which, politics impinge on foreign policy.

This essay advances four arguments. First, in general, US public opinion on North Korea and Taiwan is not strong enough to significantly constrain foreign policy decision, thereby giving policy makers enough latitude to maneuver the issues. Second, partisan politics has significantly impinged on US policies toward North Korea. The three nuclear crises—the 1994 plutonium production, the 1998 missile test, and the October 2002 uranium enrichment program—unfolded in tandem with the evolution of partisan politics in the US. Third, institutional dis-agreement between the two ends of the Pennsylvania Avenue has shaped US poli-cies toward the Taiwan Strait much more than partisan frictions do. Fourth, electoral cycle and divided government have had the effect of punctuating and compounding US policies toward North Korea, while congressional actions have tended to "fine tune" and even stabilize US policies toward the Taiwan Strait.

Section one of this essay identifies elements of domestic politics that may condition and affect US foreign policy in general. Section two examines these elements in the context of US policies toward North Korea and the Taiwan Strait. Section three explores a number of possible factors contributing to different patterns of domestic politics and draws implications for regional cooperation and conflict.

The domestic politics dimension of US foreign policy

Post-World War II American foreign policy used to be the exclusive bailiwick of the president and a few East Coast élite.[2] Congress had abdicated from it, the public was not directly involved, and the Cold War bipartisan consensus was solid. Bureaucratic turf battles remained the only domestic political game of foreign policy making, as Graham Allison's case study of the Cuban Missile Crisis vividly portrayed. But bureaucratic politics could dent foreign policy only as far as a president would permit. After all, cabinet members serve at the pleasure of president, and the buck stops at the president's office. The rational actor model crowned the Allison's tripartite analytical scheme.[3]

Foreign policy, however, has become more politicized in the wake of the Vietnam War, and especially after the end of the Cold War. Congress has reasserted its role, leading Thomas Mann to jibe that the US has two foreign policies, one toward other countries, the other toward the other end of Pennsylvania Avenue.[4] The makers of the 1789 Constitution delegated major foreign policy powers to both the president and Congress. The president is the commander-in-chief, but Congress has war declaration and budgetary powers. The president negotiates treaties and nominates foreign policy officials, but the Senate approves them. Congress also has the power to raise and support military, establish rules on immigration, regulate foreign trade, and deal with crimes on high seas. Given such a constitutional setup, there is built-in tension between the two branches of the government for the privilege of directing foreign policy; both sides may share power and cooperate, but they may wage battles.[5] Congress can impose economic sanctions, pass resolutions, attach memoranda, and hold public hearings. The administration may try to bypass Congress, such as signing agreements instead of treaties to avoid the ratification hurdle that Senate may pose, but Congress can withhold or delay appropriation to hobble the implementation of international agreements.

However, congressional activism in foreign policy making is uneven and inconsistent. At times and on some foreign policy issues, Congress can be obsessive, while at other times, and on some other issues, it can be spasmodic. Foreign policy friction between Congress and the president can be fused with partisan conflict. Under the condition of divided government (viz., when the president's party does not control both Houses), Congress may become an arena for partisan conflict. Under the condition of unified government (viz., when the president's party has majority of seats in both Houses), Congress is not necessarily the stool of the White House. To differentiate the executive-legislative cleavage from the partisan cleavage, we can analyze roll call votes in Congress and the divergence or convergence of the preferences. If the votes are cast across (versus along) the party line and if there is divergence of preference between the president and the majority of Congress, then the structure of conflict is an institutional one, rather than a partisan one.

Since the mid 1970s, "there has been a marked increase in public demand for greater engagement and more direct involvement" as the public now feels that "if ... resources and attention... are diverted to foreign policy, they will be sub-tracted from the domestic side." [6] Numerous studies show that foreign policy makers pay attention to public opinion polls.[7] But does public opinion impinge on foreign policy at all?

Conventional wisdom said that public opinion did not and should not, as public opinion was moody, mercurial, ill-informed, and lacking any structure, therefore should be molded and led through a top-down process.[8] Closely examining the interaction between foreign policy and public opinion during the Vietnam War, new literature presents three observations. First, public opinion has been generally quite stable, revolving around two fundamental considerations: whether the US should go along with others or go alone by herself, and whether the sword should be used. Second, elite opinion follows rather than leads public opinion, which changes according to events, not according to élite's opinion leadership. Third, public opinion does constrain, though not determine, major US foreign policy decisions, especially with respect to the use of force.[9] As Thomas Graham shows, if the magnitude of public support or opposition reaches the seventy per-cent level, the executive branch has extremely limited latitude in making foreign policy (see table 3.1).[10] Members of Congress, especially members of the House, are more sensitive to public opinion, especially if interest groups or expressive groups in their constituencies make a big point of it.

Does partisan politics have relevance to foreign policy making? Political party's agenda and its ideological preference have certainly been shaping the for-

Table 3.1 The impact of public opinion on foreign policy.

Opinion category	Support rate (%)	Impact on policy
nearly unanimous	80+	automatic
preponderant	70–79	substantial, deter political opposition
consensus	60–69	important, may defeat strong bureaucratic opponents
majority	50–59	problematic, impact hinges on presidential leadership
plurality	50–	insignificant

Source: Thomas W. Graham, *The Politics of Failure: Strategic Nuclear Arms Control, Public Opinion, and Domestic Politics in the United States, 1945–1980*, doctoral dissertation, M.I.T, 1989, p. 57; lecture note, 1991, University of California, San Diego.

mation and content of domestic policies. And political parties do coordinate fellow party members for policy actions, even though party discipline is weaker in the US—which has a presidential form of government, a plurality-based electoral system, and federalism—than parliamentary democracies with a list-based electoral system in a unitary state.[11]

Party politics was not as noteworthy in foreign policy issue area, given the persistence of the Cold War bipartisan consensus on the necessity of pursuing a containment policy. However, the foreign policy consensus began to break down in the wake of the Vietnam War along the liberal and conservative axis as well as the international-isolationist axis.[12] And the partisan dispute on the foreign policy approach becomes even more acute after the end of the Cold War.[13]

Partisan differences are expectedly sharpened and highlighted during the presidential campaign, typically reflected in party platform and campaign promises. Party platform and policy positions on domestic issues are generally widely monitored, and "presidents keep the promise they made as candidates," lest they be penalized at the ballot box next time around.[14] This dictum applies less to foreign policy. On foreign policy issues, candidates are not always required to take a stand. Foreign nations and nationals do not vote, exerting no electoral pressure on party candidates. And foreign policy can be altered in the name of national interest and national security. Despite all this, party platform does offer important clues to partisan differences in foreign policy, and they are meticulously parsed abroad. However, party platform typically offers overall orientation and general approach to foreign policy rather than specific policies per se. To see how partisan friction affects a specific foreign policy, we need to go beyond the words in the platform to see the deeds that may ensue.

Dynamics of US policy toward North Korea and the Taiwan Strait

With a general discussion on domestic politics and foreign policy, we now zero in to the issue of North Korea and the Taiwan Strait, beginning with American public opinion on these two issues. Public opinion surveys on North Korea and the Taiwan Strait have been conducted only sporadically, and the questions were vaguely couched, giving the administration time and latitude to fashion its policy. But such degree of freedom is less based on the paucity of opinion data as low intensity of opinion on the actions that the public endorses or opposes.

Tables 3.2a—3.2d summarize major public opinion surveys on North Korea issues. Based on these tables, we can make a few observations. First, an overwhelming majority of American public has a strong negative feeling toward North Korea and feels threatened by it, but does not regard it as an imminent threat. A majority of American public sees US having a vital interest in the Korean peninsula. Second, an overwhelming majority is in favor of pursuing some diplomatic exchange with North Korea, and, for the purpose of defusing the nuclear crisis, supports diplomatic and economic actions rather than military action. Third, if economic and diplomatic actions fail to resolve the crisis, the American public's opposition to using military action is likely to significantly weaken.

Table 3.2a Percentage (%) of polled Americans who believe that North Korea is a priority/top priority issue and the US has vital interests at stake.

Answer	February 1994	March 1994	April 1994	May 1994
Yes	45	59	62	84
No	41	34	31	14
No answer	14	7	7	2

Source: February and April 1994 surveys by Yomiuri Shimbun; the rest by Pew Research Center.

Table 3.2b Percentage (%) of Americans who think North Korea is a threat.

	February 2003	3 March 2003	10 March 2003	April 2003	July 2003	August 2003
Immediate	12	23	14	11	21	15
Long-term	67	63	73	69	61	62
No threat	11	12	8	14	15	16
No opinion	10	2	5	6	3	7

Sources: February and April 2003 surveys by CBS News; 3 March 2003 by CNN/USA Today/Gallup Poll; 10 March 2003 by the Harris Poll; July 2003 by Yomiuri Shimbun; August 2003 by Program on International Policy Attitudes/Knowledge Networks.

Table 3.2c Percentage (%) of Americans who support military force or economic/diplomatic action against North Korea.

	3 January 2003	January 2003	20 January 2003	March 2003
Military action / threats	15	6	14	15
Economic / diplomatic action	79	89	80	79
Not sure	6	5	6	6

Sources: the four surveys were done by NBC, CBS, Pew, and CNN/USA Today/Gallup, respectively.

Table 3.2d Percentage (%) of Americans who favor or oppose military action with North Korea if diplomatic and/or economic actions fail.

	Favor military action	Oppose military action	Don't know
December 1993	51	38	11
14 December 1993	33	60	7
January 1994	29	64	7
March 1994	45	51	4
April 2002	24	60	16
9 January 2003	47	48	5
30 January 2003	37	43	20
February 2003	52	36	11
16 April 2003	43	53	4

Sources: Two 1993 surveys are from Los Angeles Times and Pew Research Center, respectively. The two 1994 surveys are from NBC/Wall Street Journal and Pew, respectively. The 2002 survey is from SRI International; the 9 January and February 2003 surveys are from Program on International Policy Attitudes/Knowledge Networks. The 30 January and 16 April surveys are from SRI International and Pew Research Center, respectively.

Tables 3.3 through 3.5 summarize major public opinion surveys on the Taiwan Strait issues. Based on these tables, several observations can be made. First, the majority of American public has a consistently favorable opinion on Taiwan but an unfavorable one on post-1989 China. Respondents with an unfavorable opinion on Taiwan have never exceeded 30 percent of those who were polled. This seems to make it safe for members of Congress to join Taiwan Caucus and uncomfortable for any member to join China Caucus if it were to be formed. Having a membership in China Caucus would be "out of sync" with the public mood.

Table 3.3 The US public's attitude toward China. Is your overall opinion of China very favorable, mostly favorable, mostly unfavorable, or very unfavorable?

	Total Favorable	*Total Unfavorable*
September 1979	64	25
February–March 1985	38	51
February–March 1989	72	13
August 1989	34	54
March 1991	35	53
February 1994	40	53
March 1996	39	51
June 1997	33	50
June 1998	39	47
February 1999	39	50
March 1999	34	59
May 1999	38	56
January 2000	33	51
March 2000	35	56
November 2000	36	57
February 2001	45	48
February 2002	44	49
March 2003	45	46
February 2004	41	54

Sources: Poll Analyses, the Gallup Organization, 16 February 2001, and www.pollingreport.com/china.htm.

Table 3.4 Harris Poll asked "Do you feel that Taiwan is a close ally of the US, is friendly but not a close ally, is not friendly but not an enemy, or is unfriendly and is an enemy of the US?"

	1995	*1997*	*1998*	*2000*	*2001*	*2002*	*2003*	*2004*
Close ally	14	20	21	19	22	17	20	18
Friendly	50	41	38	34	35	36	33	33
Not friendly	22	19	22	21	17	22	20	19
Enemy	5	4	4	4	2	5	5	7
Not sure / No response	8	16	15	23	25	22	24	24

Universe of poll respondents: United States.

Table 3.5a Do you think of Taiwan as a completely separate and independent country or as part of China?

	8 August 1995	*8 March 1996*
Separate and independent	69 %	62 %
Part of China	26 %	29 %
Not sure	9 %	5 %

Source: Harris Poll.
Universe of poll respondents: United States.

Table 3.5b From what you know, or have heard, do you feel that Taiwan should eventually be reunified with mainland China under any circumstances or do you feel China and Taiwan should be reunified only if the Taiwanese want to be reunified, or should it never be reunified?

Under any circumstance	2 %
Only if Taiwanese want it to be	69 %
Never	18 %
Not sure	11 %

Source: Harris Poll, 8 March 1996.
Universe of poll respondents: United States.

Table 3.5c Supporting Taiwan's bid to become a member of the United Nations might well anger China. Should the US support Taiwan's UN bid, or not?

	8 March 1996
Yes	56 %
No	34 %
Not sure	9 %

Source: Harris Poll, 8 March 1996.
Universe of poll respondents: United States.

Table 3.5d Current US policy toward Taiwan can be summed up as, "no independence for Taiwan, and no use of force by China to compel Taiwan to rejoin mainland China." Some people say we should continue that policy. Others say since Taiwan has become a democracy, the US should support its moves toward independence, even if it provokes confrontation with China. Which is closer to your view?

	Total (%)	*Democratic (%)*	*Republican (%)*	*Independent (%)*
Continue that policy	37%	42	31	36
Support Taiwan	55	51	61	55
Don't know	8	8	8	9

Source: Democratic Leadership Council, 29 September 1999.
Universe of poll respondents: United States.

Table 3.5e If mainland China tried to invade Taiwan militarily, should America fight to defend Taiwan against China, or not?

Fight	29 %
Not fight	65 %
Not sure	5 %

Source: Harris Poll, 8 March 1996.
Universe of poll respondents: United States.

Table 3.5f China is threatening to hold military exercise off the coast of Taiwan in an attempt to influence Taiwan's first democratic presidential election in March. Should the United States send an aircraft carrier to the Taiwan Straits to try to decrease China's influence on Taiwan's election, or not?

Yes	26 %
No	68 %
Not sure	6 %

Source: Harris Poll, 8 March 1996.
Universe of poll respondents: United States.

Table 3.5g I would like you to imagine that China once again begins to make threatening gestures toward Taiwan. In this case would you favor or oppose sending US naval forces to help protect Taiwan?

Favor	50.5 %
Oppose	38.0 %
Don't know	11.5 %

Source: Project on Foreign Policy and the Public, September 1996.
Universe of poll respondents: United States.

Table 3.5h The US decided to sell advanced military equipment to Taiwan but mainland China opposes the sale. Do you favor or oppose selling US military equipment to Taiwan, even if it means a worsening of relations with China?

Favor	39 %
Oppose	41 %
No opinion	20 %

Source: Market Shares Corporation, 10 May 2001.
Universe of poll respondents: Illinois.

Second, a strong majority of American public is sympathetic to Taiwan's yearning for its own international status. Close to 70 percent of respondents regard Taiwan as separate and independent of China, and hold the view that Taiwan should be reunified with China only based on its free will. A majority of American public even hopes to see their government's support to Taiwan's bid for UN membership; even this may anger China. And another majority upholds

Taiwan's right for self-determination, and "disagrees" with the US policy of "no independence for Taiwan, no use of force for China."

Third, regarding arms sales to Taiwan, the public seems reluctant to endorse President Bush's decision to sell state of art military equipment to Taiwan. And regarding the US military operation in the Taiwan Strait, the American public is largely unwilling to support US direct involvement in actual fighting. Close to the majority of those surveyed feels that the US should do something about the Taiwan Strait, such as sending naval forces to help prevent any conflict and protect Taiwan. In other words, for the American public, deterrence is fine, so is assisting Taiwan, but there is hesitancy to get directly involved in fighting. Steven Levine concludes that US public is lukewarm about American security commitment to Taiwan.[15]

To sum up, American public opinion did strongly oppose the use of force to solve the North Korean nuclear crisis, but if diplomatic effort fails to defuse the crisis, the opposition to the use of force dropped significantly. This jibes well with the overall orientation of US policy, namely, diplomacy is given a chance, but all options are on the table. American public opinion has been favorable to Taiwan, but has been hesitant to get directly involved in defending Taiwan. However, the public hesitation is not intensive enough to dissuade the US government from selling advanced arms to Taiwan or militarily intervening in the Taiwan Strait, therefore leaving room for the government's discretion. Indeed, after China lobbed missiles to intimidate Taiwan voters during the 1996 presidential election, and in response, President Clinton sent in two carriers to deter any further action that China might take, the public opposition to the US military deployment dropped significantly.

What really impinges on US policy toward North Korea and the Taiwan Strait is not public opinion, but rather partisan politics and the executive-legislative disagreement, respectively. Three crises punctuated the evolution of US policy toward North Korea, namely, the 1993–94 plutonium production crisis, the 1998–2000 missile crisis, and the post-Oct 2002 uranium enrichment program crisis. Each one of these has triggered severe partisan disputes. There was a bipartisan criticism of the Clinton administration's handling of the second nuclear crisis in 1999, which quickly led to the passage of the North Korea Threat Reduction Act. However, political battles on US North Korea policy throughout the three nuclear crises have been largely waged along the party fault line. And party leaders—especially presidential hopefuls—wore the mantle in the battlefield. Consequently, rotation of power from one party to another following the presidential election has always resulted in a major policy shift.

Toward the end of the Cold War era, US policy toward North Korea was still one of containment, essentially in the form of empowering South Korea to deter invasion from the North. The end of the Cold War deprived North Korea of political and economic ties with Moscow as well as opportunities of playing Moscow against Beijing, thereby leading North Korea to play the nuclear card.[16] Toward the end of his tenure, George Bush (1989–92) experimented with a sort of "conditional" engagement policy by which the US seemed to be willing to hold talks with North Korea for establishing possible diplomatic ties if and only if North Korea would dismantle its nuclear program. The Bush initiatives suggested a policy that is dubbed "hawk engagement," as it requires North Korea to demonstrate willingness to cooperate before formal negotiation can start.[17] Bush's overture seemed to have some sweeteners, including a possible cancellation of annual joint military exercise (dubbed Team Spirit) with South Korea for the year 1992, as well as a plan to withdraw nuclear weapons from the Korean peninsula. North Korea responded positively, but for some reasons, a Team Spirit exercise was conducted in 1992, and International Atomic Energy Agency (IAEA) inspection was not conducted in South Korea, to the dismay of North Korea, which seemed to conclude that Bush was back to confrontation and containment again.[18]

While criticizing George Bush for cuddling human right-abusing dictators in Beijing, candidate Clinton was quite mute on North Korea issues. The 1992 Democratic Party platform did not mention North Korea's nuclear program either (in contrast, the Republican Party platform sternly defined North Korea as an outlaw state and announced that the US should not permit it to have nuclear weapons). Clinton promised to focus on domestic economy like a laser beam, if he was elected, thus North Korea and, indeed, foreign policy issues in general, were not really on his radar screen. Foreign policy issues were quickly imposed on him, however. On US policy toward China, Clinton quickly delinked human rights issue with trade issue, giving short shrift to his avowed policy shift in dealing with China. On North Korea, however, Clinton was initially inattentive and therefore simply treading Bush's policy by default. North Korea threatened to pull out of Non-Proliferation Treaty (NPT) in March 1993, to which the US responded with economic sanctions and possible military attack, and no negotiation unless North Korea complied with its NPT obligation. Once Clinton zeroed in to the emerging nuclear crisis in North Korea, he reversed the US North Korea policy, replaced containment with engagement, negotiated with North Korea, and accepted the October 1994 Agreed Framework (AF). Mark Caprio has astutely characterized Clinton's engagement policy toward North Korea as one of "negotiation for compliance" (versus Bush's North Korea policy of "compliance before negotiation.").[19]

The 1994 AF froze the DPRK's plutonium production in exchange for the US and South Korea-financed construction of two light water nuclear reactors (LWR) plus the interim heavy oil shipment to meet its energy need. The AF was not flawless as it covered Yongbyon reactor site only (notice that the IAEA can only inspect declared sites and the targeted nations, not the IAEA, are to declare the sites). In addition, LWRs could actually produce more plutonium, though these reactors would make it more difficult for North Korea to pursue diversion. But the most detrimental criticism—coming from the Republican Party—dwelt on the quintessential nature of Clinton's policy, which in the eyes of his critics, had rewarded the perpetrator of NPT and caved in to North Korea's nuclear blackmail. The critics also faulted Clinton for naively trusting North Korea's commitment to the spirit of the agreement.

Political criticism turned thunderous after the November 1994 mid-term election returned the Republicans to power in both Houses. The leading presidential hopeful of the Republican Party, Robert Dole, saw the AF as a document of appeasement (see table 3.6), while Senator John McCain predicted that North Korea would not forgo all nuclear programs. During the 1996 presidential electoral campaign, the two parties were diametrically opposed to each other regarding the US–North Korea nuclear accord. While the Democrats extolled the accomplishment of this accord, the Republicans condemned it for selling out American interest. In addition to verbal criticisms, the Republican-controlled Congress delayed the implementation of the AF. Meanwhile, the Clinton administration was distracted by his impeachment battle, and the famine in North Korea bred the speculation on possible collapse of the North Korea regime. However, Clinton kept his office, and North Korea dynasty rule stood.

Table 3.6 US political party platforms on North Korea.

Election year	Democratic party platform	Republican party platform
2004	"We should maintain the six-party talks, but we must also be prepared to talk directly with North Korea to negotiate a comprehensive agreement that addresses the full range of issues for ourselves and our allies."	"Our nation is leading the international community to speak with one voice to demand the complete, verifiable, and irreversible dismantlement of North Korea's nuclear programs... North Korea lies outside of the international system."
2000	"Our diplomacy has helped to halt North Korea's push for nuclear weapons. We got North Korea to stop testing long-range ballistic missiles and are also engaged in continuing negotiations regarding their testing and export of long-range ballistic missiles."	"We will help to deter aggression on the Korean peninsula." "North Korea ... lies outside of the international system ... The United States will stand by its commitments and will take all necessary measures to thwart, deter, and defend itself and its allies against attack, including enemy use of weapons of mass destruction."
1996	"Four years ago, the North Koreans were operating a dangerous nuclear program. Today, that program is frozen, under international inspection, and slated to be dismantled."	"We will halt Bill Clinton's efforts to appease North Korea by rewarding treaty-breaking with American taxpayer-financed oil and nuclear reactors."
1992	"A US troop presence should be maintained in South Korea as long as North Korea presents a threat to South Korea."	"We will maintain our close relationship with the Republic of Korea, helping to deter aggression from the north. North Korea remains an outlaw state and must not be permitted to acquire nuclear weapons."

Source: compiled by author.

The surprise missile test by North Korea in August 1998 shocked Northeast Asian countries that lie within its missile range and re-ignited the nuclear crisis for US policy makers. This new development triggered two high level ex-official and official (William Perry and Madeleine Albright) visits to North Korea as well as a new round of negotiation for the exchange between food aid and IAEA inspections in 1999–2000. Congress in general was alarmed, passing a North Korea Threat Reduction Act on a bipartisan basis in 2000. However, the criticism about Clinton's rewarding the perpetrators was louder from the other side of the aisle, which was clearly manifested in the 2000 electoral campaign. Vehement denouncement of Clinton's North Korea policy during the presidential election foreshadowed a policy shift afterward.

The Clinton Administration thought it had left a good diplomatic opening with North Korea for the incoming Bush administration to exploit. The new Bush Administration ordered a thorough review of Clinton's policy instead. The review even considered complete withdrawal from the AF, but eventually settled for tightening the screws: verification of North Korea's missile programs, a ban on its missile exports, and a less threatening conventional military posture. The new Administration's rhetoric on North Korea was widely known, showing distrust on authoritarian North Korea especially when it comes to verification.[20] Under the new Administration, meeting US expectation regarding the missile program would be a precondition for lifting economic sanctions and resuming negotiation for political exchange. While Secretary of State Colin Powell was willing to meet with North Korea, he drew a clear distinction between talk and negotiation. Contacts between the two sides were intermittent, but no formal talks were scheduled, Bush's "compliance before negotiation" policy evidently displaced Clinton's "negotiation for compliance" policy.

To the Bush Administration, its "compliance before negotiation" (or hawk engagement) policy was fully vindicated after the outbreak of the third nuclear crisis in October 2002. Since 1997 North Korea had secretively undertaken a uranium enrichment program (UEP), a violation of the spirit, if not the letter, of the AF, a fact that came to surface in October 2002. Not denying it, North Korea cited US hostile attitude, and the snail pace of the implementation of AF as the justification for its UEP. The US and its allies immediately suspended their AF obligations while North Korea repelled IAEA inspectors.

As the US refused to negotiate directly with North Korea, the crisis deepened and the probability of North Korea acquiring the bombs increased. The Iraq War compelled the Bush Administration to use multilateral diplomacy—the six-party talks among China, Japan, North Korea, South Korea, Russia and the US—and unspecified economic incentives to be given in the future as main tools to deal with the North Korea UEP crisis. Within the framework of six-party talk, the Bush Administration persisted in following the hawk engagement policy, meaning that North Korea should come clean first before formal negotiation for a package of carrot and stick can be hammered out. While the Powell proposal advanced on June 15, 2004 would offer some incentives, such as immediate energy assistance up front, these incentives would be conditional on DPRK's categorical commitment to terminating its nuclear program. Under this proposal, DPRK would have three months to disclose its program and have its claims verified by US intelligence. Upon verification, US would then join its allies in giving written security assurance and participate in a process that might ultimately result in direct US aid to DPRK. This proposal was still in line with the "compliance before negotiation" strategy. DPRK did not bite this bait.[21]

To Democratic Party's presidential candidate, Bush's policy toward DPRK was negligent, allowing the inspection regime to collapse and permitting DPRK to produce weapon grade plutonium. Refuting the Bush policy, Democratic Party's presidential candidate in 2004 endorsed a direct bilateral negotiation with North Korea. John Edwards, vice-presidential candidate in 2004, charged, the administration was "standing on the sidelines" while North Korea and Iran advanced their nuclear programs.[22] The partisan friction remains.

The first three rounds of six-party talks did not yield any result, and beginning in June 2004, North Korea boycotted it till July 2005. During the boycott, the US and North Korea swapped inflammatory remarks, and the US floated a variety of plans for possible sanctions and quarantine while North Korea threatened to cross a red line, namely, conducting nuclear tests. Many factors have combined to bring North Korea back to the six-party talks, including North Korea's lurking food shortage, South Korea's proposal (but not promise) to sponsor a Marshall Plan-level aid, China's brokerage, the US government's repeated statement of its harboring no intention to invade North Korea, and civility in communication. North Korea's leader was reported to have recently stated that the Joint Declaration of Denuclearization of the Korean Peninsula was still valid, and that his country's objective was not to have nuclear weapons.[23] It remains to be seen whether this stand will be codified and whether this means total eradication of nuclear *programs*. To the current Bush administration, the resumption of the talks lent support to its strategy, holding off incentives until North Korea has firmly committed to denuclearize the Korean peninsula.[24] To the Administration's critics, the Bush administration eventually and belatedly plans to negotiate North Korea's commitment to abandoning what it has developed during the past three years of stalemate.[25]

In contrast with US policy toward North Korea, there were much less partisan differences regarding US policy toward the Taiwan Strait. The overall objective of US cross-strait policy in the 1970s and the 1980s was to harmonize relations with China, largely for the purpose of outflanking the Soviet Union and inevitably at the expense of Taiwan's political interest.[26] A corollary of this overall policy was to ensure that Taiwan would not be left defenseless, and that its economic and cultural ties with the US not sacrificed. The bottom line of US policy was that Taiwan would not collapse by itself or would not be politically transferred to and militarily seized by China. The end of the Cold War drastically discounted China's strategic value to the US, but China's growing economic and political power requires that the US and, for that matter, most nations, maintain good working relations with China. On the insistence of China, South Korea and South Africa abandoned diplomatic ties with Taiwan during the 1990s, leaving Taiwan with formal ties with less than thirty, predominantly mini states.

Meanwhile, across the Strait, economic prosperity and the advent of democracy have led Taiwan to break international isolation and yearn for a viable independent and appropriate international status, expectedly to the dismay of China. The overall objective of US cross-strait policy is to prevent possible military conflict between the two sides by way of maintaining double deterrence against the use of force by China on the one hand and against a formal declaration of independence by Taiwan on the other. And the art of diplomacy is to ensure that neither side upset the status quo, that any solution to cross-strait disputes be through peaceful means, and that Taiwan's international status be achieved without jeopardizing the stability across the Strait.

Political party platforms drafted in the post-Cold War era seem to suggest some difference in the two parties' policy orientation toward the Taiwan Strait (see table 3.7). In comparison with Democratic Party's platforms, the Republican Party's have been more leery of China, more skeptical of US engagement with China, and more consistently elaborating on and signaling US commitment to Taiwan's defense and support to Taiwan's pursuit of international status. Campaign rhetoric in the 1980s also showed the Republican Party's sympathy or affection to Taiwan. Indeed, Reagan had even intended to cement official ties with Taiwan, undoing Jimmy Carter's de-recognition of Taiwan. But if we focus on deeds rather than words, we see a checkered record.

On the Democratic Party side, Jimmy Carter cut off diplomatic ties with Taiwan and was most reluctant to enact Taiwan Relations Act (TRA) in 1979, but he did insist that US continue to sell arms to Taiwan, much to the displeasure of China's patriarch, Deng Xiaoping. Clinton was the first US president to give verbal confirmation in a public forum of the three no's statement that Kissinger secretively gave to Zhou Enlai in the early 1970s.[27] In 1998, Clinton said in Shanghai, "We don't support independence for Taiwan, or two Chinas, or one Taiwan, one China ... and we don't believe that Taiwan should be a member in any organization for which statehood is a requirement." But Bill Clinton did send two aircraft carriers to the Strait in 1996 to deter China from intimidating Taiwan, and he did introduce a new ingredient to US cross-strait policy, which is that any change of Taiwan's status needs "the assent of Taiwanese people."

On the Republican Party side, Richard Nixon signed the Shanghai Communiqué in 1971 that laid the foundation for the establishment of formal US–China diplomatic ties later on, albeit the Communiqué was carefully crafted to indicate the US acknowledgement, rather than recognition or acceptance of the one-China position. Ronald Reagan signed the August 17 Communiqué with China in 1982, according to which the US would reduce and eventually end arms sale to Taiwan if China would handle the Taiwan issue only by peaceful means. George H. W. Bush decided to sell F-16s fighter jets to Taiwan in 1991, but he did secretively convey his commitment to maintaining US–China ties in spite of the imposition of economic sanctions on China after the 1989 Tiananmen massacre. George W. Bush approved sale of submarines to Taiwan and promoted military cooperation with Taiwan, but sternly warned Mr Chen Shui-bian (without using his official title, President of Taiwan) in December 2003, on the occasion

Table 3.7 US political party platforms on Taiwan.

Election Year	Democratic Party Platform	Republican Party Platform
2004	Advocated one China policy. Peaceful resolution of the cross-Strait problem that is consistent with the wishes and best interests of Taiwanese.	Taiwan classified as a democracy and a friend. Advocated one China policy; peaceful resolution of the cross-Strait problem that is consistent with the wishes and best interests of Taiwanese. Taiwan Relations Act (TRA) as the legal framework of US–Taiwan relations Committed to self-defense of Taiwan; supported arms sale and Taiwan's participation in WHO.
2000	Peaceful resolution of the cross-straits dispute consistent with the wishes of Taiwan people. TRA as the basis for US–Taiwan relations. Mentioned China's bellicose threat to Taiwan; Al Gore to fulfill responsibilities under TRA.	Taiwan classified as a friend. Peaceful resolution of the cross-Strait problem that is consistent with the wishes and best interests of Taiwanese. TRA as the legal framework for US–Taiwan relations. Committed to self-defense of Taiwan. Supported Taiwan's membership in the WTO.
1996	Highlighted the deployment of an American task force on Taiwan Straits to ensure China's military exercise did not imperil the security of the region.	TRA as the basis of US–Taiwan relations. Regarded a threat to Taiwan as a threat to US security. Supported submarine sales, Taiwan's role in theatre missile defense and in international organizations.
1992		TRA as the basis of US–Taiwan relations. Reaffirmed commitment to Taiwan's security. Regarded any attempt to alter the status by force as a threat to the entire region.

Source: compiled by author.

of Chinese Premier Wen's visit to the US, not to use referendum to upset the status quo. In addition, in his visit to China in October 2004, Secretary of State Colin Powell denied Taiwan as a sovereign state, to the surprise of China observers in the US, allegedly a statement quoted out of context and a statement that State Department spokesman later on downplayed.

Ever since the establishment of Sino–American diplomatic ties in 1979, presidential candidates from the non-incumbent party have been typically critical of the existing US cross-strait policy for being overly accommodating to China.

Ronald Reagan reprimanded the Carter Administration for betraying Taiwan (indeed, Jimmy Carter came close to vetoing the TRA). Bill Clinton faulted George H. W. Bush for coddling Beijing dictators responsible for the Tiananmen crackdown (indeed, Bush secretly sent Scowcroft to Beijing to reassure the administration's friendship to China while publicly denouncing the Beijing regime). George W. Bush criticized Clinton for misidentifying China as strategic partner rather than strategic competitor. Upon assuming office, however, new presidents, irrespective of their party affiliations, typically would moderate their critical stands toward China, work on common interests, and sidestep controversial and conflicting issues. The Reagan presidency initially intended to enhance the US–Japan alliance to redress the Asian policy under the previous three presidents, seen unduly tilting toward China.[28] And yet, during the Reagan years, the US offered China technology and even intelligence, and the Sino-American relationship reached an apogee. As soon as he began attending foreign policy issues, Clinton delinked the permanent normal trade relationship (PNTR) with human rights issues.[29] After the EP-3 incident in the early months of the Bush administration, the term strategic competitor, coined to define China during the presidential campaign, was quietly dropped. The US and China then moved to a positive mode of interaction after 9/11, and Jiang became one of the few leaders invited to Crawford, Texas.[30] By the end of George W. Bush's first term, Secretary of State Powell was able to claim that Sino–American relationship was at its best in recent history.

Policy disagreement or friction regarding the Taiwan Strait existed mainly not between the two parties, but between the executive branch and legislative branch of the US government. No matter which party is in power, it will have to deal with China in a more or less realistic way.[31] Not having to deal with China directly, but more attentive to advocacy groups in the constituencies concerned with China's human rights and religion policies as well as Taiwan's difficult international status, Congress can be more critical of China than can the executive branch.[32] Most initiatives in US China policy that affected Taiwan came from a few executive officials in each administration.[33] Congress simply reacted. However, as Robert Sutter contends, Congress reacted frequently and timely, applying the brake to reduce the thrust that the executive branch had generated. Carter's sudden decision to de-recognize Taiwan shocked members of Congress of both parties, prodding Congress—which at that time was controlled by his party—to draft the TRA in 1979. This Act passed so overwhelmingly in both Houses that Carter initially had wanted to, but could not veto it.[34] In signing the August 17 Communiqué to reduce arms sales to Taiwan, Reagan also gave Taiwan Six Assurances (including that US would not consult with China for arms sales to Taiwan, and would not compel Taiwan to negotiate with China), a balancing act that most likely had preempted the opposition from a Republican-controlled Congress.[35] Clinton's slighting of Lee Teng-hui was repudiated by a joint congressional resolution with preponderant majority in the House and near unanimity in Senate that inculcated the administration to permit Lee to visit his alma mater. In short, the executive-congressional "disagreement" has been a constant feature regarding the Taiwan Strait issue. Congress has been supportive of Taiwan, irrespective of whichever party is in power. Congressional voting records show that partisan voting was significant regarding China (Republicans were overwhelmingly for China's PNTR status, while Democrats were for human rights protection issues). But when it comes to Taiwan Strait issue, Congress tends to vote in a bipartisan way, and often to the displeasure of the administration, irrespective which party occupies the White House.

Impacts on regional cooperation and conflict

As analyzed above, partisan conflict governs US policies toward North Korea while congressional-executive disagreement colors US policies toward the Taiwan Strait. Several reasons account for this structural difference.

The first reason has to do with the availability of information on the magnitude of threat in the two flash points. The shortage of information on North Korea's nuclear capability tends to fuel rather than dampen partisan dispute over US policy toward North Korea. Lacking reliable and verifiable information, experts have to make assumptions when assessing DPRK's nuclear capability. Some would discount DPRK's claim and even call it a bluff, while others would present the worst-case scenario. For example, assuming that North Korea lacked high power motors or sufficient replacement centrifuges, Selig Harrison, in his well-known recent Foreign Affairs piece, suggested that North Korea might have only processed low enriched uranium.[36] To Harrison, the Bush administration was politically motivated to unduly overestimate North Korea's ability to produce high enriched uranium, much in the same way it inflated the threat of weapons of mass destruction in the case of Iraq. In a few weeks, and based on indirect evidence such as Libya's documents, the Bush administration suggested that DPRK might have already undertaken a moderately complex process and, possibly with the help of Pakistan, built facilities to process uranium rich enough to be marketed abroad. Different estimates of North Korea's nuclear capability thus lead one to infer North Korea's intention and interpret North Korea's international behavior in a very different light, leading the two parties to talk over rather than to each other. Different estimate about capability and different inference about the intention reinforce one's belief in one's own party's policy approach to North Korea and one's criticism of the other party's.

Information on China's missile threat and Taiwan's defense capability is quite indisputable, rarely a subject of partisan debate in the US. While confidence building mechanisms across the Strait are yet to be established, bilateral dialogues and visits for high level defense officials between Washington DC and Beijing have been long established, though occasionally interrupted, as in the case of EP-3 incidence in early 2001. US–Taiwan military consultation has also been institutionalized. The only disagreement within the policy making circle in Washington DC regarding Taiwan's security seems to be over the issue of how best to enhance Taiwan's defense without upsetting the delicate balance across the Strait. On this, Congress typically held that the more arms sales and defense assistance the US could give, the better Taiwan was able to protect itself, but the White House typically did not share this understanding for fear that unrestrained US–Taiwan military ties could spoil US–China political ties. For decades, Congress had repeatedly urged military technology transfer to Taiwan and defense cooperation with Taiwan, and eventually decided to legislate a Taiwan Security Enhancement Act (TSEA) in the late 1990s. The executive branch, irrespective of which party was in charge, had been wary of congressional requests for "over-arming" Taiwan, and had used political capital to prevent TSEA from becoming law. However, the congressional-executive friction on how best to arm Taiwan is no longer an issue. China's rapid military buildup in the new millennium (especially its deployment of 700 missiles targeted at Taiwan) and Taiwan's laggard in appropriating any budget for defense procurement to cope with this new threat have made both ends of Pennsylvania Avenue equally concerned about an under-armed Taiwan.

A second reason why partisan politics tends to taint Washington's policy toward DPRK lies in the elusive nature of regime dynamics within DPRK. The survivability of the DPRK regime is often an issue in the deliberation of Washington's policy, unlike the two regimes across the Taiwan Strait—one being a small, stable, and increasingly mature democracy, the other being an economically successful, and politically re-consolidated, authoritarian regime. The end of the Cold War at the turn of the 1990s, dynastic political succession in 1994–5, the subsequent three-year famine, led some to conjecture about a possible imminent collapse of the DPRK. And yet, the North Korean economy managed to survive and rebound, triggering a debate on whether US and other countries' food aid had prolonged the life of this anachronistic regime.[37] Then, a surprising July 2002 economic reform ignited a new round of speculation on the possibility of having a Chinese style economic transformation in North Korea. And yet, within two years of the milestone reform, cracks of the system—speculative business practices, inflation, increased refugee flow, uncontrollable spread of smuggled tapes, and defection of cadres—spurred another round of speculation on possible collapse of the North Korean regime. Uncertainty about the trajectory of regime change in the North had the effect of hardening partisan positions on US policies toward the regime. To the subscribers of the "compliance before negotiation" strategy, giving carrots first to accelerate economic transformation without demanding a full and prior compliance on nuclear issues could only reward and extend the life of an antiquated regime. On the one hand, DPRK's reform could be "merely an effort to get hard cash to prop up the economy, ease food shortages, and ultimately avoid a government collapse."[38] On the other hand, if North Korea is seriously committed to economic reform, and the regime endures and reinvigorates itself, then it will be even more unwilling to forsake nuclear program. To the advocates of "negotiation for compliance" strategy, while a regime collapse in the North cannot be ruled out, one cannot count on that to solve the nuclear crises. Moreover, the opportunity to engage North Korea in economic change can be and should be leveraged to induce its commitment to dismantle nuclear program.

While neither side of the debate on Washington's policy toward North Korea is convincing to each other, there is little controversy now about US policy to socialize China in international economic systems but keenly monitor its behavior in the realm of regional and global security (most notably its maritime activities and its arms exports). Supporting Taiwan's democracy is a bipartisan consensus, and indeed, may well be a legal obligation according to the Taiwan Relations Act, a piece of legislation passed in 1979 with an overwhelming bipartisan support. How firm and how well specified US policy needs to be in supporting Taiwan is indeed a delicate issue where the two US parties may disagree, especially when one party dislodges another party from the White House. But as contended above, neither party seems to have locked itself into any extreme position.[39] The controversy typically arises when Congress takes issue with the White House that appears to have retrenched its support to Taiwan to diminish the ire of Beijing. Responses to China's enacting of an anti-secession law against Taiwan in the spring of 2005 best illustrate the disagreement between the two branches of the US government. The anti-secession law legally defined Taiwan as a breakaway territory and codified the right to use force to prevent Taiwan's separation from China. The Bush administration indicated its disapproval of this arguably status quo disturbing legislation, but did not oppose or scorn China. Such a measured response was in contrast with President Bush's harsh treatment of Taiwan's President Chen for his introduction of national referendum to Taiwan's electoral politics in late 2003, an initiative deemed by China as status quo upsetting.[40] In mid March 2005, Congress overwhelmingly passed resolutions, requesting the administration to express "serious concern" about the anti-secession law and reiterate American position on the necessity for using peaceful means and obtaining the consent of Taiwan residents to determine the future of Taiwan.

The third reason why the structure of US domestic politics differs for the issues of North Korea and the Taiwan Strait has to do with the intrinsic nature of the game that Washington DC is engaged in these two flash points. US policy toward the Taiwan Strait is one of deterrence, preventing neither side from upsetting the equilibrium. US policy toward North Korea is one of compellence or coercive diplomacy, which requires North Korea to roll back and even eliminate nuclear programs it has already embarked on. Compellence is substantially more difficult than deterrence, because compellent actions aim at altering the behavior of the targeted nation. Moreover, compellent actions "directly engage the prestige and the passions of the put-up state... [while] deterrent threats are both easier to appear to have ignored or easier to acquiesce to without great loss of face".[41] Not only are compellence and coercive diplomacy more difficult to pursue, the leverages available to the US to execute them in the Korean peninsula are in acute short supply. The end of the Cold War has diluted, if not severely strained, the US–South Korean alliance, and eroded the "parallel interests and partnership" between Washington and Beijing, now that the Soviet Union no longer exists. South Korea's initiatives to engage North Korea in political and economic exchange with the South have compounded US policy debate on the optimal mixture and sequencing of incentives and coercion toward North Korea. China, the only remaining significant ally and the principal trade partner and oil supplier of North Korea, has hosted the six-party talks but remains an independent player rather than US ally or close partner in dealing with North Korea. (Notice that the China–DPRK alliance can be phased out only with mutual consent, unlike the US–South Korean alliance that can be dismantled only with a one-year prior notice by either party). After 9/11, the US has also been preoccupied with anti-global terrorism and the war in Iraq. Given the intractable nature of compellence and the scarcity of diplomatic, military and even economic resources that US could deploy with respect to North Korea, partisan debates over Washington policy toward North Korea easily degenerated into an uncompromising self defense and wholesale denouncement of the other side of the aisle.

Patterns of domestic politics have important implications for regional cooperation and conflict. Partisan politics in Washington compounds, and unintentionally disrupts, crisis management in the Korean peninsula. In contrast, the executive-congressional "discord" seems to have no negative externalities for security environment across the Taiwan Strait.

Partisan contention on US policy toward North Korea produced hyperbolic politics and increased noise-signal ratio, giving North Korea opportunities to irresponsibly defect from international agreement, allowing North Korea to put more roadblocks to negotiation, and shifting the time advantage to North Korea.[42] North Korean reciprocating hyperbole in turn intensifies the partisan dispute in the US, raising political cost for political elite in each party to moderate or alter an increasingly entrenched policy position. The feedback loop between domestic politics and international politics is mainly through congressional action under the condition of divided government, and through presidential electoral campaign and, in case of political power transfer, policy review and reversal. North Korea could draw upon partisan disagreement and might harbor hope that new policies might be forthcoming after each election. It is both suggestive and eerie that North Korea crises have occurred in a four-year interval. The feedback mechanism in the domestic-international linkage tends to be a vicious one, reinforcing security dilemma (to use a neo-realist term) or undermining already meager mutual trust and eroding the ability to make credible commitment (to use neo-liberal terms).

While partisan friction in US policy toward North Korea has resulted in policy discontinuity and even reversal, the executive-congressional contention has not negatively affected US policy toward the Taiwan Strait. Major foreign policy decisions made by various administrations—such as derecognition of Taiwan in 1978 by Carter and the signing of 1982 Communiqué for the reduction of weapon sales to Taiwan by Reagan—are typically non-reversible. Congress was left to take remedial measures, such as enacting the Taiwan Relations Act in 1979, and holding hearings to lead Reagan to issue Six Assurances to Taiwan. Power transfer from one party to another necessarily leads to the changing of guards for foreign policy team, and possible policy shift, but congressional membership is relatively stable, effectively restricting the limit of policy change that the executive branch may contemplate. The combination of the Executive drive and the congressional brake tends to stabilize rather than upset the equilibrium in the Taiwan Strait. Congressional hearing at T-2 following any executive initiative at T-1 can "fine tune" or "correct" any new deal that any administration cares to cut with China. The "congressional fine-tuning" closes any possible loophole that may jeopardize Taiwan's interest, but does not repudiate the deal per se. In short, Congress tinkers with but does not refute the negotiated outcome reached at the international level. The US executive branch and Beijing are thus likely to play a game of reassurance, characterized by credible commitment and incentives to cooperate, rather than a prisoner's dilemma game which is characterized by mutual suspicion and the tendency to defect. Partisan difference not being significant, US policy toward the Taiwan Strait tends to reduce any illusion on the part of China and Taiwan. Indeed the expectation is that the administration may have some surprise for Taiwan, but Congress may be expected to smooth out the edges. China, for its part, has learned to expect that whatever it can extract from the US administration will be qualified and discounted by subsequent congressional action.

Credible commitment by key players toward one another is crucial to promoting cooperation and managing crisis. A nation's credible commitment at the international level, however, is conditioned by domestic politics.[43] US policy toward North Korea suffers discontinuity and entrenched conflicting partisan positions. Policy gyrates as wildly as electoral roulettes. Partisan difference may also punctuate US policy toward the Taiwan Strait when one party dislodges another from the White House, but the policy of any new administration often quickly reverts to the well-established consensus. Congressional disagreement with the White House on US policy toward the Taiwan Strait may persist (not least for high incumbency reelection rate in the congressional race), but the interaction between the two institutions displays a highly stable pattern that even China can well predict. It is not too far fetched to conclude that US domestic politics adds uncertainty to international efforts to defuse North Korean nuclear crisis, but stability to the management of conflict in the Taiwan Strait.

Notes

1 For a few exceptions, see Robert G. Sutter, *US Policy Toward China: An Introduction to the Role of Interest Groups*, Lanham, Maryland: Rowman and Littlefield, 1998; and Kerry Dumbaugh, *US China Policy: Interest Groups and Their Influences*, Huntington, NY: Novinka, 2001.
2 Lee Hamilton, *A Creative Tension: The Foreign Policy Roles of the President and Congress*, Washington: Wilson Center Press, 2002, p. 1.
3 Graham T. Allison, *Essence of Decision*, Boston: Little Brown, 1971, conclusion.
4 Thomas E. Mann, "Making Foreign Policy: President and Congress," in Thomas E. Mann, *A Question of Balance*, Washington: Brookings, 1990, p. 7.
5 Hamilton, *A Creative Tension*, p. 6; Michael J. Glennon, *Constitutional Diplomacy*, Princeton : Princeton University Press, 1990; James M. Lindsay and Randall B. Ripley, (eds), *Congress Resurgent*, Ann Arbor: University of Michigan Press, 1993; Eugene R. Wittkopf and James M. McCormick (eds), *The Domestic Sources of American Foreign Policy*, Lanham, Maryland: Rowman & Littlefield, 1999.

6 Committee on Foreign Relations, House of Representatives, US Congress, hearing, "American Public Attitudes Toward Foreign Policy," 27 July 1994, p. 10.

7 Benjamin I. Page and Robert Y. Shapiro, *The Rational Public: Fifty Years of Trends in American's Preferences*, Chicago: University of Chicago Press, 1992; and Ole R. Holsti, *Public Opinion and American Foreign Policy,* Ann Arbor: University of Michigan Press, 1996.

8 Walter Lippmann, *Public Opinion*, New York: Harcourt, Brace and Co, 1922.

9 Richard Sobel, *The Impact of Public Opinion on US Foreign Policy*, New York: Oxford University Press, 2001.

10 Thomas W. Graham, *The Politics of Failure: Strategic Nuclear Arms Control, Public Opinion, and Domestic Politics in the United States, 1945–1980*, doctoral dissertation, MIT 1989.

11 Mathew D. McCubbins, "Party Politics, Divided Government, and Budget Deficits," in Samuel Kernell (ed.) *Parallel Politics: Economic Policymaking in he United States and Japan*, Washington: The Brookings Institution, 1991, pp. 110–117.

12 Ole R. Holsti and James N. Rosenau, *American Leadership in World Affairs: Vietnam and the Breakdown of Consensus*, Boston: Allen and Unwin, 1984.

13 Wittkopf and McCormick, *The Domestic Sources of American Foreign Policy*, p. xiv.

14 Thomas E. Patterson, *Out of Order*, New York: Vintage, 1994, p. 11.

15 Steven L. Levine, "Bathing in Lukewarm Water: American Public Opinion Regarding the US 'Security Commitment' to Taiwan," paper presented at Duke conference on security environment in the Taiwan Strait, 31 January 2004.

16 Robyn Lim, "The US-Japan Alliance in the Korean Crucible," *American Asian Review*, Vol. 21, No. 3, 2003, pp. 1–28.

17 The term is Victor Cha's, see Victor Cha and David Kang, *Nuclear North Korea*, New York: Columbia University Press, 2003.

18 See Mark E. Caprio, "US–DPRK Diplomatic Relations under the Clinton Administration: Cycles of Conflict and Resolution," *American Asian Review*, Vol. 21, No. 1, 2003, pp. 55–84, especially p. 59.

19 See ibid., p. 62.

20 International Crisis Group Asia Report, *North Korea: A Phased Negotiation Strategy*, No. 61, 2003, p. 12.

21 This package "feel short of what the North would accept" and it did not include "any clear penalties for refusing to cooperate," thus North Korea was "under little pressure to comprise." See Richard N. Haass, *The Opportunity*, New York: Public Affairs, 2005, p. 98.

22 See Vanessa Williams, "Edwards Cites Failed Foreign Policy," *Washington Post*, 30 August 2004. Think tank scholars criticize Democratic administration's approach as too tactical, while Republican administration's too inflexible. See Michael O'Hanlon and Mike Mochizuki, "Toward a Grand Bargain with North Korea," in Alexander T. J. Lennon and Camille Eiss (eds) *Reshaping Rogue States*, Cambridge, Mass: MIT Press, 2004, pp. 158–160.

23 See Glenn Kessler, "Both Sides Bend to Restart N. Korea Talks," *Washington Post Online*, 13 July 2005. Online. Available HTTP: <http://www.washingtonpost.com/wp-dyn/content/article/2005/7/13/ar2005> (accessed 14 July 2005). And "Significance of Presidential Special Envoy Chung Dong-young's Visit to North Korea," *Korea Policy Review*, July 2005, p. 12.

24 Secretary of State Condoleezza Rice reiterated on July 9, 2005 "We are not talking about enhancement of the current proposal," that is, not sweetening the US proposal advanced in June 2004. See Joel Brinkley, "Setting the Table for North Korea's Return," *New York Times Online*, 11 July 2005. Online. Available HTTP: <http://www.nytimes.com/2005/07/11/international/asia/llassess.html> (accessed 11 July 2005).

25 David E. Sanger, "US Plans to Renew Its Offer of Food Aid to North Korea," *New York Times Online,* June 23, 2005. Online. Available HTTP: <http://www.nytimes.com/2005/06/23/politics/23korea.html> (accessed 24 June 2005).

26 For an excellent summary, see Robert Sutter, "The Bush Administration and US China Policy Debate," *Issues and Studies*, Vol. 38, No. 2, 2002, pp. 1–30.

27 Edward Friedman "America's 2000 Presidential Election and China's Threat to Taiwan," *American Asian Review*, Vol. 19, No. 2, 2001, pp. 1–29.

28 See James Mann, *About Face*, New York: Knopf , 1999, ch.7.

29 Ibid., cf. chs.15 and 16.

30 EP-3 was a US plane forced to land on Hainan, China. For the change from confrontation to collaboration between the two countries in the early part of the Bush administration, see Richard Bush and Catharin Dalpino, "Introduction and Review of 2002," in Richard Bush and Catharin Dalpino (eds) *Brookings Northeast Asia Survey, 2002–2003*, p. vi.

31 This imperative is particularly clear in the post-Cold War era, see David M. Lampton, *Same Bed Different Dreams*, Berkeley: University of California Press, 2001.

32 For the effectiveness of Taiwan lobby, see Tsung Chi, "From the China Lobby to the Taiwan Lobby," in Peter Koehn and Xiao-huang Yin (eds) *The Expanding Roles of Chinese Americans in US–China Relations: Transnational Networks and Trans-Pacific Interactions*, Armonk, N.Y.: M. E. Sharpe, 2002, pp. 108–124. Congressional human rights caucuses and Taiwan caucuses overlap substantially.

33 See James Mann, *About Face*, and Ramon H. Myers, Michel C. Oksenberg, and David Shambaugh (eds) *Making China Policy*, Lanham, Maryland: Rowman & Littlefield, 2001.

34 Jaw-Ling Joanne Chang, "Managing US–Taiwan Relations: 20 Years after the Taiwan Relations Act," in Jaw-Ling Joanne Chang and William W. Boyer (eds) *United States–Taiwan Relations: Twenty Years after the Taiwan Relations Act*, Maryland Series in Contemporary Asian Studies, 2000, No. 1, p. 17.

35 Harvey Feldman, "Taiwan, Arms Sales, and the Reagan Assurances," *American Asian Review*, Vol.19, No. 3, 2001, pp. 75–102.

36 Selig S. Harrison, "Did North Korea Cheat?" *Foreign Affairs Online*, January/February 2005. Online. Available HTTP: <http://www.foreignaffairs.org/20050101faessay84109/selig-s-harrison/did-north-korea-cheat.html> (accessed 20 May 2005).

37 Nicholas Eberstadt, "North Korea's Survival Game: Understanding the Recent Past, Thinking about the Future," in Ahn Choong-yong, Nicholas Eberstadt, and Lee Young-sun (eds) *A New International Engagement Framework for North Korea?* Washington: Korea Economic Institute, 2004, pp. 64–73.

38 Norimitsu Onishi, "2 Koreas Forge Economic Ties to Ease Tensions," *New York Times Online*, 8 February 2005, Online. Available HTTP: <http://www.nytimes.com/2005/02/08/international/asia/08korea.html> (accessed 8 February 2005).

39 Nancy Bernkopf Tucker, "Strategic Ambiguity: Time for a Change?" in Tucker (ed.) *Dangerous Strait*, New York: Columbia University Press, 2005.

40 For the Bush administration's measured and low-key response, and its unevenness in treating the two sides of the Taiwan Strait, see Dan Blumenthal and Randy Scheunemann, "Tense Straits," *National Review Online*, version, January 27, 2005. Online. Available HTTP: <http://www.aei.org/publications/filter.all,pubID.21859/pub_detail.asp> (accessed 27 July 2005).

41 Robert J. Art, "To What Ends Military Power," *International Security*, Vol. 4, Spring 1980, pp. 4–55.

42 Cha and Kang, *Nuclear North Korea*, ch.5.

43   Robert Putnam, "Diplomacy and Domestic Politics: The Logic of Two-Level Game," reprinted in Peter B. Evans, Harold K. Jacobson, and Robert D. Putnam (eds) *Double-Edged Diplomacy*, Berkeley: University of California Press, 1991, pp. 431–68, especially p. 440.

4 The two Koreas in Northeast Asia: linkages between domestic, inter-Korean, and regional politics

Yong-Pyo Hong

Introduction

After North Korea withdrew from the Non-Proliferation Treaty (NPT) in March 1993, the North Korean nuclear problem became a key issue that could threaten peace and stability not only in the Korean peninsula but also in Northeast Asia. The nuclear issue may be misunderstood if the focus is put only on inter-Korean relations. On the one hand, the domestic political consideration in both North and South Korea has influenced the cause and the process of North Korean nuclear development. On the other hand, the nuclear issue is to be solved at the regional level because the US has been a key player, and other countries in Northeast Asia have also had keen interests on that issue. In particular, the regional politics in Northeast Asia gained more influence as a multilateral framework, including the US, China, Japan, Russia and the two Koreas was launched to settle the second nuclear crisis which had been initiated by Pyongyang's admission of possessing highly-enriched uranium program in October 2002.

Within this context, this paper will try to present the nuclear issue in Northeast Asia as a game in which domestic, inter-Korean and regional politics have been intertwined by utilizing Putnam's concept of two-level game.[1] This approach begins by assuming that the politics of many international negotiations can usefully be conceived as a two-level game; the national level, and the international level. According to him, neither of the two levels can be ignored by central decision-makers, so long as their countries remain interdependent, yet sovereign. In other words, statesmen are strategically positioned between two levels. Diplomatic tactics and strategies are constrained simultaneously by what other states will accept and what domestic constituencies will ratify. To conclude a negotiation successfully, the statesman must bargain on these two tables, both reaching an international agreement and securing its domestic ratification.[2]

To begin with, Seoul's relations with Pyongyang have been closely linked with domestic politics. But, until very recently, the linkage was one-sided: namely the President and a few officials monopolized any deals with North Korea, and used them for domestic reasons, while the constituency had little information on policies towards North Korea, let alone influence them. With the democratization of

South Korea, however, this trend began to change. The general public now can obtain a far larger amount of information on various government activities, including those related to the North Korean issue than before. Consequently, the populace can make, if limited, their voice heard in government's negotiation with North Korea. In this context, the two-level game approach can be applied to the inter-Korean relations as far as South Korea is concerned.

Here, one may ask whether the two-level games approach can be applied to the North Korean side, considering the fact that authority is concentrated in the hands of a single predominant leader. In the case of North Korea, it would be difficult to apply concepts such as "ratification," and "win-set."[3] But, the two-level games logic can be used in the North Korean case in the context that the approach views the relationship between the two levels through the "eyes of a single leader, or chief of government," and that it emphasizes his role as a central strategic actor.[4] According to Moravscik, strategies employed by the leader to cope with internal and external bargaining reflect: (1) the leader's interest in enhancing his domestic position; (2) an effort to mobilize an optimal response to international imperatives, regardless of domestic factors; or (3) individual policy preferences about the issues in question.[5] In this sense, the two-level games approach can be applied, however limited, to the North Korean case as Kim Jong Il's power base was not as firm as his father's on the one hand, and his perception on domestic and international environment has been reflected in his foreign policy, as will be discussed later.

In addition, in order to obtain a clearer picture of inter-Korean relations, we need to understand one more level of the game, a game to deal with constraints from the surrounding powers. Ever since the division of the Korean peninsula, which was attributable, at least in part to superpower rivalry, the fate of inter-Korean relations has never been free from influence of surrounding powers. For example, the Joint Communiqué between North and South Korea in 1972, which was the first formal agreement ever signed between the two, was heavily influenced by the Nixon Doctrine and subsequent improvement of Sino–US relations. The collapse of the Soviet Union and the Cold War system contributed to the conclusion of the Basic Agreement between the two Koreas in 1992. Recently, the American and Japanese policies towards the Korean peninsula became particularly critical in North–South Korean relations because Pyongyang has been eager to improve its relations with Washington and Tokyo. In particular, North Korea has tried to negotiate the nuclear issue with the US, rather than with South Korea.

In this respect, this paper will analyze the nuclear issue with the assumption that inter-Korean affairs can be understood as three-level games: domestic politics in North and South Korea, relationships between the two Koreas, and regional politics, especially their relations with the US. This paper will first examine changes in power distribution in both North and South Korea, and their perception of each other as well as of the US as domestic sources of internal-external linkages. Then, relationships among those domestic politics, inter-Korean relations and regional politics regarding nuclear issues will be analyzed.

Variables of internal–external linkages in the Korean peninsula

South Korea

(a) Power distribution

The primary actor in South Korea's foreign policy-making, under the constitutional provision, is the president who relies on his staff, his Foreign Minister and ministry officials. Under authoritarian regimes, the foreign policy-making was almost monopolized by the president and his core staffs. But with the democratization of Korea, the public and interest groups came to exert more pressures and influence on the process of formulating and executing foreign policy in South Korea.

At the end of 1992, Kim Young-sam was elected as president, the country's first president without a military background in more than 30 years. Thus, South Korea has lived up to the goal of establishing democracy through an orderly and peaceful transfer of power. Under the civilian government, the democratic reform progressed rapidly. With the process of democratization, civil society in South Korea became active and the autonomy of the state was correspondingly constrained. Since the regime could no longer exclude the popular sectors of the political process, it had to develop popular policies tailored to their needs to solicit their support. Intellectuals became more open in articulating their democratic values and norms, thereby exerting pressures on the regime to incorporate them in policy-making. In addition, with the middle class becoming more vocal and attentive, the government was pressured more to promote and protect the interest of a large number of constituencies and interest groups. With an activated civil society, the government begun to accommodate a large number of demands placed by interest groups for participation in the process of policy-making, including the policy toward North Korea.[6]

This tendency was reinforced with the advent of the Kim Dae-Jung government in 1998. Kim was the first president from the opposition party in Korea's constitutional history. Moreover, he stood for Cholla province which had been discriminated by the authoritarian regimes based in Kyongsang province. Accordingly, President Kim's policies, including the Sunshine Policy[7] toward North Korea, were continuously opposed and criticized by the establishments which were relatively conservative.

In 2003, Roh Moo-hyun from Kim Dae-Jung's party was elected as new president. During the election campaign, Roh was strongly supported by the young generation who was relatively progressive, and wanted fresh changes in Korean politics. After election, President Roh publicly tried to overcome the authoritarian legacy, and encourage the activity of NGOs, identifying himself as progressive. Thus, the public and the civilian sectors came to play a greater role in the formation of South Korea's foreign policy while the criticism from the conservative establishments became stronger. Moreover, the new generation of leaders, known as the "386 generation," assumed important positions in the government and the ruling party.[8] The new leaders, by and large, have critical views of the US while emphasizing the necessity of cooperation with North Korea.

(b) Changing perceptions of the US and North Korea

Traditionally, South Korean perception of the United States and North Korea, the major objectives of its foreign policy, had been symbolized as "pro-Americanism, and anti-Communism." Ever since the Korean War, in which the US protected South Korea from being communized by North Korea, the US and South Korea had maintained a close alliance system to cope with the threat from the North. But this perception began to change with the end of the Cold War externally, and with the democratization internally.

First of all, the collapse of the socialist systems in Eastern Europe, together with the political and economic development of South Korea, made Seoul confident in its competition with Pyongyang. Thus, the former began to emphasize exchange and cooperation with the latter. The first initiative was taken by President Roh Tae-woo who proposed a comprehensive policy for reconciliation with North Korea. This move resulted in the conclusion of the Basic Agreement between North and South Korea in 1991.

President Kim Young-sam went further to declare in his inauguration speech of February 1993 that "ideology" or "system" could not take precedence over "nation." In addition, President Kim first named Han Wan-sang, a relatively progressive figure regarding relations with North Korea, as deputy prime minister in charge of unification affairs. But Han quickly came under heavy ideological attack from conservative critics and he was eventually dismissed. Meanwhile, as the nuclear crisis was heightened by North Korea, President Kim could not but take a hard-line stance toward the North.

President Kim Dae-Jung had more positive perceptions of North Korea, considering Kim Jong Il as a reasonable and negotiable partner. In this context, President Kim's Sunshine Policy toward North Korea was designed to induce North Korea to open up and institute reforms through reconciliation and cooperation, in contrast to past hard-line policies. The Sunshine Policy made it clear that South Korea would not try to absorb the North. In addition, President Kim kept this reconciliatory policy direction despite such events as the intrusion of a North Korean submarine in 1998 and the conflict in the yellow sea between North and South Korean warships in 1999.[9]

The Roh Moo-hyun government developed the Sunshine Policy into the "Peace and Prosperity" policy. The perception of the Roh government on North Korea seems to be even more positive than that of the Kim Dae-Jung government. Such a perception can be symbolically found in the fact that the Roh government stopped identifying North Korea as the "main enemy" of South Korea,[10] and that it has been trying to abolish the National Security Law which regards North Korea as an anti-state group.

While South Korean perception on North Korea has been changing positively, South Korea and the US came to have difficulties in coordinating their policies vis-à-vis North Korea. During the Cold War period, the two allies had the same goal as far as North Korean affairs was concerned, the goal of containing the Communists. With the end of the Cold War, however, South Korea and the US came to pursue different objectives regarding North Korea; the reconciliation with North Korea for the former and the prohibition of the proliferation of weapons of mass destruction for the latter. In particular, the advent of the Bush administration and the September 11 attacks in New York made the US emphasize security issues, taking a hard-line posture toward North Korea while South Korea sought eagerly to improve its relations with North Korea, encouraged by the North–South summit of June 2000. Thus the perception gap between the two has deepened.

Moreover, as relatively progressive forces gained power, unfavorable views of the US increased. The "386 generation" is known for being ideologically opposed to close relations with the United States. They also cite historical reasons for their distrust of the United States. They typically regard the US as less the country that fought in the Korean War, than as the country that backed past military dictators. In this vein, they seek to have more equitable relationships with the US, as reflected in President Roh's inaugural speech on February 2003: "We will see to it that the alliance matures into a more reciprocal and equitable relationship."[11] Negative perception of the US is increasing among the public, too. For example, a recent survey asked people what country they believe most threatens Korea's security. Of the respondents to the survey, 33 percent named North Korea as the biggest threat to security, while 39 percent named the United States. Perhaps even more intriguing, among people in their 20s, 58 percent named the United States as the greatest threat to security, while only 20 percent cited the North.[12]

North Korea

(a) Power consolidation

The Kim Jong Il era opened in earnest with the power succession from his father in September 1998. The Kim Jong Il system, however, was still under the shadow of the late Kim Il Sung at that time. For example, at the meeting of the Supreme Peoples' Assembly in 1998, Kim Jong Il did not make his own speech, suggesting that Kim Il Sung's speech made eight years ago should be "implemented as programmatic guidelines." Moreover, the new Constitution, which claims to uphold the late Kim as the "eternal President," was named "the Kim Il Sung Constitution."[13]

In fact, since Kim Il Sung's death in 1994, North Korea had been ruled by "the late Kim's teachings" with such a slogan as "Great Leader Kim Il Sung is forever with us." One of the major reasons why Kim Jong Il utilized his father's behest can be found in Kim Jong Il's search for regime stability.[14] First, it would be necessary for Kim to pay his respect for his father in order to justify the hereditary succession. Second, more importantly, given Kim Jong Il's relatively weak legitimacy, he sought to succeed to the late Kim's charisma, and thereby to secure the kind of authority his father had maintained.[15] Such an intention was sufficiently reflected in the popular slogan, "Kim Il Sung is Kim Jong Il, and Kim Jong Il is Kim Il Sung."[16] Third, in a pragmatic sense, Kim Jong Il might have figured that it was better to push ahead with his father's policies because it was difficult to devise new policies for reviving the sagging economy and for cheering up the North Korean residents plunged into despair. In addition, he probably intended to avoid the responsibility for economic failure.

Although Kim Jong Il's power base became more stable with the formal power succession in September 1998, he still had serious problems in terms of political consolidation. His foremost difficulty lay with the economy. The economic diffi-culties have been a critical threat to the Communist regime in the context that 'self-reliance in economy' has been one of the pillars of the *Chuch'e* ideology. A severe food shortage may emerge as a decisive factor instigating distrust of the Kim Jong Il regime. The food rationing system in North Korea had already been paralyzed due to the lack of food from early 1990s, and the masses were being compelled to procure food on their own through black markets or elsewhere, thus creating social confusion. For overcoming this problem, North Korea introduced new economic steps which partly accepted the market system. But they proved insufficient to solve the economic difficulties.[17]

Given the situation, Kim Jong Il faced a dilemma. In order to overcome diplo-matic isolation and economic difficulties, North Korea needed to open its door. But the opening will surely be accompanied by the flow of outside information which can awake the North Korean populace to the problems of the Chuch'e sys-tem, as well as to the illegitimacy of Kim Jong Il's hereditary succession of power. In this respect, it can be argued that Kim Jong Il put his policy focus on overcoming the dilemma between state security and regime security.[18] And this influences the direction of North Korean foreign policy.

Another problem Kim Jong Il should deal with internally is the military. Kim Jong Il has valued the role of the military under the flag of "military-first poli-tics." According to a North Korean source, the "military-first politics" "depends on the People's Army as a pillar of our revolution, enabling the entire people, including workers and peasants, to wage their struggle armed with a revolution-ary army spirit; this is a powerful and refined socialist political method that radi-ates brilliantly."[19] Kim Jong Il's own remarks reflect how heavily he relies on the North Korean armed forces, as when he noted: "My strength comes from the mil-itary. There are two sources of my strength: the people united in oneness and the military. Even if we should fare well with other countries, we will always need military strength. In relations with foreign countries, strength comes from the military, and my strength too stems from the military. We should have adequate military strength even when we maintain friendly relations with foreign coun-tries." In fact, the military emerged as the most influential group in North Korea under "military-first politics."

In North Korea, Kim Jong Il is supposed to maintain monolithic power. But, as long as he relies on the military for his strength, it would be difficult for Kim Jong Il to disregard the opinion of the military in making foreign policy.

(b) Changing perception on the US and South Korea

Ever since North Korea's desire to unify Korea on its terms was frustrated by the firm American military response during the Korea War, North Korean leaders have regarded the US as "archenemy" while fearing its formidable power experienced during the war. During the Cold War era, shouting the slogan of "anti-imperialism and anti-Americanism," North Korea could cope with the potential threat from the US by relying on the Soviet Union and China.

The collapse of the socialist system in the Soviet Union and East Europe brought about a new strategic environment for the North. Now the North Koreans needed to face the US threat directly for themselves. Thus, the question of 'survival' in the dimension of both the state and the regime has emerged as a more important factor than the principle of "anti-imperialism."[20] Pyongyang's security concern had increased dramatically as a result of Seoul's successful *Nordpolitik*. In addition, due to the ever-widening gap of national power between the two Koreas in favor of the South, the prospect of a German-style reunification, i.e., integration by absorption, was hard to exclude completely. Given the circumstances, Kim Il Sung tried to reduce the perceived threat from South Korea by concluding the "North–South Joint Declaration of the Denuclearization of the Korean Peninsula" and the "North–South Basic Agreement" in 1992.

For North Korea, probably the utmost task to resolve its security crisis was to deal with the US. Thus, Pyongyang sought to negotiate directly with Washington, aiming at obtaining US security assurances, and ultimately at improving relations between the two. And, by effectively using its "nuclear card," North Korea could successfully conclude the Geneva Agreement in 1994.

Unlike its positive attitude towards the US, the Kim Jong Il regime took a negative posture towards South Korea until 1997. This tendency was also related to Kim Jong Il's political necessity to maintain such a stance. First, North Korea attempted to mobilize the people and consolidate internal unity by using South Korea as a "scapegoat." In particular, as North Korea was trying to improve its relations with the US, its long-time sworn enemy, there arose an acute need to designate South Korea as its main enemy in place of the US.[21] Second, it seems that Kim Jong Il took into account the fact that the wave of openness stemming from improved relations with South Korea might threaten his political stand. He was also afraid of the possibility of the South's absorption of the North.[22]

In contrast with the need to retain strained relations with South Korea for the sake of his regime security, Kim Jong Il found himself in an awkward situation in which he could not completely reject contacts with South Korean authorities. Without progress in North–South dialogue, it was difficult for Pyongyang to improve its relations with the US to the extent it wished because of the cooperation between Seoul and Washington. Besides, South Korea has played the largest role in the provision of outside support for North Korean economic difficulties. Given the situation, North Korea had no way but to step forward, if limited, for inter-Korean contacts. In particular, with the summit of June 2000, North Korea began to take a more positive posture towards inter-Korean dialogue. But the weight was still put on its relations with the US.

The nuclear issue in domestic, inter-Korean, and regional linkages

The first nuclear crisis: 1993–1997

North Korea's foreign policies had been designed fundamentally to nurture international supportive forces to help it unify the South under communism. The collapse of the socialist camp, however, deprived it of such chances. Now Pyongyang was compelled to work out new policies to cope with the post-Cold War situation. Thus, North Korea sought to improve relations with the US and Japan in order to overcome security crisis, diplomatic isolation, and economic difficulties.

In a desperate effort to cope with the regime crisis, North Korea in March 1993 declared that it would withdraw from the NPT. This move inevitably caused crisis in the Korean peninsula, as well as in Northeast Asia. The Kim Young-sam government, which had taken a soft-line policy toward the North, began to change its posture, and the implementation of the Basic Agreement between the two Koreas, concluded in 1992, was at danger. The negotiation between North Korea and Japan to normalize diplomatic relationships was also postponed.

By launching brinkmanship diplomacy with the nuclear card, however, Pyongyang could establish a bilateral dialogue channel with the US. The main aims of North Korea in the negotiations with the US were obtaining the guarantee that the US would not use military forces against North Korea, and that the US must recognize the existing regime in Pyongyang. After a series of difficult negotiations, North Korea finally concluded the Geneva Agreement with the US in October 1994. Through the agreement, Pyongyang could achieve security, political, and economic benefits in return for its promise to freeze and eventually dismantle its nuclear weapons program. This agreement enabled Kim Jong Il not only to strengthen his political foothold on the domestic scene but also to obtain a nuclear security assurance that the US would not use nuclear weapons against North Korea.

Since then, Pyongyang has sought to institutionalize peaceful relations with Washington to assure its survival by demanding the conclusion of a peace agreement between the US and the DPRK. North Korea also tried to maintain bilateral dialogue channels with the US through negotiations on such agenda as exchanging liaison offices, repatriating American remains from the Korean War and controlling North Korean long-range missiles. Although the Pyongyang government wished to improve its relationship with the Washington government, however, it also needed to continue its anti-American campaigns as a means of ensuring internal unity for a political purpose.[23] Consequently, this practice hampered improving Pyongyang's relations with Washington.

While North Korea was eager to negotiate with the US to obtain a guarantee for survival by using the nuclear card, it maintained hostility and a confrontational attitude toward South Korea, rejecting any dialogue. Washington also sought to deal with Pyongyang, not within the context of South–North Korean relations as Seoul desired, but rather in response to the North Korean challenge to the NPT, a mainstay of post-Cold War US foreign policy. Accordingly, the South Koreans have been worrying about a rapid improvement in Washington–Pyongyang relations without matching development of Seoul–Pyongyang dialogue. Furthermore, South Korea was excluded from the negotiations to provide the light-water reactors (LWRs) to the North while the US dealt directly with North Korea.

The fact that South Korea was kept from participating in the talks, even though Seoul would be footing the bill for the LWRs, has aggravated South Korean public opinion and sown distrust of US policies and intentions. Given this situation, the Kim Young-sam government in the South tried to recover its initiative in relations with the North.

In June 1995, Pyongyang and Seoul had a series of contacts in Beijing, in which the former demanded food in the form of civilian assistance. South Korea wanted to make this occasion a breakthrough of its relations with the North. Accordingly the South insisted on labeling the contacts as a formal meeting to discuss rice aid between the authorities of the two sides. At last, the two agreed on South Korea's grant-type aid of rice amounting to 150,000 tons without any political strings. The Beijing negotiations followed a peculiar pattern, as it was the donor that found itself in the awkward position. This awkwardness was because President Kim Young-sam was so eager to provide food aid to North Korea and resume a formal dialogue with the North. President Kim even stated that, if needed, he was willing to import rice for additional assistance to the North. It appeared that President Kim hoped to increase public support for him and his party through successful rice diplomacy, facing the local elections due to be held in June, which was Korea's first in more than three decades. There were indications that the government hastily launched the first shipment of rice to North Korea on June 25 for a propaganda effect on election day. Nevertheless, the ruling party lost the local elections.

While President Kim had his desire to improve North–South relations by using the rice assistance, and thereby to increase his popularity at home and his influence abroad, North Korea feared, because of regime security, that the South Korean government would develop the rice talks into fully-fledged inter-Korean cooperation. Probably for this reason, the North locked up a South Korean rice-carrying vessel with the allegation of "spying activities," which indeed aggravated North–South relations. The Beijing rice talks finally broke down in September 1995 as the North continued to reject the principle of 'government official talks' the South wanted. The North Korean position was eloquently explained by the head of North Korean delegation when he said, "we will not sacrifice our political independence because of rice." [24] North Korea continued such strategy as 'negotiating with the US while isolating South Korea' virtually until the end of the Kim Young-sam government.

Reconciliatory period: 1998–2000

With the election of Kim Dae-Jung as new President of South Korea at the end of 1997, however, North Korea refrained from slandering the new government, taking a 'wait-and-see' approach.[25] In fact, President Kim suggested a forward-looking North Korea policy, so-called 'Sunshine Policy.' Borrowed from an Aesop fable that to get a passerby to take off his coat, sunshine is more effective than a strong wind, this policy sought to, in President Kim's own words, "lead North Korea down a path toward peace, reform and openness through reconciliation, interaction and cooperation with the South." President Kim also emphasized that the two sides would expand cultural, academic, and economic exchanges on the basis of separating economics from politics.[26]

Probably encouraged by South Korea's soft-line posture, the Pyongyang government participated in the vice-ministerial conference for fertilizer with the Seoul government in April 1998. In particular, Kim Jong Il presented on April 18 his new "Five-point Guidelines on Greater National Unity," where he emphasized, among others, "the improvement of North–South relations."[27] Since then, North Korea continued its contacts with the Southern government, despite ups and downs in the relationship. Eventually, the two Koreas held the summit between Kim Dae-Jung and Kim Jong Il on 13–15 June 2000, issuing the Joint Declaration.[28] Subsequently, various types of dialogue between North and South Korea were held, centering on ministerial level talks.

Unlike the previous period, the improvement of DPRK–US relations coincided with that of DPRK–South Korea relations around this time. As North Korea tested the Taepodong missile, a medium-range delivery system, in August 1999, President Clinton appointed former Secretary of Defense William Perry as Special Coordinator for Korean policy, who then launched a six-month review of US policy toward North Korea. Consequently, so-called "the Perry Process," which sought to offer North Korea a new way forward in ties with the US, was implemented. In November 1999, North Korea agreed with the US to suspend its plan to test another ballistic missile in return for lifting part of the American economic ban against North Korea.

Most of all, in October 2000, First Vice Marshall Jo Myong Rok visited Washington as Kim Jong Il's special envoy and announced the US–DPRK Joint Communiqué. It stated that "neither government would have hostile intent towards the other and confirmed the commitment of both governments to make every effort in the future to build a new relationship free from past enmity." This was indeed an encouraging statement for Kim Jong Il, who had been anxious to obtain a security guarantee from the US. In return for Jo's visit to Washington, Secretary of State Madeleine Albright visited Pyongyang. In addition, it was suggested that President Clinton himself might also visit North Korea, although it was not realized.

The second nuclear crisis: 2001–present

The inauguration of the Bush administration has reversed the conciliatory atmosphere. In early 2001, after a review of North Korea Policy, the Bush government took a hard-line posture, concluding that: The policies of the Clinton administration were appeasing in orientation; the Geneva Agreement fell short of exercising binding power to deter the North from developing nuclear weapons. In June, although President Bush stated that the US would reopen dialogue with North Korea, he still expressed his pessimistic view of the Kim Jong Il regime. Accordingly, North Korea criticized Bush's hard-line policy, and even postponed its contacts with South Korea.

US–DPRK relationships were aggravated in January 2002 when President Bush branded North Korea an "axis of evil," together with Iran and Iraq, after the terrorist attack of September 11. Furthermore, President Bush often displayed his personal dislike of Kim Jong Il. When he visited Seoul on February 2002, President Bush, harshly criticizing the North Korean leader, said that he doubted whether Kim Jong Il represented the will of the North Korean people, and implied that the US would separately deal with the North Korean regime through its own people for regime change. In addition, in March 2002, the Nuclear Posture Review (NPR) laid out recommendations for the US nuclear policy that included the development of new nuclear weapons and a list of potential targets of nuclear strikes, including North Korea. Along with the NPR, Bush's subsequent emphasis on the potential need for preemptive action against terrorist groups and rogue states armed with weapons of mass destruction led to considerable speculation about whether North Korea might be subject to attack after the US invasion of Iraq.

Pyongyang reacted with outrage to President Bush's rhetoric of the "axis of evil," arguing that it was virtually a declaration of war. Without saying a word, the Kim Jong Il regime, which had worried about its survivability, expressed even harsher reaction against Bush's remarks on the possibility of regime change in the northern part of Korea.

On October 3, 2002, Assistant Secretary James Kelly visited North Korea as a special envoy of President Bush. In the meeting between Kelly and North Korean officials, North Korea acknowledged its uranium enrichment program in response to the evidence of that plan presented by Kelly. A spokesman for North Korea's Ministry of Foreign Affairs stated: "We clearly mentioned that in order to protect our national sovereignty and right to survival from the nuclear threat posed by the US, and we are entitled to possess not only nuclear weapons, but also more powerful weapons than that," which made it clear that Pyongyang had a plan to develop nuclear weapons.[29] Thus, the North Korean nuclear issue entered a new phase.

After North Korea admitted to its nuclear program, tension increased as Washington and Pyongyang faced off for an offensive and defensive battle. Thanks to Chinese efforts to make a multilateral framework to settle the nuclear issue, the three-party talks among the US, China, and North Korea were held in April 2003. It was followed by three rounds of six-party talks including South

Korea, Japan, and Russia, together with the above three countries from August 2003 to June 2004. During these meetings, North Korea consistently claimed the renunciation of US antagonistic policy towards North Korea as a condition for the dismantlement of its unclear program. In particular, Pyongyang enumerated specific items for American security assurance; confirmation of non-aggression towards North Korea, diplomatic normalization between the US and North Korea, and lifting economic sanctions against North Korea. On the contrary, the US has stuck to its previous position as it suggested the possibility of a security guarantee to North Korea after the complete, verifiable, and irreversible dismantlement (CVID) of all forms of nuclear programs in North Korea.

Given the situation, the South Korean government under President Roh Moo-hyun tried to narrow the gap between the US and the DPRK, being supposed to play a mediating role. But a close look at President Roh's policy toward nuclear issue suggests that he has been supportive of the North Korean position rather than keeping up with American policy, partly reflecting the fact that his power has been based on relatively progressive forces which has a critical view on the US.

After North Korea's nuclear weapons problem was highlighted in October 2002, President Roh Moo-hyun, even as a presidential candidate, constantly emphasized the importance of resolving issues through peaceful dialogue, and he promoted talks with Pyongyang over pressure tactics. Especially when the so-called strategy of "tailored containment" was carried in the US press in December 2002, Roh Moo-hyun, president-elect at that time, expressed concerns over the strategy. He also emphasized that such a matter should no longer be simply announced by Washington and then accepted by Seoul, as it may have been in the past, but should be announced jointly after the two parties had reached a collective decision in the spirit of the South Korea–US alliance.[30]

President Roh also consistently argued that South Korea sought to resolve North Korea's nuclear weapons program while fostering inter-Korean economic cooperation at the same time, and he stressed the importance of reconciliation and cooperation with the North. He continued to support exchange and cooperation with North Korea despite escalating tensions over the nuclear weapons program.

But such an attitude was negatively responded to by the US. In addition, domestically, there were critics that Roh's stance would harm the relationships with the US, which in turn could cause negative impact on the South Korean economy. Partly influenced by these internal and external pressures, the Roh government's policy of peaceful resolution through dialogue seemed to have weakened since the South Korea–US summit in May 2003. In particular, President Roh agreed with President Bush to take "further steps" to prepare for increased threats from North Korea and gave tacit permission on Washington's additional pressure to North Korea.

While the results of the summit were praised by the conservatives, the progressives, the supporters of President Roh criticized them. In addition, North Korea complained about such cooperation between South Korea and the US, requesting South Korea to cooperate with North Korea (Minjok kongjo).

As the first six-party talks got under way, opening channels for dialogue with the North, Roh's government once again placed more weight on peacefully resolving the issue than pressuring the North. In the course of policy consultations among high level officials of South Korea, the US, and Japan, South Korea proposed a detailed roadmap for North Korea and consistently requested that the US present an offer to Pyongyang so that progress could be made in negotiations. In addition, shortly before the talks, when North Korea indicated it might not attend the Daegu Universidad, and also demanded an official apology for the incident in which the North Korean flag was damaged, President Roh, against widespread opposition and criticism, quickly expressed his regrets in hopes of maintaining the momentum for dialogue.

In November of 2004, President Roh went one step further by saying that there was some validity to the North's argument that its nuclear and missile programs are intended to deter outside threats. Calling on America to understand North Korea and to accommodate Pyongyang's requests, he said that North Korea would eventually give up its nuclear weapons when it sees hope for security assurance and success in economic reforms.

In sum, President Roh seemed to pose himself as a mediator between the US and North Korea. However, in fact, he appeared to understand more about the position of Pyongyang than that of Washington. While progressive forces at home welcomed such a stance taken by President Roh, those who held traditional views on the security of the Korean peninsula might feel skeptical about his position. In addition, Roh's position on maintaining a cooperative relationship with Pyongyang was so firm that it raised concerns about weakening the ties with the US, which has been fighting the proliferation of nuclear arms as its top mission.

Conclusion

The nuclear issue has been a typical example in which inter-Korean relations closely intertwined not only with the domestic politics but also with regional politics, especially those including the United States.

One of the main causes of the first nuclear crisis of 1993–4 was Kim Jong Il's domestic consideration for regime security. North Korea also took a negative posture vis-à-vis South Korea while improving its relations with the US because of its domestic concern. This practice on the part of North Korea also reflected its changing perception of the US and South Korea. Meanwhile, the lack of progress in inter-Korean relations made the South Korean government anxious for dialogue with the North, complaining of the rapid improvement of US–DPRK relations.

During the second nuclear crisis, North Korean concern for regime security also played a key role. As the Bush administration openly indicated the possibility of regime change in North Korea, the Kim Jong Il regime harshly reacted to such a move, and stubbornly maintained its position that the US first provide security assurance before North Korean dismantlement of its nuclear program. This stance of North Korea, in turn, hampered the settlement of the nuclear issue in the six-party talks among Northeast Asian countries.

Unlike in the first nuclear crisis, the South Korean government tried to play a mediating role in the second crisis. In doing so, the Roh Moo-hyun government raised its own voice, which was different from that of the US, reflecting changes in its perception on the US. This tendency was also attributable to the growth of NGOs which had a negative view of the US. But conservative forces criticized President Roh's posture toward the US. It is said that democratization weakens central authority and introduced new populist actors into decision-making, generating uncertainty regarding national purpose. Through the domestic uncertainty that democratization generates, it undermines the transnational credibility, or reputation of national security elites with one another, by casting doubt on their ability to deliver promised results.[31] The situation in South Korea to some extent followed this phenomenon. In other words, the weakening of central authority with the growth of civil society, the widening of the political spectrum encouraged by the democratization in South Korea partly made policy coordination with the US difficult, a coordination which is a necessary, if not sufficient, condition for the effective settlement of the nuclear issue through cooperation among Northeast Asian countries.

Notes

1 Robert Putnam, "Diplomacy and Domestic Politics: The Logic of Two-Level Games," *International Organization,* Vol. 42, Summer 1988, pp. 427–60. For a comprehensive review of literature on the link between internal and external affairs, see Joe D. Hagan, "Domestic Political Explanations in the Analysis of Foreign Policy," in Laura Neack, Jeanne A. K. Hey, & Patrick J. Haney (eds) *Foreign Policy Analysis: Continuity and Change in Its Second Generation,* Englewood Cliffs: Prentice Hall, 1995, pp. 118–21.

2 Andrew Moravcsik, "Introduction: Integrating International and Domestic Theories of International Bargaining," in Peter B. Evans, Harold K. Jacobson, and Robert D. Putnam (eds) *Double-Edged Diplomacy: International Bargaining and Domestic Politics,* Berkeley: University of California Press, 1993, p. 4. In the two-level games, ratification at the domestic level not only entails a formal voting procedure, but also refers to any decision-process that is required to endorse or implement an agreement at the international level, whether formally or informally. In addition, the actors, who are supposed to ratify it, are not confined to parliament. They may represent bureaucratic agencies, interest groups, social classes, or even public opinion. Putnam, "Diplomacy and Domestic Politics," pp. 436–7.

3 "Win-set" refers to the set of potential agreements that would be ratified by domestic constituencies.

4 In this sense, the political leader is imaged as "Janus-faced," who, as the mythological guardian of doorways with two faces to look both forwards and backwards, should deal with both international and domestic concerns. Moravcsik, "Introduction," in Evans, Jacobson, and Putnam, *Double-Edged Diplomacy,* pp. 16–23.

5 Ibid., p. 30.

6 Young Whan Kihl, "Democratisation and Foreign Policy," in James Cotton (ed.) *Politics and Policy in the New Korean State,* Melbourne: Longman, 1995, pp. 110–12.

7 The Sunshine Policy is a soft-line policy which emphasizes reconciliation and exchange with North Korea. Detailed contents of the policy will be discussed later.

8 The 386 generation refers to those in their 30s (in fact including early 40s), went to college and fought in pro-democracy movements in the 1980s, and were born in the 1960s. The 386 generation leaders and those who share views of the new generation

took core position in the presidential office under the Roh government. They are play-ing a key role in the National Security Council, which has been virtually leading South Korean foreign policy including North Korean affairs. In the 17th general election of 2004, 58 candidates in the age from 30 to 45 were elected, compared to 34 in the 16th election of 2000. National Election Commission, "Statistics of the 17th General Election." Online. Available HTTP: <http://www.nec.go.kr/necis/index.html> (accessed 1 September 2005).

9 For a detailed analysis of the policy, see Chung-in Moon, "The Sunshine Policy and Ending of the Cold War Structure," in Chung-in Moon, *et. al.* (eds) *Ending the Cold War in Korea: Theoretical and Historical Perspectives*, Seoul: Yonsei University Press, 2001, pp. 279–318.

10 In the *2004 Defense Whitepaper,* published by the Defense Ministry in January 2005, the term "main enemy" which had been used in defining North Korea since 1995 was deleted. Instead, it noted that "North Korea has been posing direct threat to South Korea."

11 "A New Takeoff toward an Age Peace and Prosperity," Address by President Roh Moo-hyun at the 16th Inaugural Ceremony. Online. Available HTTP: <http://english.president.go.kr/warp/app/en_speeches> (accessed 1 September 2005).

12 *Chosun Ilbo,* 14 January 2004.

13 *Naewoe Press*, No. 11328, 7 September 1998.

14 For this point, see Yong-Pyo Hong, "North Korea's First 50 Years and the Opening of the Kim Jong-Il Era," *Korea and World Affairs*, Vol. 22, No. 4, Winter 1998, pp. 558–9.

15 Although Kim Jong Il has long been worshiped as the successor, he is considered to lack legitimacy compared with Kim Il Sung. According to a study based on interview with North Korean defectors, popular support for Kim Jong Il is lower than his father who established a charismatic leadership through his "anti-Japanese activity, founda-tion of North Korea, and struggle against the American imperialism." Byung-ro Kim, *The Internalization of the Chuch'e Idea*, Seoul: Korea Institute for National Unification, 1994, pp. 87–92 (in Korean).

16 For example, see *Rodong Shinmun*, 1 January 1995.

17 For comprehensive analyses of North Korean food shortage, its impact, and the pos-sibility of North Korean economic improvement, see Philo Kim, "The Sociopolitical Impact of Food Crisis in North Korea," *Korea and World Affairs*, Vol. 23, No. 2, Summer 1999, pp. 207–24; Kongdan Oh and Ralph C. Hassig, *North Korea: Through the Looking Glass*, Washington D.C.: Brookings, 2000, Chapter 3.

18 According to studies on security issues in the Third World, political leaders who lack legitimacy tend to regard the issue of state security and regime security as the most important factor to put into consideration in the promotion of internal and external policies. See Mohammed Ayoob, *The Third World Security Predicament: State Making, Regional Conflict, and the International System*, London: Rienner, 1995, pp. 14–17. In a similar context, B. C. Koh argues that North Korean foreign policy can be explained in terms of its quest for three interrelated goals: security, legitimacy, and development. See his "Trends in North Korean Foreign Policy," *Journal of Northeast Asian Studies*, Vol. 13, No. 2 (Summer 1994).

19 *Rodong Shinmun*, 1 January 2000.

20 It is not easy to differentiate the "state" and "regime" in the North Korean case in which Kim Il Sung and his successor Kim Jong Il have maintained monolithic power identifying themselves with the state. But in the context that the collapse of the Kim Jong Il regime does not necessarily mean that of North Korea as a state, it can be said that regime security is one thing and state security another in North Korea.

21 For its survival, a totalitarian system needs an archenemy, without which the system's *raison d'etre* may be threatened. Michael Howard, "Lessons of the Cold War," *Survival*, Vol. 36, No. 4, Winter 1994–5, p. 163.

22 See *Rodong Shinmun*, 18 August 1994; *Pyongyang Broadcasting*, 25 October 1995.
23 For example, regardless of developments in US-North Korean relationships, Kim Jong Il continued to warn of the dangers of "American imperialism."
24 *Chung-ang Press*, 2 October 1995.
25 For example, see New Year's editorial in *Rodong Shinmun*, 1 January 1998.
26 Address by President Kim Dae-Jung at the School of Oriental and African Studies, London, 4 April 1998. The Sunshine Policy was based on 'three principles': (1) South Korea will never tolerate any armed provocation by North Korea; (2) South Korea does not have any intention to undermine or absorb North Korea; and (3) South Korea will actively pursue reconciliation and cooperation with North Korea beginning with those areas that can be made available.
27 The other four points are (1) upholding the principle of national independence, (2) seeking unity based on patriotism, (3) opposition to foreign domination and anti-unification forces, and (4) stepping up national contacts, dialogue, solidarity and unity.
28 The Joint Declaration included five points: (1) North and South Korea agreed to pursue national unification based on the principle of independence; (2) The two Koreas recognized the commonality between the confederation proposed by the South and the federation at the lower level proposed by the North; (3) North and South Korea agreed to make efforts to reunite family members separated by the Korean War, and for the South to repatriate "unconverted" North Korean spies who had finished their respective jail terms; (4) North and South Korea agreed to promote the "balanced development of the national economy" through economic cooperation, and to stimulate exchanges in civil, cultural, health, environment, and all other areas; (5) The two Koreas agreed to hold a dialogue between relevant authorities to implement the above agreements expeditiously. In addition to these five points, South Korea has also extended an invitation to Kim Jong Il to visit Seoul, which he accepted.
29 *Korean Central News Agency*, 25 October 2002.
30 *Yonhap News*, 31 December 2002.
31 Kend E. Calder, "Security and Democratization in East Asia," *The Korean Journal of International Relations,* Vol. 44, No. 5, 2004, pp. 152–3.

5 The transformation of Chinese foreign policy

Lowell Dittmer

The advent of the policy of "reform and opening to the outside world" at the historic third Plenum of the eleventh Party Congress in December 1978 was accompanied by a groundbreaking reassessment of Chinese foreign policy. While retaining certain elements of continuity, such as the more balanced, triangular relationship to the two superpowers Mao had introduced in the early 1970s (after taking China to the brink of war with the USSR), there were a number of profound differences. One of the biggest was the de facto abandonment of world revolution as a high priority foreign policy goal in favor of the maximization of China's national interest. Though some have argued that China's revolutionary foreign policy in the 1950s and 1960s was merely an ideological expression of China's national interest, there were in fact serious contradictions: China's frequent endorsement of "wars of national liberation" and other such efforts had a destabilizing impact in the Third World and antagonized both the US and the USSR (for different reasons), pitching China's foreign policy in a dangerously provocative direction. And China's simultaneous opposition to both superpowers seriously jeopardized national security, particularly in the event of Soviet–American collusion (as appeared possible with the advent of détente and arms control talks in the late 1960s). Hence, although China's Communist revolution was never repudiated and "Mao Zedong Thought" has remained an ideological cornerstone of the People's Republic, the official construal now eviscerated its radical foreign policy implications. The export of revolution gave way to a "peace and development" line (meaning in effect that China would support whomever was in its economic interest to support). Fresh analyses of the international correlation of forces resulted in the discovery that war was not inevitable, leading to reconciliation with a no longer "revisionist" USSR, to a steady reduction in military spending from the end of the war with Vietnam through the end of the decade, "a search for consensus while reserving points of contention." During the 1980s China began to exploit its opening to the United Nations network of organizations (particularly the financial organizations), while also taking advantage of the gradual arousal of interest in Taiwan in closer economic and social links to the mainland, but the primary focus remained on domestic economic development, attempting to equilibrate a tumultuous business cycle and an approach-avoidance complex concerning its own public sphere.

These oscillating patterns of economic boom and bust, investment binge-led inflation followed by tight money policy, intellectual *fang* and *shou*, and the spasmodic introduction of price reform and industrial reorganization, all culminated in the April–May 1989 protests at Tiananmen mushrooming out to other cities, precipitating the regime's savage crackdown on 4 June. The international reaction to this well-publicized bloodbath was the invocation of sanctions and diplomatic ostracism, which, in combination with the collapse of socialist regimes in Eastern Europe and ultimately the Soviet Union, deeply concerned the Chinese Communist Party (CCP) leadership. The consequent emphasis on "peaceful evolution" bespoke a basic reevaluation of the opening policy, leading to the formulation of "identity realism": economic opening was profitable and would continue, but the Chinese people must be inoculated against such spiritual pollution with greater emphasis on patriotic education, including reincorporation of pre-Revolutionary Chinese history in a version that shifted the focus from the glorious communist revolution to the foregoing national humiliation [*guochi*].[1] Yet the impact on foreign policy was neither immediate nor obvious, as Deng led China gradually back into international society — and toward Asia in particular — via a revival of economic reform and high growth rates in the context of a relatively low-profile national identity referred to domestically as *tao guang yang hui* [hide brightness and nourish obscurity] and *bu chu tou* [keep your head down]. That is, neither China's national feelings nor its ideological goals as the last credible representative of the Communist bloc were widely advertised at this point. The foreign policy making process became more institutionalized, there was a resurgence of rapid economic growth (and high inflation rates) amid continuing economic reform, and China shifted from great power politics to the cultivation of its near abroad [*zhoubian waijiao*], i.e., the Asian regional community, and the Third World.

The purpose of this paper is to analyze the transformation of Chinese foreign policy that followed its recovery from international ostracism to reclaim a position as a major world power by the turn of the millennium. The first section reviews the structure and process of foreign policy making, with special attention to recent institutional reforms. In the second section, the evolution of the major foreign policy themes during this period will be considered. In the third section we assess the impact of the recent transformation of Chinese foreign policy, weighing relative continuity and change, strength and weakness, emerging difficulties, and the likely implications of these for China and the major players with whom China is engaged. Our preliminary assessment is that China's pursuit of its national interest, the polestar of foreign policy making since the advent of reform and opening, is informed by China's underlying conception of its national identity, which has been undergoing a process of evolution over time. Since the collapse of Marxism-Leninism as a plausible contender for international ideological leadership, for example, China has redefined its identity as an "Asian" state, with a consequent policy prioritization of the Asian region.

Organization of foreign policy

As in all aspects of politics and administration during the reform era, foreign policy making has been the beneficiary of increasing institutionalization of the division of labor, higher educational preparation of officials, and a greater emphasis on collective consensus building in the policy process. The three main institutional participants in the foreign policy process are the same: they are CCP, the State, and the People's Liberation Army (PLA); supplemented by several other organs with auxiliary roles, such as the intelligence services.[2]

Given its constitutionally sanctioned "leading role," the Party has a dominant role over both State and army in this as in all political decision-making. Formally speaking, the leading decision-making forum is the Central Committee (CC), which in turn delegates power to the 24-person (and one alternate) Politburo and hence to its still tinier (currently 9-member) Standing Committee (in the early 1950s, and again briefly in the mid 1980s, the Secretariat eclipsed the Standing Committee, but since 1989 the leading role of the Politburo Standing Committee (PBSC) has been reaffirmed). Yet even the PBSC is deemed too large and cumbersome to make foreign policy decisions: during the Maoist era these were made by the team of Mao Zedong and Zhou Enlai (with Zhou increasingly relegated to the position of implementer). In the reform era the ambit was widened somewhat to a "leading nuclear circle" initially consisting of Deng, Chen Yun, Hu Yaobang and Zhao Ziyang (1979–89), then of Deng, Yang Shangkun, Li Peng, and Jiang Zemin (1990–93), and finally of Jiang Zemin and Li Peng.[3] Currently, Hu Jintao having at last consolidated successorship as "core" (as Party Secretary, Chief of State, and finally CMC Chair), seems to be forming another such leadership axis with Premier Wen Jiabao.[4] This "core" is given informal institutional status via the CCP Central (Committee) Foreign Affairs Leading Small Group (LSG), consisting of key members of the PBSC and of government and party foreign affairs agencies. Inasmuch as this is a non-standing committee with no permanent staff, the Central Processing Unit (CPU, or guikou) for the implementation of its decisions is the Foreign Affairs Office of the State Council. Owing to its special status and problems, Taiwan alone does not fall under the jurisdiction of this guikou; in 1987, a CCP Taiwan Affairs LSG was created, initially headed by Yang Shangkun; now chaired by Zeng Qinghong (the only LSG not chaired by Hu Jintao); its CPU is the Taiwan Affairs Office of the State Council. These two committees have eclipsed what was for a long time the dominant non-standing foreign affairs committee, the CC International Liaison Department [ILD, *duiwai lianluobu*], with eight regional bureaus as well as functionally organized "movement" sections (union issues, peace commission, youth organizations and women's leagues). But since the fall of the International Communist Movement in the early 1990s the ILD has fallen into desuetude. Now chaired by Wang Jiarui, a former mayor of Qingdao, the ILD has been relegated to the task of maintaining liaison with other political parties — at one time this meant communist parties, but since the collapse of the International Communist Movement in 1991 the ambit was broadened to include first socialist parties and eventually virtually all parties.⁵ Other LSGs involved in foreign policy (all now convened and chaired by Hu Jintao) are the Finance and Economy Leading Group (Deputy Director, Wen Jiabao), the Taiwan Work Leading Group (Deputy Director Jia Qinglin, Chair of the Chinese People's Political Consultative Conference), the recently revived Hong Kong and Macao Coordinating Group (chaired by Zeng Qinghong, and the National Security Council of China a very recent and still somewhat controversial organ, which duplicates the FALSG and the Central Military Commission (CMC) functionally and to some extent in personnel (vice chair, Zeng Qinghong), designed to cope with such national security crises as the 1999 Belgrade embassy bombing or the 2003 transnational severe acute respiratory syndrome (SARS) epidemic. All of these leading groups convene at the pleasure of the General Secretary to advise the center (i.e., the PBSC) on foreign affairs issues within their functional purview.

Of the seven organs of the State listed in the 1982 Constitution, which has remained authoritative with only piecemeal amendment throughout the reform era, three are formally relevant to foreign policy making: the National People's Congress (in its capacity to ratify treaties), the restored (in 1982) position of chief of state (who receives and delegates ambassadorial personnel), and the State Council. As the first two are essentially ceremonial we focus on the State Council, which actually runs China's foreign policy apparatus. Four of the State Council's current complement of 29 ministries and 4 commissions (as of March 1998) are concerned with foreign policy: the Ministry of Commerce (which since the 16th Congress has absorbed the Ministry of Foreign Trade and Economic Cooperation (MOFTEC) and as such focuses on foreign trade and investment); the Ministry of Foreign Affairs (MFA), the Defense Ministry, and (in specialized cases) the People's Bank, which has ministerial rank. Although MOFTEC (formerly MOFERT), hitherto considered the second most powerful ministry, by dint of the People's Republic of China (PRC)'s prioritization of GDP growth, its consolidation (under former People's Bank Chair Bo Xilai, son of Bo Yibo) into a foreign-domestic superministry may dilute its foreign policy impact. The MFA [*waijiaobu*], the queen (and largest) of the ministries by dint of its long favored position under Zhou Enlai, is similar in structure to foreign ministries in many other countries. It comprises a General Office (consisting of a Secretariat and a Confidential Communications Bureau), five internal affairs departments, and 18 external affairs departments.⁶ The internal departments are functionally organized to manage personnel and direct information traffic. The external affairs departments include both regional departments (e.g., Africa, North America and Oceania, Taiwan Affairs, Western Europe, Hong Kong and Macao, Latin America) and functional departments (e.g., protocol, consular, international organizations, policy research, translation). Below the departments are divisions, such as the US Affairs division under North American and Oceanic Affairs Department. Leading MFA personnel include the Foreign Minister, a series of vice foreign ministers [*fuwaizhang*], a score of assistants [*waijiao buzhang zhuli*], and the MFA spokesman [*waijiaobu fayanren*]; below them is a small army of ambassadors, general consuls [*zongling shi*], consuls [*lingshi*], charges d'affaires [*linshi daiban*], etc. These are career officials, with remarkable stability of tenure: fully 87 percent of all officials at or above ambassadorial rank in 1966 survived through 1979. Chinese diplomatic personnel are typically area specialists rather than generalists, often with excellent language training and cultural sensitivity to "their" area. The reform era has witnessed a turnover of four foreign ministers: Wu Xueqian (November 1982 until being forced out in the wake of his son's involvement in the Tiananmen protests), Qian Qichen (1989–1998), Tang Jiaxuan (1998–2002) and Li Zhaoxing (2002–present). Only Qian could be considered a political heavyweight, one of three post-Liberation FMs (after Zhou Enlai and Chen Yi) to be promoted to the Politburo (in 1992); though he yielded his position as FM to Tang in 1997, he retained Politburo membership and a visible presence in the foreign policy process until the 16th Party Congress, at which point he yielded his senior advisory role to take Tang Jiaxuan as a protégé.[7] Tang is a well-educated career MFA official with a grounding in Sino–Japanese affairs — who as erstwhile ambassador to Japan was temporarily damaged by Jiang Zemin's disappointing November 1998 Tokyo summit visit.

Though the PLA, legatee of an historically close relationship with the CCP, has seen its political influence wax and wane over the years, since 1989 it seems to have been in the ascendancy. Whereas active military officers are eligible for any governmental or Party positions (two currently serve on the Politburo), the highest venue for their official political influence is the CC's Central Military Commission. Somewhat unexpectedly, Jiang Zemin has been able to exert his command over this organ since his appointment as chair in the fall of 1989 despite his total lack of military experience — due to the unequivocal support of Deng Xiaoping, the 1992 elimination of the "Yang family army" (and the absence of political rivals with superior military credentials), and Jiang's own skill in exercising his appointment powers. Yet the PLA's political power base is extensive, enabling it virtually to articulate its own foreign policy. In 1997 alone, the PLA received over 150 delegations from 67 countries and all 5 continents on visits to China, including 23 defense ministers; about 100 PLA delegations traveled to 70 foreign countries. Since being urged by Deng to go into business in the 1980s to compensate for steadily diminishing budget allocations, the military has accrued its own interests, and these are not only strategic. The foreign policy input of the military has in fact increasingly reflected vested business interests — whether China should join the Missile Technology Control Regime (MTCR) or sign the Non-Proliferation Treaty (NPT) or sell missile or nuclear technology to Pakistan — it is perhaps no coincidence that China cast a rare UN Security Council veto (one of a handful since 1972) to prevent any public criticism or sanctions against Pakistan when the latter conducted underground nuclear tests after India tested in May 1998. This may change following the PLA's involuntary forfeiture of economic interests in 1998, but it is important to recognize that this surprisingly swift divestiture involved only services and not the national defense industrial sector. The PLA had many contacts with their US counterparts in the 1980s, broken off after Tiananmen and not resumed until 1997, only to be broken off in the wake of the April 2001 EP-3 incident and not resumed. Meanwhile, the military's interests with the Russian Federation have overshadowed those with the US: since 1991 Russia has become the major weapons supplier to the PRC, selling tanks (T62s), supersonic fighters (Su-27s), submarines and high-tech destroyers, even a couple of old aircraft carriers (apparently non-operational). The military is officially represented in some high-level negotiations, such as the series of five-power talks on frontier security with former Soviet republics after 1991, leading to the April 1996 border treaty and the April 1997 treaty stipulating mutual demilitarization and confidence-building measures.

In 1994, Deng, in the context of eliminating the Yang appointees, made a systematic effort to reduce military influence in politics. In June of that year Jiang Zemin, who shared an interest in that goal, appointed 19 new generals, giving the PLA leadership his own imprimatur. But in order to protect and perhaps control his militarily inexperienced successor Deng appointed two powerful senior military officials to the CMC, Liu Huaqing and Zhang Zhen, and the remainder of the CMC membership remained unchanged through Deng's death (Jiang replaced both at the 15th Congress). Though zealous military officers reportedly played a key role in the decision to employ coercive diplomacy against Taiwan in 1995–96, military influence in political decision making seems to have waned since that time—partly because of the somewhat disappointing outcome of that exercise, partly because of perceived military implication in illegal commerce, and partly because the history of military intervention in Chinese politics (martial law in 1949–1954, military intervention in the Cultural Revolution, the Tiananmen crackdown) has not endeared them to the civilian populace.[8] Military participation in controlling the summer 1998 Yangtze flood, widely publicized in the media, helped to alleviate that image somewhat, but their impact on foreign policy has continued to fade.

The role of China's secret service organs in the foreign policy process is for obvious reasons not well advertised. Most relevant is the Ministry of State Security (MSS), China's counterpart of the Central Intelligence Agency and the Federal Bureau of Investigation, currently chaired by Xue Yongyue. Its main tasks are to counter espionage, gather intelligence, and conduct analysis to safeguard the state from enemy spies and dissidents, while at the same time gathering and assessing intelligence vital to the national interest. Since the advent of reform its purview has broadened to include commercially relevant "high-tech." As in the US and many other countries, the PLA also has foreign policy relevant security organs: the 2nd and 3rd Directorates of the PLA General Staff Department (the former concerned with human-source intelligence, the latter with signal and imagery intelligence gathering) and the so-called Liaison Directorate [*zhongzheng lianluo bu*] of the General Political Department all appear to be involved in collecting information relevant to military security, including high-tech weapons data. The most important source of unfiltered information to the foreign affairs establishment is the New China News Agency [*Xinhua She*], which publishes a series of news digests of varying degrees of confidentiality (e.g., *Cankao Ziliao, Guoji Neican, Cankao Xiaoxi*). Analytically processed information is routed through the foreign affairs research institutes or think tanks, of which there are now three categories. First are the mainstream think tanks with direct links to the formal policy process: the Institute of International Studies is the official research arm of the MFA, which submits confidential briefing papers and also publishes *Guoji Wenti Yanjiu* [Journal of International Studies]; others include the Chinese Institute for Contemporary International Relations, or CICIR (the research arm of the Bureau of Investigation, under the MSS), the China Institute of International Strategic Studies (established in 1979 under the General Staff Department of the PLA), and the Strategic Research Institute of the National Defense University. The second is the more academic think tanks, which includes the Chinese Academy of Social Sciences (under the State Council), the Shanghai Academy of Social Sciences and the Shanghai Institute of International Studies, both under the Shanghai municipal government. The third category is the somewhat more informal network of information gathering agencies that operate under the auspices of the secretaries and staffs of individual leaders, or under the foreign policy-relevant LSGs —thus the State Council Foreign Affairs Office has its Policy Research Department (headed by Gong Xiaosheng since 1998), and the MFA has a Policy Planning Office comprising some 50 researchers.[9]

Although the greater impact of public opinion on the foreign policy process has been noted, as exemplified by the riots against the American and Japanese embassies in 1999 and 2005 respectively, and whereas this is no doubt true, it is not yet entirely clear to what extent these were spontaneous expressions of public opinion and to what extent a mass response to elite signaling that may have gotten out of hand, thanks to such technological innovations as email and intertext messaging. In any event it can be said that the fiery nationalist thrust of such eruptions is not only an expression of public opinion but of the selective elite licensing of such expression. More transparent and sustained has been the effort by the leadership, using consultative tactics, to solicit and aggregate elite interests into the policy process. Jiang Zemin appointed a council of wise men consisting largely of retired MFA officials and solicited their input from time to time, and Hu Jintao has proceeded to convene meetings of academics and researchers beyond the formal apparatus. These "study sessions," to which the cabinet and the entire Politburo are invited, reportedly convene on a monthly basis, typically beginning with a presentation by a leading authority lasting perhaps 90 minutes followed by a question-and-answer period. There have been increasingly open public discussions of such issues as the North Korean problem or missile defense on TV talk shows and in leading media outlets such as *People's Daily, Global Times* [*huanqiu shibao*] or *Southern Weekend* [*nanfang zhoumou*]. The government helps to whet public interest in foreign affairs via the regular publication of "white papers" on controversial topics such as Tibet, Taiwan, and national defense (there are now more than 30 such documents, all publicly available on the web).[10]

Despite the growing salience and complexity of formal organization in the Chinese foreign policy process, the personal equation remains highly relevant, as manifest in the influence of informal groups in decision making and the occasional discrepancy between formal position and actual power. The organization of informal influence is a notoriously elusive quarry for research, as it is expressly forbidden and denied; thus one must rely on the elite grapevine and occasional leaks. The nodes of informal networks are a combination of ascriptive and associational attributes, and although networks are often stable over long periods membership is by no means mutually exclusive and in a given showdown members always have an option whether to participate and in what manner. In the context of reform the old nodes (e.g., the PLA Field Armies) have tended to become less relevant, replaced by new nodes. To the extent that factionalism still has an organizational locus, it appears to have taken root in two directions: first, despite elite countermeasures, there is a longstanding tendency to carve out quasi-autonomous institutional niches in the central apparatus to function as a base, from Lin Biao's reorganization of the PLA in the early 1960s to the "petro-leum faction" (*shiyou pai*) in the heavy industrial and planning ministries in the early 1980s. The three most potent current exemplars are: (1) Echoing the role of the *genro* (*yuanlao*) in Japan's Meiji restoration, the retired senior officials con-tinue to function as a bloc in defense of a perceived interest in maintaining ideo-logical values and traditions (though this now includes the age and term limits that forced their own retirements). Though deprived of a formal base by the dis-solution of the Central Advisory Commission at the 15th Congress and by Hu Jintao's discontinuation of the annual summer meetings at Beidaiho, the so-called immortals retain the formal rank last held before their retirement, plus "class 1 guard service," access to classified documents and the right to be consulted by still active Politburocrats (or participate in expanded meetings, at the discretion of the convener).[11] (2) The "Youth League group" (*tuan pai*), a younger faction consisting of those who served under Hu Yaobang (as did Hu Jintao) or later under Hu Jintao, share an interest in bureaucratic rejuvenation and generational turnover.[12] (3) the National People's Congress (NPC), whose distinct institutional profile first emerged under Peng Zhen in 1983 (Peng stemmed from the factional network of Liu Shaoqi, a distinct pedigree from those of either Deng Xiaoping or Chen Yun) and continued under Qiao Shi , has come to stand for reform qua the rule of law. The long-term thrust of the NPC (and to a lesser degree the Chinese People's Political Consultative Conference) has been to become an institutional counterweight to the Party's Central Committee in a more "democratic" central government. The second major emerging factional base has been geographic, e.g., the "Shanghai gang," the "Beijing gang," etc.—not as a primordial datum (place of origin, *tongxiang*), but as a shared experience at a formative phase in one's career. The goal of the geographically-based faction is to capture the center and convert it into a national model (e.g., Jiang's "Shanghai miracle"). To the extent that regional bases overlap with general economic interests, we may see emerging an east coast grouping committed to rapid and relatively free market economic modernization bespeaking the interests of the entrepreneurial elite ver-sus a central-western-northeastern grouping committed to a revival of socialist ideals and the redistribution of the material benefits of reform to those left behind.[13] But with an established political base in the capital, a clear monopoly of formal authority in the Party-state apparatus and no apparent disagreement with the bureaucratic conventional wisdom, the Hu–Wen axis would have an interest in foreclosing any such informal polarization and ruling solely via the formal levers of power, which is in fact what they have been doing since 2002.

We can draw two preliminary conclusions from this series of institutional changes: First, without changing the overall Party-State-PLA institutional framework, channels of decision-making have become increasingly diversified and complex—we find, for example, that the circle of decision-makers has grown progressively wider, as new talent and new ideas have been incorporated via the LSGs, the host of research institutes and think tanks, and study sessions with academic scholars. Second, the influence of the PLA over foreign policy, which for understandable reasons gained temporary salience after the June 4 crackdown at Tiananmen, has tended to decline, particularly since the 1995–96 Taiwan Strait crisis. This is true in general, but even with regard to the Taiwan issue and Sino–US relations, where the PLA continues to claim an indispensable advisory role.

Evolution of foreign policy during reform

The evolution of China's foreign policy since Tiananmen may be roughly subdivided into three periods: China's post-Cold War reintegration into the international community (1989–95), the bid for great power status under partnership diplomacy (1995–99), and the readjustment of that policy from the late 1990s to the present that has been translated alternately as "peaceful rise" or "peaceful development" [*heping jueqi*]. During each period, without departing significantly from the "peace and development" line articulated at the outset of the reform era, Beijing undertook significant policy adjustments in the ongoing dialectic between domestic needs and the international environment; some of these adjustments characterized the period as a whole, whereas others were specific to only one phase. Thus in the following overview, we begin by summarizing the features relatively distinctive to each phase, followed by a more extended consideration of the features that characterized the period as a whole.

Unobtrusive re-entry, 1989–95

The censorious international reaction to China's brutal suppression of the Tiananmen protest seems to have caught CCP leaders off guard. The coincidence of the crackdown with the collapse of European communist regimes led many in the West to presume that the fall of the PRC could not be far behind, leading not only to the imposition of sanctions but to the sudden withdrawal of private capital, contributing to an economic hard landing in China. The Soviet Union's collapse eliminated the third leg of the strategic triangle, with the result that Sino–American friction was no longer offset by either Washington's strategic need for Beijing nor Beijing's strategic need for Washington, and the Clinton administration attempted in 1993–94 to extort human rights reform by threatening withdrawal of most favored nation trade status. China's sudden relief from visible threats to its national security with the collapse of the Soviet Union could not fully be appreciated in the context of a legitimacy crisis *cum* ideological vacuum, and military expenditures began to escalate annually by double digits after nearly a decade of annual reductions.[14]

Yet Beijing was able to rise to the foreign policy challenge by making four policy adjustments. First, given the unprecedented absence of great power threats, Beijing for the first time lowered its sights from great power global diplomacy to the regional arena. In the early 1990s Beijing normalized relations with all remaining Association of Southeast Asian Nations (ASEAN) members on the basis of the Five Principles of Peaceful Coexistence (and non-recognition of Taiwan), and China's regional neighbors reciprocated by moving into the vacuum left by the flight of Western investors. Hong Kong, Taiwanese, and South Korean investment capital flooded into southern China in record quantities beginning in 1989. Japan was the first major power to make steps toward reconciliation: on August 11, 1989 Premier Toshiki Kaifu announced that cooperation with China would continue in accord with the joint Sino–Japanese declaration of 1972, and (in response to Chinese urging) Japan the following year remitted the frozen yen loan promised by Takeshita in late 1988. This prepared the stage for the Kaifu visit in 1991 (the first visit by the leader of a leading industrialized democracy since the crackdown), and the visit of the emperor himself in 1992, commemorating the 20th anniversary of normalization (and providing a long-sought apology for Japanese war crimes). The target of numerous Chinese complaints in the 1980s (Japanese investors had been frightened by Baoshan and other such abrupt Chinese economic reversals), by the mid 1990s Japan had become China's second largest foreign trade partner and largest investor.

Second, though barely avoiding a diplomatic faux pas when they considered recognizing the abortive hard-line coup in August 1991, China quickly overcame its reservations about the collapse of the Soviet Union and the inauguration of Yeltsin and normalized relations with the Russian Federation and all 14 other former Soviet Republics, and in the fullness of time the initially suspicious relationship was to develop into a quite warm one: by 1991 China had become Russia's leading arms market (compensating for declining international sales in the wake of the triumph of US "smart" munitions in the Gulf War). China's embrace in turn facilitated Moscow's backdoor participation in the thriving Asian economic market in the wake of its exclusion from an expanding North Atlantic Treaty Organization. Border talks with a diplomatic team consisting of all four former Soviet Republics (Russia, Kazakhstan, Kyrgyzstan, and Tajikistan) culminated in successful border treaties and agreements on frontier demilitarization and confidence-building measures jointly signed in 1996–97, and in 1998 the demarcation of the Sino–Russian border was finally completed. True, the economic relationship, after a promising beginning in the early 1990s, has fallen somewhat short of early predictions, but by evoking the old Sino–Soviet "bloc" without actually reviving any of its constraining commitments the relationship improved both countries' diplomatic leverage at no visible cost.

Third, without in the least apologizing for its overreaction to the student demonstrations, Beijing for the time being quietly adopted a somewhat more ingratiating stance toward the West, facilitating a massive influx of foreign direct investment (FDI) hoping to take advantage of China's potentially enormous market following Deng's 1992 "southern voyage" [*nanxun*]. Further political reforms having been for the time being deferred, China's officialdom and middle classes "plunged into the sea" [*xia hai*] of commerce with a vengeance, and the economy rebounded with double digit growth (and initial high rates of inflation). While continuing to articulate its polemic against superpower hegemonism in international forums, China demonstrated growing willingness to play by Western rules: it finally (after a final series of underground nuclear tests ending in 1996) joined the NPT and the Comprehensive Test Ban Treaty, as well as the Chemical Weapons Convention and Biological Weapons Convention, and vowed to abide by the MTCR.[15] Beijing even began to respond more diplomatically to human rights concerns, preparing a series of white papers rationalizing China's position; particularly during annual Congressional deliberation of China's trade status, Beijing was always willing to release a·few dissidents and purchase more American imports.

Fourth, as in previous periods when great power relations frayed (e.g., the 1960s), Beijing revived its diplomatic contacts with the developing countries — none of whom had imposed sanctions or joined the chorus of recrimination. Thus a mid 1989 Politburo directive announced that "from now on China will put more effort into resuming and developing relations with old friends (in Africa) and Third World countries."[16] "In the past several years we have concentrated too much on one part of the world and neglected the other," Deng reflected during his summer 1990 vacation at Beidaihe. "The USA and other Western nations invoked sanctions against us but those who are truly sympathetic and support us are some old friends in the developing countries... This course may not be altered for 20 years."[17] A series of high-level visits (by Yang Shangkun, Qian Qichen, Li Peng) was conducted in 1989–90. China joined Malaysia, Singapore and assorted others in a defense of "Asian values" and developing countries' right to immunity from superpower intervention in the name of Western values. China also supported the Third World proposal to launch a new international economic order. China's support for Third World causes remained rhetorical, as it declined to join most Third World organizations and in those mainstream groups that it did join it participated in debates but shied away from the functional committees and subsidiary bodies where business is transacted.[18]

Thus by 1995, marking the beginning of Jiang Zemin's solo leadership stint (Deng lived on until February 1997, but made no public appearances and was reportedly on life support), China seemed to have reintegrated itself into the international community far more successfully than seemed conceivable in 1989. Deng, though primarily responsible for the public relations disaster that led to China's ostracism in the first place, can take considerable credit for this rapid recovery of international status, urging colleagues not to panic but calmly to persevere in their work, staunching a revival of Sino–Soviet polemics urged by some during the Eastern European collapse in 1989–91, successfully regenerating reform momentum with his 1992 *nanxun*, and, last but not least, finally setting forth and adhering to a stable and reasonably transparent succession regime.

Great power diplomacy, 1995–2001

Filially hoisting the flag of Deng Xiaoping's Theory and lauding his predecessor's reform course, Jiang made no claim to foreign policy innovation. Indeed, the fundamental reform line of peace and development was retained, the primacy of domestic political economy with foreign policy in an auxiliary role,[19] the continued deradicalization of ideological rhetoric (as in Jiang's "three represents" definition of what the CCP stood for). Yet Chinese foreign policy under Jiang's leadership has shown certain distinctive features—partly due to China's altered circumstances. After all, as the nation responded to resurgence of economic reform with the world's fastest GDP growth rate, the PRC was no longer a scorned pariah but a widely admired paradigm of market transition. This resulted in three foreign policy innovations identifiable with the "Jiang era." First, China rejoined great power diplomacy, now riding the vehicle of "partnerships." Second, China has, despite profuse denials, shifted from Deng's policy of demilitarization to one of military modernization. Third, as if in compensation for the budgetary outlay on behalf of a national security state, China embraced a "new security concept" based not solely on traditional strategic assets but on a calculus of "comprehensive national power" that included economic capacity and a cultural dimension ("soft" power) as well.

What exactly is a "partnership?" It is not an alliance, not even a "friendship" alliance, it is decidedly not a "military bloc," nor is it a "united front" (opposition to a third party is explicitly disavowed); it is rather a vaguely privileged bilateral relationship based upon comprehensive cooperation. The first "partnership" was proclaimed with the Russian Federation on April 23, 1997, followed quickly by a partnership with France (May 16, 1997), and later by partnerships with Pakistan, the United States, South Korea, the European Union, even Japan (no socialist countries, oddly enough), all of which were hailed in similar rhetoric, aiming grandiosely toward the 21st century. At the center of such "comprehensive" cooperation within partnerships is "consultation" [*xieshang*], which seems to feature building a strong personal relationship with other leaders—thus the proliferation of bilateral "summit" visits, and the Sino–Russian and Sino–American partnerships included construction of "hot lines" to the Kremlin and the White House. It was said to be instrumental to realization of China's vision of a "new international order" [*jianli guoji xin zhixu*] through "multipolarization" [*shijie duojihua*], and the concomitant rejection of "hegemonism, power politics, conflict and confrontation." This new international order would consist of a series of carefully cultivated, discrete bilateral links based on reciprocal advantage; thus a wheel, as it were, with China at the center. The logic of these partnerships seems to be essentially that of the triangle, with Beijing in the "pivot" position, but now extended to an unlimited number of "wing" players.

China's post-Tiananmen military modernization and its budgetary accounting has been the focus of several studies with conflicting results, partly because the official budget figures do not include all expenditures that would be included in Western arms budgets (for example, foreign arms purchases are excluded), and the magnitude of unrecorded expenditures is inherently uncertain.[20] Less important in this context than the adequacy of the official budget figures is the trend line: following a decade of spending decreases, spending began to increase in the 1990s, according to the official figures, by 11–18 percent per year. Initially this could understandably be attributed to the tenuous situation after Tiananmen, but over a decade later, domestic tranquility has presumably returned (and in any case responsibility has been transferred to the People's Armed Police). During the early 1990s high budget figures could be rationalized by double digit inflation, but in the past few years inflation has been all but eliminated while military budgets continue to rise at the same annual rate. The official Chinese defense budget more than doubled in real terms (adjusted for inflation) between 1989 and 2000, growing an additional 17 percent in 2001, 17.7 percent in 2002, and 9.6 percent in 2003 (its lowest in 13 years).[21]

The CCP leadership introduced the "new security concept" with its broadened definition of security in the early 1990s, accompanied by the concept of Comprehensive National Power (CNP) and even a methodology for calculating a given nation's CNP score. Economic growth and development were to be given higher priority, as well as cultural assets constituting "soft power." The operational impact was not immediately noticeable: it is certainly true that China has had one of the world's highest growth rates since the advent of reform and opening in the early 1980s, but this was domestically generated without a conscious mechanism linking it to foreign policy and it was unclear what purpose such a linkage would serve beyond advertising China's spectacular growth rate. The impact of China's emphasis on soft power has been somewhat controversial — some see strong evidence of China's exertion of soft power, particularly in Southeast Asia and perhaps elsewhere in the Third World, while others have argued this merely bespeaks rational prudence to avoid calling attention to China's growing hard power.

Peaceful rising, 2002–5

Hu Jintao's smooth succession to Jiang Zemin seems to have been modeled after Jiang's succession to Deng, consisting of such a painstakingly seamless continuation of Jiang's ideological (e.g., his "Three Representations") and policy innovations that the retiring incumbent could find no pretext to reinsert himself into the policy process. Thus the emphasis on multilateral regional diplomacy continued, as did the double-digit military buildup (largely vis-à-vis Taiwan), the Sino–Russian partnership *cum* friendship alliance, the New Security Concept, all the planks of the Jiang Zemin platform have remained firmly in place. Thus it is more accurate to periodize this phase beginning with the turn of the millennium rather than the 16th Party Congress, deriving as it did from a summary of leadership experience conducted in the late 1990s. The central datum on which that reassessment was based was that the United States, which had emerged as the lone superpower amid the collapse of the Soviet bloc and the uncertain foreign policy cohesion of the European Union, had not faded into some sort of pentagonal multipolar system as predicted in the early 1990s but has rather continued to strengthen its relative position economically, strategically, and culturally, and that this posed a serious risk to China's debut in Great Power Diplomacy. If the United States deemed China's rise to be threatening to its hegemony (the much decried "China threat" theory), it might simply nip it in the bud—the rise and ruin of Germany and Japan early in the 20th century stood as warning precedents. The practical lesson was that China must diffuse such hegemonic paranoia. Thus has given rise to a rhetorical emphasis on China's "peaceful rise" [*heping jueqi*], sometimes translated "peaceful development," and its determination to play the role of a "responsible great power." Thus, Vice Premier Qian Qichen, in internal meetings in January 2001, emphasized that Beijing should place cooperation above contradiction in relations with Washington, putting "national economic development" above the "unification of the motherland," for example. This entailed not only a lower prioritization on resolving the Taiwan question (unless provoked by movements toward independence on the island), but lesser emphasis on good relations with Tokyo: the US was key, Sino–Japanese friendship was not essential, so long as bilateral economic relations remained strong.

Hu Jintao's foreign policy initiatives have been consistent with this new emphasis. Although Hu was the first Chinese leader to participate in the G-8 world economic summit in 2003 (as an observer), the Great Power Diplomacy typically associated with Jiang Zemin's summitry and partnership agreements has faded from view, and despite a frosty beginning of relations with the incoming Bush administration amid the rhetoric of "strategic competition" and the EP-3 incident, since September 11 both countries have toned down inflammatory rhetoric and found areas in which they could usefully cooperate. China volunteered to cooperate with the Global War on Terror (using this as a pretext to suppress Uighur dissent in Xinjiang), and in April 2003 China launched tripartite diplomacy to initiate negotiations with the Democratic People's Republic of Korea, which had withdrawn from the nuclear nonproliferation treaty and reactivated nuclear facilities to build a bomb, leading in August to the Six-Party Talks on that issue that have since convened several times before being unilaterally suspended by Pyongyang; if these talks have not yet solved the North Korean problem they did at least contain it for the time being, much to the gratitude of the Bush administration. The Hu-Wen administration undertook no significant new concessions or policy demarches vis-à-vis Taiwan, but they toned down the cross-Strait rhetoric and showed tactical adroitness in manipulating Washington to discipline Chen Shui-bian during the 2004 presidential campaign rather than whipping up an anti-PRC backlash on the island with direct threats. With regard to Japan, political relations have remained essentially frozen since Jiang Zemin's stormy 1998 summit visit, partly to be sure because of Prime Minister Koizumi's painfully mnemonic annual visits to the Yasukuni shrine where Japanese war dead lie buried. The new regime also demonstrated tactical flexibility with regard to Hong Kong: although Jiang's proposal to reconfirm Chief Executive Tung Chee Hwa (whom he had appointed) in 2002 was dutifully endorsed, when Tung's popularity continued to plummet, culminating in a massive popular demonstration against his proposed anti-sedition law on 1 July 2003, Hu publicly criticized Tung at a December 2004 Hong Kong meeting, setting the stage for the latter's early resignation in March 2005. In sum, the fourth generation leadership has made no new contribution to grand strategy, but offers a display of pragmatic intelligence and subtlety in the choice of tactics.

Assessment

In this section we attempt to weigh the relative strengths and weaknesses, continuities and discontinuities of Chinese foreign policy. The Chinese policy making process is quite deliberately value-added, punctuated by a series of internal critiques in which policies deemed unsuccessful are typically discarded (often accompanied by the purge of their sponsors), while even policies deemed relatively successful may be adjusted. In this collective learning process, policy continuity can be taken to mean successful and progressive, while discontinuity represents failure and a negative verdict (the "trash bin of history")—at least in the self-critical eyes of the CCP leadership.

The Tiananmen "incident" resulted in a purge of the reform coalition and forged an ideological and policy consensus among elite survivors that steeled the CCP leadership against subsequent political vicissitudes and has survived with surprising tenacity right up to the present. Included in this consensus is Chinese foreign policy. The basic tenets of this foreign policy consensus, which have either been maintained intact or cumulatively intensified, include the following:

1. Since weathering the sort of massive popular dissent that led to the toppling of communist regimes in many other countries in which socialism seemed far more powerful and deeply rooted than in China, the CCP leadership has proceeded to *construct a national security state*. The chief beneficiary of this effort has been the PLA, which jumped from last place to first in budgetary priority among China's four modernizations. Though relieved of imminent national security threats by the collapse of the Soviet Union, military spending has since 1993 outpaced inflation, and since 1996 has outpaced even China's unusually high GDP growth rate, although the PLA has simultaneously been downsized in terms of numbers (still the world's largest, at 2.3 million troops). This is true even if we limit our purview to official figures—those estimates that include off-budget expenditures such as foreign arms purchases vary by from two to twelve times as much as the official figure. (To be sure, according to the most recent RAND study, China's arms budget remains only about 15 percent of that of the US and may be approaching parity with that of Japan.[22]) China's domestic security apparatus, including the People's Armed Police, has also benefited budgetarily from this new focus.

This focus has locked Beijing into an arms purchasing arrangement with Russia, as both Europe and the US discontinued arms sales after Tiananmen: China has displaced India as Russia's biggest arms customer; indeed, since 2000 China has been the world's biggest arms purchaser. In 2001, more than half of all Russian exports totaling US$4 billion are believed to have gone to the PRC.[23] And the chief target of such sales has since 1989 been Taiwan, toward whom China's policy has become one of inflexible international isolation and threat (of tactically variable intensity), alleviated by growing cross-Strait economic integration and by the occasional public relations gesture (the 1998 Koo visit, the 2005 reception of "pan-blue" leaders Lien Chan and James Soong).[24]

2. Paradoxically coexisting with the PRC as paranoid monitor and disciplinarian of the Chinese masses has been China as one of the large countries most open to foreign trade, investment and tourism, and a consistent advocate of greater international pluralism, including "multipolarity." China's *conversion to multilateral diplomacy*, cross-cutting China's historically embedded realist traditions, emerged only gradually, moving from economic to security multilateralism and from universal to regional multilateralism. The first step was as free rider in various UN agencies after winning admission to the Security Council in the early 1970s, joining the International Monetary Fund, World Bank, Asian Developmental Bank, International Atomic Energy Association, UN Conference on Trade and Development, UN Children's Fund, UN Educational, Scientific and Cultural Organization, World Health Organization, MFA and over 200 international agencies concerned with the development of science and technology. Beijing participated in the activities of the UN Disarmament Commission, in 1982–87 attending 7 of the 11 conferences of the Commission in Geneva, contributing its critique of superpower nuclear arsenals. In the late 1990s, seeing the rise of multilateralism in Southeast Asia apparently designed to balance against the growing power of the PRC in the wake of the Taiwan Strait missile crisis, China astutely agreed to join and thus neutralize these fora in what it called "good neighborly diplomacy" [*zhoubian waijiao*]: in 1994, China joined the ASEAN Regional Forum, in 1996 the Asia–Europe Meetings, in 1997 organizing ASEAN Plus Three—China, Japan, and South Korea—followed by the organization of ASEAN + 1 (viz., China) in November 2001, slated to become the world's largest free trade agreement (FTA) upon the scheduled elimination of all internal tariffs by 2010. Also in 2001 China converted its post-Soviet negotiating arrangement with border state successors of the Soviet Union (viz., Kazakhstan, Kyrgyzstan, Tajikistan, Russia, and now Uzbekistan) into the world's only security organization in which the US is not involved, the Shanghai Cooperation Organization. And in 2002, in the interest of neutralizing the Spratleys dispute with several countries in Southeast Asia, China signed the ASEAN Code of Conduct, and the following year at Bali signed the group's Treaty of Amity and Cooperation and proposed a China-ASEAN Strategic

Partnership to increase communication among Asian militaries.[25] As noted above, China played a seminal role in inaugurating Six-Party Talks in 2003 to tackle the issue of nuclear proliferation to North Korea. Meanwhile, China also stepped up cooperation with various UN activities, increasing its participation in peace-keeping activities (first approved in principle for Cyprus in 1981, China became involved in peacekeeping operations in 1990 in Cambodia, East Timor, and Somalia).

While Chinese foreign policy behavior has definitely shifted in favor of more multilateral cooperation since the Deng Xiaoping period, it is not yet clear how it should be interpreted. On the one hand it may be argued that as China has opened economically to the outside world to an unprecedented degree it makes a lot of sense for it to support a policy of multilateral international cooperation (which is, after all, consistent with the five principles of peaceful coexistence). On the other hand, one can also take a realist position toward multilateral organizations, and China's new policy can be considered a subtle and effective counter to recent American foreign policies of "congagement" (a combination of containment and engagement) frequently caricatured in China as hegemonism or unilateralism. China's willingness to join intergovernmental organizations (IGOs), involvement with which it previously avoided, bespeaks a new confidence that as the most populous and economically dynamic member (and one of the world's biggest traders), it can steer the association in directions compatible with its national interests.

3. As noted at length above, China's *foreign policy process* has become increasingly *complex, institutionalized, well-educated, and transparent* (to the extent that the foreign policy process in any country is transparent). Although the passage of an anti-secession law by China's NPC was clearly a foreign policy error under the circumstances, procedurally speaking the attempt to encode foreign policy into law represents another manifestation of this tendency: China's public arena has since the 1970s shifted from spontaneous, bottom-up dramatization to painstakingly staged ritual. The impact of this has been greater consistency and rationality in decision-making—with perhaps still a certain lag in responding appropriately to national security crises such as the April 2005 anti-Japanese riots.

4. *Nationalism* has since 1989 virtually displaced Marxism-Leninism as the *new civil religion* among the Chinese masses (though not among the CCP elite), to the extent that a Party born in the May Fourth Movement that once scorned the "Confucius shop" (and tried to root it out during the Cultural Revolution) has resolved to set up a chain of Chinese culture and language centers throughout the world to be named Confucius Institutes. There are many manifestations of this new nationalism, such as the deification of Zeng Guofan and the reversal of verdicts on Hong Xiuquan (now as embarrassing as the Red Guards). Although internet chatrooms cannot be considered representative samplings of public opinion, they do suggest that Chinese nationalism has considerable domestic appeal. Embracing Chinese nationalism could also have a multiplier effect on China's "soft power" abroad, e.g., in

Hong Kong, Southeast Asia, or the overseas Chinese communities in the West, which have been receptive to Chinese popular film and TV—certainly more so than to Marxism-Leninism—even "socialism with Chinese characteristics"—whose international plausibility does not seem to have survived the Cold War. Yet nationalism is a powerful, iconoclastic emotion and reliance on it poses some risks, particularly in the absence of any well-institutionalized channels for the calm expression of public opinion. Clearly there is a sharp stylistic contrast between expressions of mass nationalism and the rationalization of the foreign policy process prized by China's increasingly cultivated elite, and the former may sometimes disrupt the latter.

If a national security state, multipolarity, foreign policy rationalization, and nationalism have been consistent manifestations of Chinese foreign policy since Tiananmen, why have we broken that period into several phases? Partly as a convenient periodization, but also because Chinese foreign policy continues to change over time, giving each phase its distinctive features. These changes occur in those policy areas still marked by uncertainty, permitting foreign policy making elites to arrive at different verdicts. These areas of uncertainty and change seem to be concentrated in two broad areas: with regard to China's national identity, and with regard to the nature of the enemy. As the leadership's conceptualization of these two phenomena has evolved over time, so has its definition of the national interest and foreign policy agenda.

During the period of reentry into the international community after the Tiananmen "incident," China's national identity was, even if we assume the CCP leadership was absolutely certain of the historical correctness of its decision to suppress what were then considered unruly masses whose outrageous antics were beyond the pale, not displayed with pride but cultivated in reserve. The national identity was at this time stripped of its communist aspect, at least for public consumption, indeed the contemporaneous revival of interest in China's century of national humiliation may have been a displaced expression of the mournful feelings of the elite about China's place in a world of post-Tiananmen sanctions. The nature of the enemy, on the other hand, was fairly clear: the enemy was the non-communist West, led by the United States, whose concerted and insidious campaign had succeeded in precipitating the "peaceful evolution" of the entire Soviet bloc into political oblivion and was now focusing on the few remaining survivors. The Deng Xiaoping leadership deserves considerable commendation for their remarkable cool-headedness in the teeth of what they clearly perceived to be a life-or-death struggle for political (or even physical) survival.

During the period of promiscuous partnerships, summitry and great power diplomacy, China's leadership exhibited visible pride in their national identity: China had not only survived on the brink of destruction, but had made considerable progress toward a *xiaokang shehui* and was one of the most demonstrably successful economic models in the developing world. As China overcame its most favored nation quandary and signed partnerships with Russia, the US, India, Japan, and all other former enemies, and recovered Hong Kong in 1997 and

Macao in 1998, the enemy became increasingly pinpointed as Taiwan, whose perverse democratization was pulling that renegade province into a position increasingly adverse to Chinese interests and anathema to a fully integrated Chinese national identity. Thus Beijing sought to employ its newly built national security apparatus in a demonstration of coercive diplomacy against the island state, with results that included growing respect for China's power but distrust of its motives. Taiwan was however also useful as a scapegoat, letting the leadership argue that China's arms spending was focused on an unresolved "domestic" problem and not a threat to its neighbors.

During the period of peaceful rise, China's leadership had a new sense of fragility about their national identity, although the reasons for this are not fully clear: officials in the Bush administration congratulate themselves on impressing the Chinese with their bluff, no-nonsense definition of red lines, though the more cautious Chinese reassessment of Sino–American relations seems to have antedated the electoral victory of George W. Bush. As in the US, there seems to have been a basic policy review of Sino–American relations in Beijing in the wake of the Taiwan Strait crisis at the end of the 1990s, in which the leadership recognized that China could not afford such a confrontation and must ensure that it does not recur. For at least the time being, China needed the US for its continued peaceful rise, could not take Taiwan yet anyhow, and should avoid unnecessary provocation. The new national identity hence focused on China as a mature and responsible pillar of the international status quo, a model participant in all the important decision-making fora of world order. Taiwan was still a problem, but with the tacit cooperation of US diplomacy there was growing confidence that Chen Shui-bian could be contained, that long-term trends integrating Taiwan economically were very much in the mainland's favor, so a policy of quiet arms buildup and international isolation would suffice until the Democratic Progressive Party passed from the scene. The rise of right-wing nationalism in Japan, on the other hand, need not be tolerated; Japan was a mere puppet of the US that could be publicly lambasted so long as Sino–US relations were kept intact.

The evolution of Chinese foreign policy behavior cannot be entirely be attributed to areas of uncertainty and abiding ambivalence allowing periodic changes of elite opinion. There are after all new and unexpected developments in the world with which any reasonably pragmatic foreign policy must be expected to cope. Among these emergent problems are those arising from China's pell-mell industrialization; take for example China's ravenous appetite for energy and raw materials, which having exhausted much of the easily available domestic supply, has created a lucrative international import market. Petroleum has been one of the most urgently desired imports: whereas thanks to a strategic decision by Deng Xiaoping early in China's modernization process, China's energy consumption doubled from 1980 to 2000 while the Chinese economy quadrupled in size, since 2000 China's energy consumption has been growing faster than its GDP growth rate. Thus China has become, with India, the world's fastest growing new market for oil products; according to a study by the East-West Center, Asia accounted for

92 percent of global net growth in oil consumption in 2000, and in 2004 China overtook the US as the world's leading consumer of most industrial materials and displaced Japan as the second largest oil consumer (after the US). As a former centrally planned economy, China has not been content to meet these needs via piecemeal purchases at market or to leave supply to its trading companies, but has increasingly functioned as "China, Inc." in the formation of FTAs, in the construction of transnational pipelines, direct investment in oil and raw material development projects (e.g., a nickel mine in Papua New Guinea, iron ore in Australia). Although the government's proactive involvement in such projects is a mere replay of the East Asian practice of "industrial policy," it has the effect of politicizing, even nationalizing, what would otherwise be regarded as mere business competition. Thus the recent arrest and conviction of Russian oil oligarch Khodorkovsky of Yukos Oil for tax evasion played into the story of a competition between Japan and China for a pipeline deal from Angarsk, which Japan seems to have "won" with a late but more munificent bid. The foreign policy implications of this competition for resources seems to have been to improve China's relations with prospective resource sellers (thus many developing countries in Africa and Latin America have struck lucrative deals with Chinese purchasers—for which they are particularly grateful when under sanction by the West for human rights abuses) while complicating relations with competing resource buyers (such as Japan, or the US).

Conclusions

Chinese foreign policy during reform and opening may in general be considered highly successful, in contrast with the more dramatic aspirations and methods but meager results of the Maoist era. While striving for less, China has achieved far more: a stable and peaceful environment in which to pursue modernization, the restoration *[huigui]* of Hong Kong and Macao, and an improved relationship with Southeast Asia. China has been absolved of national security threats and enjoys reasonably good relations with all powers capable of posing such a threat. Adhering to the same fundamental principles, Chinese foreign policy, we have attempted to show, displayed different tactics during the phases of its evolution. Deng Xiaoping's basic method was first to stabilize relations with the major powers (that is, those potentially of threatening the PRC's national security) and then to make further gains at the margins. First he succeeded in shifting China's position in the Strategic Triangle to the pivot, allowing Beijing to "play" the triangle to its own advantage. When the Triangle disintegrated upon the collapse of the Soviet Union and the West sanctioned and ostracized China, Deng avoided any return to Maoist bipolarity or ideological grandstanding (as was urged by some communist ideologues) and coolly recovered lost international status while resuming the economic reforms on which he had staked his reputation. To resolve the Hong Kong and Taiwan dilemmas he made parallel offers to both of unprecedented magnanimity, which Hong Kong accepted, while Taiwan, in an inherently stronger position, equivocated.

Jiang Zemin, from an unprepossessing and frequently scorned beginning, was able to consolidate his leadership and to put his own mark on Chinese foreign policy within an amazingly short time. With "partnership diplomacy," China was able to build a series of relationships with the other major powers to enhance China's attractiveness as a partner without impairing its flexibility to realign with another state or group of states. Thus, instead of building a new bloc to resist hegemonism, China became an equal opportunity strategic partner. While partnership diplomacy was essentially a defensive strategy to allay threats from the great powers, China's offensive strategy now focused on integrating itself with the world's most economically dynamic region. Identifying itself now as an Asian state, China moved from regional isolation to active involvement in the proliferating number of post-Cold War regional IGOs, often taking the initiative, sometimes playing a leadership role, as the US became preoccupied with the War on Terror and seemingly lost interest in multilateral diplomacy (except insofar as it could be involved in the War on Terror).

The advent of "peaceful rising" diplomacy represents a deliberately lowered profile, as China's foreign policy feedback mechanism informed the leadership that such incidents as the Strait Crisis or Mischief Reef could not be quarantined from China's peace and development line. Without reducing spending on its security apparatus, China began to focus on building Comprehensive National Power by emphasizing economic growth and multilateral diplomacy. China would be the world's model citizen, joining various IGOs and FTAs, regional and global, participating in peacekeeping operations, signing environmental and human rights manifestos—only when the CCP's domestic security is directly at stake is there any visible hesitation about such eleemosynary commitments. Beijing's positive contributions to world peace in its new role, though inherently limited by perceived national interests (e.g., opposition to UN Security Council reform), should by no means be stinted for that reason.

We have tried to show that China's foreign policy continues to be characterized by periodic shifts of direction, if no longer such abrupt course reversals as during the period of continuing revolution. As an organizational legacy of a policy-making practice cultivated since revolutionary days, China's leadership undergoes a disciplined organizational learning process punctuated by a regular pauses for "criticism and self-criticism" and "summaries of experience" to reflect upon mistaken initiatives and adopt a new and improved set of policies. These have since Tiananmen resulted in the deepening and increased sophistication of the leadership's understanding of how to realize China's national interests, leading it more or less to abandon ideological trammels and open itself to the dynamic Asian regional economy, expanding cooperation through multilateral organizations, avoiding unnecessary contradictions with the US (its biggest market but also its biggest threat) and playing a proactive diplomatic role, as seen for example in its role in the Six-Party Talks. We have suggested however that the leadership remains somewhat flummoxed about two areas: its own national identity, and its enemies. With regard to the former, it has not entirely resolved whether China is still a revolutionary power in some sense or whether it simply wishes to embrace Chinese tradition, whether China is still a humiliated victim or whether it has finally arrived and can proudly embrace its achievements. This uncertainty about national identity is a new phenomenon—certainly during the Maoist period, whether during the era of "two camps" or "three worlds," there was no lack of clarity about who China was and what it stood for. With regard to its image of the enemy, China also shows considerable disorientation since abandoning its Marxist conspiracy theories about world capitalism. At some moments it seems China has no enemies at all, that China has a foreign policy of peace and friendship at all azimuths. At other times the Chinese seem convinced they are beset by enemies bent on their national destruction, as after the American bombing of the Belgrade embassy in 1999 or in the anti-Japanese riots in April 2005. The enemy selection process is somewhat strange, reportedly resulting in thousands of intelligence agents being dispatched worldwide to keep tabs of a religious exercise cult. At the moment, Taiwan and Japan seem to be consensus candidates for this unenviable role, though other countries may qualify. To repeat, these are relatively minor problem areas in a foreign policy that has in most other respects been a brilliant success story.

Notes

1 Alastair Iain Johnston, "Realism(s) and Chinese Security Policy in the Post-Cold War Period," in Ethan B. Kapstein and Michael Mastanduno (eds) *Unipolar Politics: Realism and State Strategies after the Cold War*, New York: Columbia University Press, 1999, pp. 261–318. There were no books on this topic before 1990, but since that time there have been about 120 books and 190 scholarly articles published on the topic of *guochi*.
2 For an excellent overview of the structure of the Chinese foreign policy making establishment, see Robert G. Sutter, *Shaping China's Future in World Affairs*, Boulder: Westview, 1996.
3 See Lu Ning's outstanding study, *The Dynamics of Foreign-Policy Decisionmaking in China*, Boulder: Westview, 1997, pp. 21–31 et passim.
4 Although the two men are not part of the same "faction," they have much in common: both are the same age, spent much of their careers in Gansu, and have had a smooth working relationship since the sixteenth Party Congress. Wen Jiabao holds administrative leadership of the Ministry of Foreign Affairs and his forays abroad have been considered quite successful: he attended an ASEAN summit conference on SARS in Bangkok and made an important trip to Washington in the fall of 2003, at which time China was able to publicly involve the US in disciplining Taiwan.
5 By late 1998, the ILD had established party to party relations with some 300 political parties and organizations from 130 countries and regions on 5 continents; following the June 1998 Clinton visit, overtures were made to the American Democratic and Republican parties.
6 Lu, *Dynamics*, pp. 20–40.
7 Especially in 1994, Qian Qichen was reproached in a public letter from the National Defense University of "right deviationism," specifically for being too conciliatory toward the United States and in the negotiations with Britain over the retrocession of Hong Kong. See *Zheng Ming*, 1 May 1994, pp. 10–12. To thus proceed against a Politburo member and one of China's four vice ministers indicates that his critics must have had a base at least as high as the Central Committee. Since 1995 Qian's public foreign policy pronouncements have been harder line.

8 Thus for the first time in more than twenty years, the military has no representation on the Standing Committee of the Politburo (though Generals Chi Haotian and Zhang Wannian have full Politburo membership). Military intervention in the economy is a different matter, as indicated by widespread popular support for the PLA's yeoman service during 1998s disastrous floods.

9 Lu, *Dynamics*, pp. 107–43.

10 See Evan S. Medeiros and M. Taylor Fravel, "China's New Diplomacy," *Foreign Affairs*, November/December 2003.

11 In order of rank, the top senior officials after completion of the succession process at the March 2003 NPC are: Jiang Zemin, Li Peng, Wan Li, Qiao Shi, Zhu Rongji, Song Ping, Liu Huaqing, Wei Jianxing, Li Lanqing, Rong Yiren, Bo Yibo, and Song Renqiong. Andrew J. Nathan and Bruce Gilley, *China's New Rulers: The Secret Files*, New York: The New York Review of Books, 2002, p. 140.

12 This grouping includes Zhou Qiang, 42, secretary of the Central Committee of the CYL; Li Keqiang, 47, governor of Henan Province; Xi Jinping, 48, governor of Fujian Province (and son of Party veteran Xi Zhongxun); Zhao Leji, 44, governor of Qinghai Province; Quan Zhezhu, alternate member of the 15th Central Committee and executive vice governor of Jilin Province; and Wu Aiying, alternate member of the 15th Central Committee and deputy secretary of the Shandong Provincial Party Committee. Zhou Qiang is current CYL first secretary and Li Keqiang was his predecessor; both Liu Peng, executive deputy head of the Central Propaganda Department, and Zhao Shi, deputy director of the State Administration of Radio, Film, and Television, were CYL secretaries. Li Keqiang, Liu Peng and Zhao Shi all worked under Hu Jintao when he was CYL first secretary; Zhou Qiang was personally selected by Hu to chair the CYL from his vantage point in the Politburo Standing Committee. Other *tuan pai* members who once worked with Hu include Fujian party secretary Song Defu and Minister of Justice Zhang Fusen. See *Cheng Ming*, July 2002.

13 Lowell Dittmer, "Chinese Factional Politics under Jiang Zemin," *Journal of East Asian Studies*, No. 3, 2003, pp. 97–128.

14 From 1980–9, China's military spending dropped from 16.9 percent of Gross Domestic Product to 8.34 percent. Jian, *Restructuring*, p. 147. In 1990, it rose by 15.2 percent (vs. an increase of 4.8 percent for the budget as a whole). *The Military Balance 1990–1991*, London: Institute for Strategic Studies, 1990, p. 148.

15 Samuel S. Kim, "Chinese Foreign Policy in Theory and Practice," in Kim (ed.) *China and the World: Chinese Foreign Policy Faces the New Millennium*, Boulder: Westview, 1998.

16 *Foreign Broadcast Information Service-China*, October 3, 1989, p. 3 (hereinafter FBIS).

17 As quoted in *Zheng Ming*, August 1990, p. 15.

18 Samuel S. Kim, "International Organizational Behavior," in Thomas Robinson and David Shambaugh (eds) *Ideas and Interpretations in Chinese Foreign Policy*, New York: Oxford University Press, 1993, p. 9.

19 For example, China's trade dependency ratio had by 1997 reached 40 percent, which is quite high for a large continental power with its own domestic market. By 1994 China had become the largest creditor of the World Bank.

20 For example, cf. Richard A. Bitzinger and Chong-Pin Lin, *The Defense Budget of the People's Republic of China*, Washington, D. C.: Defense Budget Project, 1994; and Shaoguang Wang, "Estimating China's Defence Expenditure: Some Evidence from Chinese Sources," *China Quarterly*, No. 147, September 1996, pp. 889–911.

21 Institute of International Strategic Studies, 2002, p. 298, as cited by Bates Gill, "China as a Regional Military Power," in David W. Lovell (ed.) *Asia-Pacific Security: Policy Challenges*, Singapore: Institute of Southeast Asian Studies, 2003, pp. 124–42.

22 Keith Crane, et al., *Modernizing China's Military: Opportunities and Constraints*, Santa Monica, CA: RAND Corp., 2005. The 2005 Pentagon estimate that China's

budget is now 3rd in the world behind that of the US and Russia is at the high range of estimates that include unofficial expenditures. According to Crane et al., the PLA's budget is still below that of the US, Russia, Japan and France (in 2003).

23 Kay Moeller, "China's Strategic Objectives and Policies," in Erich Reiter and Peter Hazdra (eds) *The Impact of Asian Power on Global Developments*, Vienna: Physica-Verlag, 2004, pp. 135–41.

24 Whereas up to 1996 the arms budgets of the two "China's" remained roughly comparable, since that time China's arms spending has overtaken and by 2002 more than doubled that of Taiwan. Crane et al., *Modernizing China's Military*, p. 134.

25 See Medeiros and Fravel, "China's New Diplomacy."

6 The fragility of China's regional cooperation

Edward Friedman

The future of regional cooperation in Northeast Asia rests on the policies and politics of China. Will China be able or not to transform Asia in China's image, authoritarian and Sinocentric? Muthiah Alagappa relies on the ASEAN way of regional integration to prevent that outcome.[1] In the ASEAN way, mutual economic success provides societal stability and trumps irredentist mobilizations for war about territorial claims. Regional peace and prosperity are then perpetuated. Without impeding any party's sovereignty, the ASEAN way facilitates a uniquely successful form of regional cooperation that socializes China to the status quo. Samuel Kim is even more optimistic.[2] He sees the rise of China greatly intensifying these win-win regional arrangements.

A contrasting view is more impressed that the Chinese Communist Party's (CCP) policy of restoring China to its rightful, glorious position in Asia can win. This CCP vision is informed by an irredentist nationalism. In Asia, the CCP rejects a multipolarity which would enhance Russia, India, the Association of Southeast Asian Nations (ASEAN) and Japan and facilitate cooperation among sovereign equals. Given CCP objectives, regional peaceful prosperity is not guaranteed. Maintaining the status quo requires China–Japan reconciliation and a peaceful resolution to China–Taiwan tensions. The CCP does not embrace Alagappa's ASEAN model. Instead,

> China wants to be seen as the only Asian ... power to speak on equal terms with and potentially to challenge the United States. China is the only regional power in the world to have placed herself in open and global competition with the US. The danger of this strategy has been to antagonize the US and its allies in the region and increase rather than decrease America's military presence in and concern for the region.[3]

Is the ever more robust cooperation that Alagappa and Kim highlight threatened by the Chinese attempt to subordinate Japan, incorporate Taiwan, and make the rest of the region serve China's hegemonic ambitions, as when the CCP demands support for its annexation of Taiwan as the price of good relations? How fragile is Asian regional cooperation as a result of Chinese territorial ambitions, including an insistence that, before the CCP negotiates sharing South China Sea oil,

ASEAN states must first recognize China's sovereignty in the territory? In 2005, Singapore's senior statesman, Lee Kuan Yew, made public his worries on this matter.

China's robust regional cooperation

By the 1990s, the People's Republic of China (PRC) clearly enhanced regional and global cooperation. It courted ASEAN nations with generous economic deals. It was supported by the smaller nations of South Asia for membership in that India-dominated region's organization, the South Asian Association for Regional Cooperation. The PRC began regular talks with the North Atlantic Treaty Organization (NATO) and the Muslim Gulf Cooperation Council. Because China's rulers did not want neighbors to their south in the ASEAN to be dependent on China's regional and global rivals, India, Japan, and America, CCP leaders became active in regional fora so as to keep international conflicts from serving American interests. The CCP's enemy was American democracy.

To China's west, among new Islamic republics, the PRC promoted a Shanghai Co-operation Organization (SCO) to deny aid to China's Muslim separatists who sought succor in the Central Asian republics and to counter "agents of ... democratization" and "to show the political preferences of Central Asian governments" to back China on policies such as Taiwan.[4] Opposition to democracy and support for Chinese irredentism were the price for CCP cooperation.

China's government-organized non-governmental organizations (GONGOs) became more active within international non-governmental organizations (INGOs). Its annual Boai Forum in Hainan attracts Asia's elites to discuss the region's future. By almost any measure, China had turned strongly in the direction of regional and international cooperation that is compatible with Chinese interests as defined by the CCP dictatorship. Given the ham-handedness of the Bush Administration, China became a far more attractive pole to many in Asia than was America.[5] Early twenty-first century polls in most countries showed more people seeing China playing a positive role in the world than George W. Bush's America.

China entered the World Trade Organization (WTO). In the WTO, it joined with Brazil, India, and South Africa to make HIV/AIDS drugs more available to diseased people in poor countries.

The CCP ended Mao era policies which had harmed the people and national interests of China.[6] It courted nations Mao had turned into enemies—Vietnam, India, Mongolia, and Russia. The CCP's tamping down of regional tensions sparked by Mao's dogmatism helped foster a regional environment that was more conducive to mutually beneficial economic exchanges. The PRC made rapid economic growth, based on acting on a world market-regarding logic, a very high priority. Nations welcomed China's cooperative efforts. The people of the whole region benefited. Mutual prosperity was privileged.

The United Nations (UN) was no longer treated by the CCP as a tool of American imperialism. Instead, it was used to further Chinese interests by holding up peace-keeping missions to Haiti or Guatemala unless these governments broke relations with Taiwan. China participated in UN Peacekeeping Operations (PKO) in Kampuchea and East Timor.

The key concern of the CCP was not to end up like the Communist Party of the Soviet Union, that is, ousted from power. The CCP's top interest is survival. Its major adversaries are the forces of democratization. In this domestically driven CCP analysis of the world, Moscow erred in allowing a power vacuum to grow around it, from East Europe to Central Asia. Therefore, the CCP welcomed opportunities to get its forces involved and its voice heard, focusing its PKO efforts in Asia. If the PRC does not participate, then, the CCP fears the US will impose democratization. The CCP wants to avoid democratization. "China opposes America's view, [that] it may be reasonable to use military forces to spread the values of the West."[7] The 2005 democratic revolution in the Ukraine was experienced as a threat by the CCP. Consequently, although China opposed NATO's effort to stop the ethnic cleansing of Muslims in Kosovo by China's friend, the Milosovic regime, right after the NATO victory, the PRC joined the UN PKO in Kosovo, furthering "neutrality" instead of democracy.

Preventing democratization is so important that China, which seldom funds UN efforts, set up a PKO training base in Langfang, Hebei, welcomed police from Indonesia, Thailand, South Korea, Malaysia, and the Philippines to PKO courses in Beijing, and cooperated with the Central Asian governments in the SCO to the same purpose.[8] International cooperation to block American democracy, that is, democratization serving American interests, was strengthened during the 1997–8 Asian Financial Crisis which led to the fall of Indonesia's Suharto regime and democratization. Seeing the US block Japan's effort to create an Asian financial mechanism to cushion such crises, the CCP found that regional financial cooperation could stop American democracy. It therefore promoted regional financial cooperation.

Whatever the rationales, China's cooperative regional participation should be welcomed. It erodes doctrines of non-intervention and absolute sovereignty which precluded UN intervention in the genocide in Rwanda, although it remains taboo in China to mention that the machetes used by the Hutu in their slaughter of the Tutsi and moderate Hutu were imported from China.[9] Whatever CCP motives, regional cooperation serves humane purposes, as with America's 1960s commitment to an Asian Development Bank (ADB) so America in Asia would not be defined by its war in Vietnam at that time. Long after the war ended, the ADB continued to do good work.

But the main conclusion of Chinese analyst Tang Yongsheng is that China's domestic political system, an authoritarianism opposed to democratization, limits China's cooperation. Domestic Chinese politics hurt Northeast Asian regional cooperation. As long as the CCP regime's actions lead it to be seen in terms of "Tibet, Taiwan, and human rights violations," China can not readily win deep trust from its neighbors. In addition, however idealistic are young Chinese, without political reform they cannot fully participate in NGOs and INGOs which are crucial to grappling with pressing problems in this age of deepened globalization.

Instead, in spring 2005, they turned their idealistic energies into chauvinistic Japan-bashing, not promoting conciliation and cooperation.

While ASEAN began as a grouping which cooperated regardless of internal politics, subsequently Thailand, the Philippines and Indonesia democratized, while limits on freedom were reduced in Malaysia and Singapore. ASEAN has recently spoken out on behalf of democracy leader Aung San Suu Kyi in the military dictatorship of Burma. In contrast, China buttresses that Burmese tyranny, as well as the one in North Korea. The CCP works to prevent democratization in the region. How far can the CCP cooperate or lead the largely democratic region when most of the region's people suffering from dictatorial rule are Chinese?

Given the outstanding efforts of China's fledgling civil society in responding to the Indian Ocean 2005 tsunami disaster, clearly a free China would be a major contributor to humane purposes. But the CCP does not trust the Chinese people. China therefore has yet to fulfill the hope of the modern Confucian thinker Liang Qichao of creating new citizens whose energies would dynamize a Chinese Confucian national community. To obscure its opposition to democracy and to win "soft" power to enhance its comprehensive power, the PRC funds Chinese language learning all over the region and claims to struggle for international democratization, meaning the CCP opposes the influence of America and its allies and friends, especially Japan and Taiwan. The PRC actually blocks international democratization. It opposes democratizing UN reforms.[10] The CCP enjoys representing one of only five veto-wielding permanent members of the Security Council and opposes reforms which would dilute China's big power status. Although its propaganda line is to identify China as weak and poor, similar to other developing countries, actually China is a rising big power. The CCP wants to maximize its global influence, heedless of the impact on non-Chinese. "China is downright hostile [to UN sanctions on the *genocidaires* in the Sudan], playing the same supportive role for the Darfur genocide that it did for the Khmer Rouge genocide."[11] From the Sudan and Iran, to Burma and Cambodia, to Venezuela and Pakistan, the CCP resists liberal, democratic, and rights-oriented forces. China's international cooperation embodies a particular politics.

The quality and character of China's cooperation regionally also reflects its national identity. Presenting itself as weak and poor, a victim of the international system, Chinese ruling groups cannot see how China does not contribute as would befit a nuclear-armed state with veto power on the UN Security Council whose economy has been rising at high rates for over a quarter of a century, such that industry and investment flee from its neighbors who worry about hollowing out. Given the goals and identity of the CCP, its cooperation with ASEAN is merely tactical. Drawing Burma, Laos, Vietnam and North Korea into its orbit, China intends to transform ASEAN rather than be transformed by ASEAN, as Alagappa hopes.

ASEAN was formed during the Vietnam War in response to a threat from the spread of Stalinist forces backed by Mao's China. To survive, ASEAN governments shelved territorial disputes. But in China's nationalism, the goal is incorporating every piece of claimed territory so as to return China to its historic place in Asia, the regional hegemon. The CCP works for a hierarchical regional cooperation serving Chinese purposes.

Does the PRC vision of cooperation guarantee ASEAN-style reconciliation and peace? The CCP armed the *genocidaires* in Serbia, in Rwanda, and in the Sudan and sold weapons to global hot spots in West Asia and South Asia. It provides crucial support for major human rights violators in its region, warmly welcoming Uzbeki tyrant Islam Karimov upon his slaughtering of peaceful demonstrators. It silences discussion in China of the PRC's role in initiating the Korean War in 1950, of China's launching of an all-out assault on the Indian military in 1962, of China's supporting the genocidal Khmer Rouge in Cambodia. The CCP will not face up to its role in alienating Japan[12] and in keeping alive military tensions in the Taiwan Strait region. Despite seeking regional economic cooperation, the CCP created hostility toward Taiwan, Japan, and America in ways that made regional cooperation fragile.

China rejects cooperation

A non-cooperative posture was manifest in the CCP's go-it-alone actions on energy security. China's leaders would not agree to mutually beneficial ways to share the energy resources of the South China Sea, also claimed by nations in ASEAN.[13] It and India competed over Burmese and Bangladesh energy, ignoring Indian requests for cooperation. China pressured Russia not to run an oil pipeline to Japan. It would not compromise or cooperate with Japan in order to equitably resolve conflicting claims to East China Sea energy resources. Fairly sharing the energy of the East China Sea and the South China Sea would promote cooperation and strengthen forces of peace and prosperity.

Instead, China treated Taiwan, an island nation at the north end of the South China Sea and the south end of the East China Sea, as a place to be incorporated so that the PRC could dominate the energy resources of neighboring ocean territories.[14] China also invested in a naval build-up to have the might to impose its will on littoral neighboring regions. It seems to be seeking port access in Burma and Pakistan. China would turn itself into a maritime power. In general, CCP leaders, moved by a nationalism legitimating regional predominance acted heedless of the imperatives of ASEAN-style regional cooperation.

PRC policy toward Taiwan illuminates the CCP policy of restoring Chinese glory at the cost of regional cooperation. It blocks any Taiwanese contribution to the international community. China isolates Taiwan, excluding it from international organizations and fora that do not even require *de jure* statehood as a prerequisite for membership.[15] China has denied Taiwan membership in the World Health Organization (WHO), even as a mere observer called a "health entity." As a result, WHO's help on severe acute respiratory syndrome (SARS) came late, facilitating the spread of SARS in the region.[16] Given how avian flu, AIDS, SARS and other diseases can spread in a globalized world, the PRC's isolation of Taiwan does not make for a healthy region.

The CCP has blocked Taiwan from helping people in need, whether it is earthquake relief in Turkey or medical supplies to sub-Saharan Africa. In so many arenas where cooperation with Taiwan, the world's 14th largest economy, can be a positive force for human improvement (gender, indigenous peoples, environment, development), China has not even allowed Taiwan NGOs to participate and contribute.[17] The CCP even joins fora and organizations to not allow peace-oriented second channel groups or INGOs dedicated to preventing armed conflict from discussing a peaceful resolution of cross-Strait tensions. A statement by a government in the region that it is interested in a peaceful resolution is treated by the CCP as a hostile act. The CCP prevents regional cooperation to maintain the peace.

The Chinese nationalism which legitimates irredentism and absolute opposition to "American democracy" is a recent construction. It does not embody some deep Chinese essence. Panicking in 1989–91, when much of the Soviet bloc disintegrated and democratized, CCP leaders imagined Taiwan's democracy as threatening the survival of CCP state power and slowing a Han return to global glory. PRC ruling groups demonized Taiwan's democratic presidents for undermining the stability and unity of China.

The CCP was traumatized by the events of 1989 to 1991, the nationwide 1989 democracy movement in China and its bloody suppression on June 4, the fall of the Berlin Wall in November and the subsequent democratization of former Soviet socialist bloc countries, culminating in a failed August 1991 reactionary coup in Russia and the subsequent implosion of the Soviet Union. These eruptions made the CCP worry about its own future. The anxiety reshaped Chinese national identity so that Taiwan was suddenly re-defined as an ultimate enemy, even though Taiwan, which democratized in 1988, did nothing to threaten China and sought mutual benefit from economic interchange. How, after all, could little Taiwan, whose military budget has been declining while China's has been rising at double-digit rates, threaten great power China?

Prior to those 1989–91 events, Chinese policy toward Taiwan had a peace-prone thrust. Paramount leader Deng Xiaoping privileged a peaceful regional environment to facilitate growth out of Mao-era stagnation. To make money on missile sales to Saudi Arabia in 1986–7, the PRC did not insist that the Saudis break official diplomatic ties with Taiwan.[18] China invited in Taiwan traders and investors. By the late 1980s the two sides were finding *modus vivendi* facilitating peaceful co-existence. Taiwan rejoined both the Olympic Games and the Asian Table Tennis Association as Chinese Taipei and stayed in the Asian Development Bank as Taipei, Taiwan.

When Deng ordered the June 4 massacre, France led the industrialized democracies to sanction China for mass murders of unarmed people. Taiwanese investment then rushed in. Rather than trying to undermine the shaky dictatorship by massively supporting Chinese democrats in exile, democratic Taiwan, led by President Lee Teng-hui, facilitated a surge of mutually beneficial economic relations with Deng's China, thereby helping Deng in January 1992 to re-ignite economic reform. Taiwan President Lee was "reaching out to the PRC, sending secret emissaries to arrange discussions of how to improve cross-strait relations."[19] In the early 1990s front organizations for Taipei and Beijing began talks on improving Taiwan-China relations.

To counteract the international sanctions imposed after the CCP's June 4, 1989 massacre in Beijing, Deng sought to conciliate Taiwan, America, and others. He weighed how to respond to President George H. W. Bush's mid-1992 decision to sell advanced weapons to Taiwan so as to provide jobs for workers in an electorally important state in the Bush race for presidential re-election against challenger Bill Clinton. "[T]he MFA's [Ministry of Foreign Affairs] original proposal to retaliate openly against Bush's decision to sell 150 F-16 advanced fighter aircraft to Taiwan during the US president elections ... was overruled by Deng."[20] As with Mao's earlier prioritizing, for Deng, too, Taiwan was, on the one hand, used to drum up patriotic passions in support of the CCP regime, yet, on the other hand, in international and domestic politics, little, weak Taiwan was of far lesser importance than many, many other matters. Taiwan, after all, really was a small, unthreatening island in the chain running south from Sakhalin Island and eventually out into the South Pacific islands.

Yet by 1995–96, China used weaponry to terrorize Taiwan. The CCP stopped talking to elected Taiwanese leaders. It militarized relations with Taiwan.[21] How had national identity and politics changed so the economic imperative, however vital, no longer easily trumped a new nationalist agenda and a new survivalist notion of preventing democratization in the region?

First, a new, self-serving nationalist mythos of the CCP, after so many Soviet bloc dictatorships democratized, saw democratic Taiwan as a threat, despite Taiwan's efforts to be helpful to the post-June 4 Deng regime, re-imagining Taiwan as a pawn in an American plot to subvert socialist regimes. The Deng-led CCP, after the Soviet Union imploded into many ethnic and religious nations, and Czechoslovakia split, and East Germany (the DDR) disappeared, saw ethnic splitists as a dire threat to Communist Party rule everywhere, including China. A multicultural Taiwan with a separate identity (which the newly democratic Taiwan was) made Chinese ruling groups anxious. Political and ideational changes and concerns in Beijing turned a democratic and friendly Taiwan into an existential enemy for the CCP, despite Taiwan's best efforts to seek mutually beneficial relations.

That is, extraordinary 1989–91 events led to a rupture in how Chinese rulers imagined the world, suddenly moving them to interpret a multicultural democratic Taiwan as an ultimate threat to the very survival of the CCP regime. The CCP abandoned Mao's attacks on Chinese culture as feudal and backward and instead promoted Confucian conservatism, spread a national essence fever, and made national heroes of conservative stabilizers, such as Zeng Guofan who slaughtered revolutionaries in order to maintain the *ancien regime*.[22] China's policy toward Taiwan, in accord with the CCP's reimagined national identity, was militarized. China thereby undermines the core of ASEAN-style cooperation by threatening to use military means to settle territorial disputes.

Nonetheless, in opposition to Organization for Economic Co-operation and Development economic sanctions against China, Taiwan worked for China's development. While many tried after June 4 to get America's Clinton Administration to end the PRC's Most Favored Nation (MFN) status for trade, "The Taipei government never sought to curb China's MFN benefits, because many Taiwan-based companies were running factories in mainland China, earning handsome profits by exporting their products to the United States."[23] Yet Chinese were taught to see Taiwan's democratically elected presidents as troublemakers.

Second, the new generation of CCP leaders had been brought up in an age of patriotic anti-Taiwan narratives. They imagined Taiwan, as Tibet, as historically part of China and central to China's anti-imperialist mission. The revolutionary generation of Mao and Deng, in contrast, had never heard such a historical narrative in its youth, when Chinese accepted that Taiwan was not part of China. Only in 1942–3, as America seemed set to defeat Japan (Taiwan's colonial master since 1895) was Taiwan reimagined by Chinese as always part of China. Deng's successor, Jiang Zemin, made annexing Taiwan a sacred duty, finally to end a century of imperialist humiliation and to wipe away the shame of the Opium War. This victimization narrative still appeals to Chinese despite the extraordinary rise of post-Mao China to great power status.

Obscuring millennia of expansionism, making invisible the subordination or incorporation of neighbors,[24] Chinese nationalists believe China and the Chinese, uniquely among large nations, are not expansionist but innocent victims. Conquered peoples were pictured as having volunteered to enjoy the blessings of Sinic civilization. To Chinese chauvinists, Taiwanese who promote a separate Taiwanese identity in the new era of multicultural Taiwanese democracy are crazy as well as unpatriotic and subversive. The potential aggressor sees the targeted victim, Taiwan, as the instigator. This mythos of Chinese national identity rested on a distorted notion of the Qing dynasty. The Qing, a world leader in territorial expansion and settler colonialism, was treated singularly by the CCP as the victim of Opium War style imperialism. After 1991, the CCP, silent about the massacres involved, embraced Manchu Qing conquests as Chinese[25] and incorporated a new anti-Taiwan narrative into the old Mao-era victimization nationalism.

Third, a new international situation allowed President Jiang's administration to focus militarily on Taiwan. In the 1970s, the Chinese were worried about a Soviet invasion, and thus "anti-tank weapons were made the top priority for development."[26] With the Soviet Union no longer the threat Mao had made it, post-Mao China could focus on weapons purchases suited to victory over Taiwan. Deng's normalizing endeavors left China free of threats to its continental borders. Conquering Taiwan became the Chinese military's major preoccupation. This is reflected in weapons purchases, military production, and planning aimed at conquering Taiwan.

After the military on June 4, 1989 saved the authoritarian Deng regime from a popular Chinese democratic movement and after the Soviet Union imploded in 1991 when the Red Army did not defend the regime, CCP ruling groups found a yet greater need for a loyal military to defend the ruling party and suppress purportedly splitist forces. Taiwan was reimagined as part of splitist forces in Lama

Buddhist Tibet and Uighur Muslim Xinjiang. Didn't Baltic independence lead to the implosion of the Soviet Union? Subsequent events strengthened this CCP notion that, without ethnic unity, China could not hold together and rise to glory. Didn't Kosovo imperil Yugoslavia? Didn't East Timor imperil Indonesia? The Chinese military now took Taiwan as "its main focus."[27]

Given this demonization of Taiwan, in 1991–2 the CCP decided to build and deploy missiles to intimidate Taiwan. In 1992–3 the CCP leadership opted for "greater pressure (including military coercion)."[28] The consensus was that only intimidation would keep Taiwan from *de jure* independence.[29]

"China's domestic policy situation made it impractical to consider revising its Taiwan policy... on which the People's Liberation Army (PLA) had to be consulted... because... the party leadership was beholden to the army for saving their mandate to rule in 1989" and "because the PLA saw Taiwan as the key challenge for the future," although it is inconceivable that the Taiwan military could challenge China's. Consequently, in China, "the armed forces would continue to... receive a higher proportion of national budgetary resources"[30] to make the threat to Taiwan credible. The policy consequences of the new Chinese nationalism brought a negation of the ASEAN way of regional cooperation premised on abjuring irredentist claims.

The Deng era priority of economic growth, however, kept President Jiang from acting on the military option. In response, in 1994 retired generals joined to attack Jiang as soft. They demanded "a staged escalation of military pressure on Taiwan over a twenty-year period." Military "pressure to be 'tough' on the Taiwan issue" "limited his [President Jiang's] policy flexibility."[31] Eventually Jiang had to criticize himself.

Although the CCP's "one-China principle," a claim that Taiwan is but a regional unit of the CCP's China, is a non-starter in mainstream Taiwan politics, when Taiwan rejected a 1995 overture of President Jiang Zemin to surrender to the one-China principle, other Chinese leaders painted Jiang as "dovish to the point of capitulation."[32] Senior and retired Chinese military leaders could then force President Jiang to act militarily in 1995–6 by claiming that Taiwan's unchallenged separation is shameful. Taiwan policy bled into CCP politics, making Taiwan a litmus test for those who aspire to leadership in Beijing.[33] "China's hardline option will probably hold center stage in its Taiwan policy for some time."[34]

China's threat to Taiwan makes regional peace and cooperation fragile. Is there anything the regional community can do to move China's rulers back toward peaceful cooperation instead of a military unilateralism in which Chinese are taught to hate Japan and America for opposing China's armed annexation of Taiwan?

China's rulers prefer to use means other than war to incorporate Taiwan. First, they sought to make Taiwan dependent on China so Taiwanese tycoons, to keep making money, would betray Taiwan's democratic autonomy. Next they interfered in Taiwanese politics, hoping to split the Green Camp which promoted a separate Taiwan identity and to strengthen the old guard of the Blue Camp which hated de-Sinicization. Meanwhile, the military build-up by China against Taiwan continues unabated. The irredentist agenda has not changed.

Although a Chinese military success against Taiwan would cement China's rise to regional hegemony,[35] something not desired by most nations in Asia, the tendency of the international community is to heed China's story and to stigmatize Taiwan. Blaming the victim is normal. Power, and China is again a great power, attracts admirers and sycophants. In addition, many international reporters are stationed in China because China's actions constitute major international news events. Few journalists reside in a Taiwan whose deeds are insignificant for international power politics. Consequently, commentators are exposed to the official CCP line on Taiwan and almost never have an empathetic experience of democratic Taiwan as endangered because of Chinese policies and patriotic passions. Although Taiwan has no intention of declaring an independent Republic of Taiwan, and repeatedly says so, international analysts give credence to the CCP view that a provocative Taiwan is about to declare independence and must be brought into line.[36] Few criticize the PRC for ignoring Taiwan President Chen's offers for conciliation. The actual source of regional instability is an irredentist China.

While the CCP's legitimacy is promoted both by regional cooperation furthering economic growth in China as well as by China's new nationalism, naturally, the large and positive changes from its regional cooperation should be welcomed. Yet, because of its domestic political system and the content of its nationalism, China also acts in ways which undermine democracy, peace, and regional cooperation. The big policy question then is, what can regional actors do to strengthen the positive tendencies and weaken the negative tendencies that make cooperation fragile? The question leads to a discussion of reconciliation with Japan, engagement and democratization.

Extending regional cooperation with China

"[W]ithout true reconciliation [between China and Japan] there can be no guarantee of long range regional stability."[37] Why then won't Beijing reconcile with Tokyo? It is not because Japan does not apologize for 1937–45 aggression and crimes against humanity. Britain and France reached out to a democratizing Germany right after World War Two, hoping to integrate Germany into a peaceful and democratic Europe long before 1968 when the socialists were in power in Germany and a younger generation of Germans finally forced the nation to face up to its Nazi past. Reconciliation did not end when neo-Nazism and racism rose in the early 1990s in eastern Germany or at the outset of the twenty-first century when Germans focused on how they were the victims of criminal American and British bombing of civilians and no longer wanted to be treated singularly as war criminals. Indeed, on the 60th anniversary of Victory in Europe Day, the German ambassador to Britain asked "the British to forget their obsession with Hitler and concentrate instead on the achievements of post-war Germany."[38] What prevents reconciliation and limits regional cooperation in Asia, in contrast, is that authoritarian China is not a democracy looking to integrate Japan into a democratic Asia and that CCP foreign policymakers wish to pillory and marginalize Japan so as to legitimate China's regional ascendancy. Cooperation is made fragile by China's politics and policies.

Can ever deeper and broader engagement change the CCP's nationalistic attitudes and alienating practices? Critics of engagement, a policy of maximally promoting exchanges, find that, with China, as with North Korea, engagement is welcomed by Leninist regimes to buttress the dictatorship, both by building its military prowess and also by enhancing its popular legitimacy by raising standards of living.[39] American intelligence analyst Kenneth Pollack criticizes deep engagement with China that builds a market economy and mutual dependency, "arguing that the removal of economic obstacles in China has only allowed its leaders to ignore pressure for political change by emphasizing the country's economic development."[40] Critics of engagement oppose the policy because they see no good in militarily and politically strengthening dictatorial regimes which may become wartime enemies of America, Japan, and Taiwan.

These critics of engagement may be factually correct, but they are wrong about policy. Engagement of course strengthens the CCP. Why else would it embrace engagement? There is a problem, however, with ending one's analysis at that point. One ignores the real world of politics, the actual and worse alternatives to engagement. The political realm of international relations is not a struggle of pure good and evil. Political leaders are compelled to choose lesser evils. Whatever the negative externalities of engagement, the negative consequences of hostile containment toward China (or North Korea) are far nastier and more explosive. Engagement at least offers some hope of a better future that is impossible should regional nations choose a policy of hostile containment. So while naïve promoters of engagement who expect it soon to produce societal openness, political democracy, and progress in human rights are bound to be disappointed and to appear to more realistic observers as naïve, this is not because engagement, as with Ostpolitik in Europe, was an error, or because unremitting hostility to North Korea or China would guarantee a peaceful future for Northeast Asia.

Ostpolitik, begun in 1969, did not stop Brezhnev's militarism in the 1970s. Engagement with Soviet bloc Europe could not prevent Poland's General Jaruzelski from crushing the nationwide democratic movement known as Solidarity. But over a long period of time, engagement did strengthen reformist forces in the Soviet Union and elsewhere in the bloc. It even helped reform elements among ruling groups to become accepting of democratization.

In the same way, engagement with China enhances the weight of regions and peoples in China who benefit from the world market and openness, people whose greatly increased wealth and knowledge strengthen their clout in Chinese politics in clashes with more chauvinistic and war-prone forces.[41] The trading coastal south opposes war with Taiwan, Major General Peng Guangqian of the Academy of Military Science found, because "the coastal areas in the southeast may be affected by the flames of war and suffer casualties and losses to property."[42]

The gradual gains for forces of peace from engagement may not seem like much. They do not guarantee that China must take the path of peace, democracy, and cooperation. But they do weaken forces which are war-prone. It may not be much, but one should not exaggerate happy consequences from external pressures. China's future will still be decided by politics in China. It is best for other nations not to act in ways which are likely to unleash a chauvinist backlash in China.

Outsiders lack the clout to democratize China, which is a great and independent country. In fact, heavy-handed intervention on human rights matters is likely to boomerang among the legion of Chinese patriots, who, on their own, privately, may rail against the inhumanities of the pervasively corrupt CCP, but who, as proud patriots, hate having China ridiculed by powerful, threatening, distant foreigners, imagined as ill-willed meddlers intervening "into Chinese internal affairs."[43]

The best the democracies in the region can do is, after institutionalizing an agenda of full engagement, to build a regional organization to act on behalf of human rights in the region which does *not* single-out China, but, instead, focuses first on worst offenders, Burma and North Korea. Taiwan does its best to promote a Democratic Pacific Assembly on behalf of such goals.[44] But China has isolated Taiwan. Its voice is not heard.

There are a few small efforts among Indians and Japanese to achieve cooperation among regional democracies on behalf of promoting human rights. Nations in the region should embrace India within its future community, which the Indians have dubbed "JACIK," or "Japan, ASEAN, China, India, and Korea." Northeast Asia will do best as part of a larger democratic, Asian region. It is possible to construct the region as a democratic one so that authoritarian Chinese see the CCP as the odd government out, an authoritarian island in an ocean of democracies.

This regional effort is discredited by the CCP by a pillorying of rulers in Tokyo as the unrepentant legatees of Imperial era invaders. Japan, of course, has been a democracy since the end of World War Two. In the post-War era, it has strongly supported the UN's mission of peace and cooperation. It has been the largest supplier of aid funds in Asia and to China. The CCP goal is to obliterate Japan's good works and make the PRC the only legitimate moral leader of Asia. Therefore, the CCP rejects reconciliation with Japan.

Actually, the region (India, Mongolia, Indonesia, Taiwan, Thailand, Japan, the Philippines, Bangladesh, South Korea) is democratic. But, as an economically rising great power, China acts as if it should be the regional leader. But where would China lead? A maintenance of the region's peaceful pluralism of sovereign equals may require that the democracies build regional institutions supporting regional human rights and democracy. But the CCP blocks that agenda. For China's rise to promote peaceful cooperation "will demand profound changes in the way China is governed."[45]

Democracy and peaceful cooperation, in the democratic peace hypothesis, are closely linked. The point is not that democracies do not start wars. They do. The point is not that among democracies there are no serious disputes. There are. But, overwhelmingly, the likelihood that democracies will, among themselves, settle those disputes by war is so very much lower than between dictatorships and democracies.

Engagement therefore can contribute somewhat both to forces working for democracy and also for peace, both of which enhance the likelihood of regional cooperation to solve common problems. Engagement also holds the possibility of strengthening forces inside China which oppose the CCP's war-prone chauvinistic national identity that facilitates military mobilization against Japan, America, and Taiwan so that the CCP can maintain its dictatorial grasp on power. Engagement, even as it strengthens the CCP domestically, is also a force on the side of international peace, cooperation, and prosperity.

Northeast Asian nations, however, can not impose an agenda on China. The Chinese will make their own future. But they will not make it in the image of the ASEAN way unless there is a change in China's nationalism and the project it legitimates.

The victimization Maoist nationalism of anti-imperialism began to be challenged by reform leader Deng Xiaoping. He needed to legitimate foreign investment, joint ventures and trade. Deng found that the Ming-Qing decline down to the feeble condition where a fleet from small and distant England could crush the great Qing dynasty's shore defenses around 1839 in the Opium War was brought on by the rulers' arrogant rejection of global best practices. Deng's view challenged Mao's victim-revenge nationalism narrative. The empire's decline, for Deng, began when Ming dynasty rulers abjured scientific and technical knowledge, destroying shipyards and executing astronomers who would learn from foreigners to advance their science.[46] Today, openness to best global practices helps China rise. Benefiting from open cooperation with the world, China is a great power again, even as CCP leaders pretend the nation is still weak and a victim. The victimization identity which legitimates vengeful military action in the region need not be permanent. Nationalism can change—indeed, the 1989–91 dangerous nationalism sketched in this work, referred to as Beijing nationalism, is already being challenged by a Shanghai nationalism which sees time on China's side, with no need to risk China's rise by promoting hatred or initiating a war.

As engagement succeeds, Deng's narrative, which privileges mutually beneficial international exchange, makes more sense. Engagement may be strengthening some better cultural forces in China while weakening vengeful myths. Engagement, in comparison to hostile containment, holds the promise of furthering peace, prosperity and regional cooperation. But it would be innocent to believe that twenty-first century China has already abandoned the myths of the Mao era which delegitimated reconciliation. Instead, the CCP's old nationalism has been refurbished to target Taiwan, Japan, and America, thereby rendering peace and cooperation fragile.

The best path to peace and reconciliation in Taiwan–China relations and then to stable and mutually beneficial regional cooperation would be the democratization of China. The conventional wisdom, however, is that, with Chinese privileg-

ing a raising of standards of living over political reform and with the rise of commercial families dependent on connections to the politicized state, there is no
independent (bourgeois) force in society to democratize the nation. Consequently,
the CCP will continue to hold power, largely unchallenged.

But in France's 1789 revolution, the same venal relationship held between
commerce and the state as in China entering the 21st century. What was wanted
then, as now in China, is fairness, opportunity, careers open to talents, and an end
to unjust corruption that entrenches the families of the already privileged at the
cost of great suffering to the vulnerable. So it was with the overthrow of the
Manchu empire in 1911. One already sees in China demands for political reform
in this freer, fairer direction.

There is no reason why the logic of modernization, professionalization, merit,
fairness, and opportunity will not continue to transform the consciousness even
of ruling groups in China, making them believers in promoting a project of gradual political reform. The alternative, the succession crisis inherent in authoritarianism, is instability. The alternative to a relatively fair and open merit-based
democratic society is a continuation and worsening of a brutal and venal system
of secret and arbitrary power that an injured and innocent Chinese populace
already rails against and riots over in huge numbers. In the interest of social stability and a fair shot for families to see their children have opportunities to rise,
democracy can come to seem irresistible.

Such a transition, of course, is not actually inevitable. But certainly it is best
if neighboring nations act so as not to undermine the prospects of those healthier
forces. This potential can and should be strengthened by engagement and regional
cooperation.

China's nationalistic and vengeful victim consciousness which facilitates anti-
democratic power for the CCP is contestable and mutable. There seems to be
some anxiety at the top, a finding that pro-democracy feeling is growing, not only
in China but even among its Asian neighbors. That is much more difficult to dis-
miss and damn than American human rights efforts which can be demonized in
China as imperialist attempts to weaken China and spread chaos. Regional cooperation matters. It has what the literature refers to as a neighborhood effect.

The CCP regime, opposing the democratizing of the Asian region, has been
fostering a national mindset to get the Chinese people to see democracy as alien
to their Confucian mores[47] and not to notice the flourishing democracies in neighboring Confucian South Korea, Taiwan, and Japan. Research institutes and journals in China propagate this Confucian authoritarian view. In one statement of
this anti-democratic and Confucianized nationalistic appeal, by National Essence
Research Center analyst Kang Xiaoguang, an argument is made that empires (and
China is said to be an empire by Kang) such as Russia or Austria-Hungary break
up when forces of democratization rise. If Chinese do not act in an ethically
Confucian way to limit ever-worsening corruption, inequality, and instability,
then China too may see democratic forces rise because "China is an isolated
island. We live in an ocean of democracy where we either ... prove our existence
[through Confucianism] or change ourselves into what other people [that is, the

democratic nations of Asia] look like."[48] In other words, because regional cooperation especially among democracies can have an impact, China's authoritarian
rulers worry about it.

While friends of peace and cooperation in the region lack the capacity deci-
sively to influence the political choices of the proudly independent Chinese people, a deepened policy of engagement and cooperative institution-building in
Northeast Asia holds the best possibilities for strengthening already emerging
peaceful and progressive forces inside China. This regional cooperation makes
democracy, the system Chinese visitors will experience in Japan, Taiwan, South
Korea, Thailand, India, Malaysia, Australia, the US, etc. seem normal.
Democracy's stability—something Chinese much desire—will become obvious.
A peaceful transfer of power out of the hands of unpopular ruling groups is a good
anywhere. But given the surge of Chinese tourists and other exchanges, one way
for regional democracies to help these better forces in Chinese society is for the
democracies both to be open to China and to fulfill their own democratic promise at home. Acting unilaterally as a "bull in a china shop" to force China to
change, however, will backfire.

Nothing, of course, is guaranteed in the political realm. It is a contingent arena.
A hegemonic China could win. Or a war, with unforeseeable consequences, could
be initiated by China. But the safest way ahead for regional cooperation is to
advance policies so that Chinese too come to want the benefits of multilateral
regional cooperation that Alagappa wisely touts as the ASEAN way and the benefits of democratic stability and fairness domestically that are the only solid basis
for that cooperation. Ultimately, however, the fate of peaceful regional cooperation will be decided by political action at home by a rising and great China. The
region's future turns on the political system and domestic politics of China.

A key question deciding whether peaceful regional cooperation can be institutionalized is: can a peaceful *modus vivendi* be reached with Taiwan? Yes, if the CCP
rulers recognize that a democratic, multicultural Taiwan does not threaten China's
return to glory. It surely does not. But such a Chinese recognition requires the CCP
to end its threats to Taiwan and maximize its positive exchanges with Taiwan so as
to remove Taiwanese, Japanese and American concerns over the growing Chinese
military build-up. Evidence suggests that China's Hu Jintao administration knows
this. But the policy impact of that awareness, using carrots to court Taiwan, is
negated by the ever-intensifying threatening posture of the Chinese military toward
Taiwan, and by the imperatives of China's post 1989–91 nationalistic mindset, and
by the PRC's demeaning isolation of Taiwan internationally.

China should remove its missiles across from Taiwan. It might get in return
Taiwan ending America's intelligence basing on Taiwan and Taiwan's ending its
participation in a theater missile defense system aimed at China. If trust were to
prevail, Taiwanese would eventually not want to purchase expensive American
weapons systems instead of spending scarce tax monies on domestic needs on
Taiwan.

The key to building trust in Beijing–Taipei relations is for China to respect
Taiwan's separate identity. A central issue, therefore, is the content of Chinese

nationalism which channels patriotic energies. For China to build trust with Taiwan requires the CCP to stop promoting the 1989–91 national identity which defines Taiwan as a threat because it is democratic and multicultural, an envisioning of Taiwan in terms of the Opium War mythos of a weak China endlessly victimized and humiliated by imperialism. China cannot win the confidence of the Taiwanese people while it educates Chinese people into believing that Taiwan has always been a part of China and that it is the sacred duty of the Chinese people to end the supposed humiliation of a *de facto* independent Taiwan.

The CCP regime has surrendered the Qing dynasty claim to Mongolia. It has surrendered contested territory to Burma and Russia to achieve a deepened cooperation. The CCP can be flexible with Taiwan too, but, perhaps, only if a different nationalism redefines national interests. If Russia could change *vis-à-vis* Finland, if England could change *vis-à-vis* Ireland, then China should be able to change *vis-à-vis* Taiwan. This is a matter for internal Chinese politics.

Given how much China's regional cooperation to date has already achieved, given how much China's leadership would be more welcome in the region were the PRC to abandon its war-prone passions and policies, surely ending the obstacles to full cooperation would be a blessing. First and foremost, benefits would accrue to the peoples of China and Taiwan. But the large benefits for the entire region would also be profoundly significant. The benefits would include strong and solid regional cooperation in the interest of peace and mutual prosperity.

Notes

1 Muthiah Alagappa (ed.), *Asian Security Order*, Stanford, Stanford University Press, 2003.
2 Samuel Kim (ed.), *The International Relations of Northeast Asia*, New York, Rowman and Littlefield, 2004.
3 Jean-Pierre Cabestan, "The Chinese Factor," in Gilles Boquerat and Frederic Grafe (eds) *India, China, Russia*, Singapore, Indian Research Press, pp. 86, 87, 106.
4 Chien-peng Chung, "The Shanghai Co-operation Organization," *China Quarterly*, No. 180, December 2004, pp. 993 and 997.
5 Joshua Kurlantzick, "China's Chance," *Prospect*, No. 109, March 2005.
6 Edward Friedman, "Wounding the Chinese Nation," *Journal of Contemporary China*, Vol. 13, No. 40, August 2004, pp. 601–6.
7 Yongsheng Tang, "China's Participation in UN Peacekeeping Regime," in Wang Yizhou (ed.) *Construction Within Contradiction*, Beijing, China Development Publishing House, 2003, p. 99.
8 Ibid., pp. 73–99.
9 The other weapons for the *genocidaires* came from France.
10 Dongyan Li, "A Chinese Perspective on U.N. Security Council Reform," in Wong Yizhou, (ed.) *Construction Within Contradiction*, Beijing, China Development Publishing House, 2003, pp. 100–27.
11 Nicholas Kristof, "The American Witness," *The New York Times*, 2 March 2005.
12 In 2004, two Chinese analysts who published analyses of how to improve relations with Japan were silenced.
13 An offer for reconciliation was a mere stratagem. Alistair Iain Johnston, "China's International Relations," in Samuel Kim (ed.), *The International Relations of Northeast Asia*, New York, Rowman and Littlefield, 2004, p. 93.

14 Jiann-fa Yan, "Taiwan's Asia-Pacific Geo-Strategic Value," in Edward Friedman (ed.) *China's Rise, Taiwan's Dilemmas, and International Peace*, New York, Routledge, 2005, ch. 10.
15 Vincent Wang, "Taiwan's Participation in International Organizations," in Edward Friedman, (ed.) *China's Rise, Taiwan's Dilemmas, and International Peace*, New York, Routledge, 2005, ch. 9.
16 Dennis Hickey, "The High Cost of Excluding Taiwan from the WHO," in Edward Friedman, (ed.) *China's Rise, Taiwan's Dilemmas, and International Peace*, New York, Routledge, 2005, ch. 4.
17 Jie Chen, "Civil Society, Grassroots Aspirations and Diplomatic Isolation," in Edward Friedman, (ed.) *China's Rise, Taiwan's Dilemmas, and International Peace*, New York, Routledge, 2005, ch. 6.
18 Ning Lu, *The Dynamics of Foreign Policy Decision-Making in China*, Boulder, CO, Westview, 1997, p. 157
19 Robert Suettinger, *Beyond Tiananmen*, Washington, D.C., Brookings Institution Press, 2003, p. 201.
20 Lu, *The Dynamics of Foreign Policy Decision-Making in China*, p. 160.
21 Edward Friedman, "China's Dilemma on Using Military Force," in Edward Friedman (ed.) *China's Rise, Taiwan's Dilemmas, and International Peace*, New York, Routledge, 2005, ch. 11.
22 Yingjie Guo, *Cultural Nationalism in Contemporary China*, New York, RoutledgeCurzon, 2004, pp. 52, 62, 73, 97, and 125.
23 James Mann, *About Face*, New York, Knopf, 1999, p. 244.
24 Nicola di Cosmo, *Ancient China and Its Enemies*, New York, Cambridge University Press, 2002; Peter Perdue, *China Marches West*, Stanford, Stanford University Press, 2005.
25 Guo, *Cultural Nationalism in Contemporary China*, ch. 3.
26 Wuzheng Qi, "China's Artillery Development," in Michael Pillsbury (ed.) *Chinese Views of Future Warfare*, Washington, D.C., National Defense University Press, 1998, p. 177.
27 Lu, *The Dynamics of Foreign Policy Decision-Making in China*, p. 124.
28 Michael Swaine, "Chinese Decision-Making Regarding Taiwan," in David Lampton (ed.) *The Making of Chinese Foreign and Security Policy in the Era of Reform, 1979–2003*, Stanford, Stanford University Press, 2002, p. 316.
29 Jianhai Bi, "The Role of the Military in PRC Taiwan Policymaking," *Journal of Contemporary China*, Vol. 11, No. 32, 2002, p. 568.
30 Suettinger, *Beyond Tiananmen*, pp. 203 and 137.
31 Ibid., pp. 208, 210.
32 Ibid., p. 224.
33 David Lampton, *Same Bed, Different Dreams*, Berkeley, University of California Press, 2001, p. 106.
34 You Ji, *The Armed Forces of China*, New York, I. B. Tauris, 1999, p. 211.
35 See Yan, "Taiwan's Asia-Pacific Geo-Strategic Value," in Friedman, *China's Rise, Taiwan's Dilemmas, and International Peace*.
36 Typical is the report of 23 November 2004, "Chen wants new charter declaring independence," in Singapore's *Straits Times International* in which Taiwan President Chen dangerously rejects China's supposedly reasonable position. Despite the headline, President Chen did not want to declare independence and, of course, did not.
37 Stanley Crossick, "Toward a China-Europe Alliance," *Far Eastern Economic Review*, May 2005, p. 48.
38 Vernon Bogdanor, "Fortunes of war – still the stuff of nightmares," *Financial Times*, 28–29 May 2005.
39 Natan Sharansky, *The Case for Democracy*, New York, Public Affairs, 2004.
40 Reza Aslan, "Misunderstanding Iran," *The Nation*, 28 February 2005, p. 30.

41 Johnston, "China's International Relations," in Kim, *The International Relations of Northeast Asia*, p. 83.

42 "Two High-Ranking PLA Military Experts on 'Taiwan Independence,' Price of a War," Beijing Renmin Wang, 3 December 2003, translated by the Foreign Broadcast Information Service, as quoted in a manuscript by Alan Wachman.

43 Qi Zhou, "Conflicts Over Human Rights Between China and the US," *Human Rights Quarterly*, No. 27, 2005, p. 40.

44 Tim Culpan, "The Democratic Dream," *Taiwan Review*, October 2004, pp. 16–21.

45 Isabel Hinton, "Reaching beyond the myth of Mao," *The Guardian*, 4 June 2005.

46 A similar "know-nothing" xenophobia hastened the decline of the Ottoman Empire.

47 Guo, *Cultural Nationalism in Contemporary China*, pp. 113, 119, 122, 125 and 129–130.

48 Chuanwei Sun, "Scholar Kang Xiaoguang: China's Democratization Means a Calamitous Choice for the Country and the People," *Lianhe Zaobao*, Singapore, 8 November 2004. Also see Guo, *Cultural Nationalism in Contemporary China*, pp. 113, 119, 122, 125 and 129–30.

7 State consolidation and foreign policy in Russia

Leszek Buszynski

Introduction

This chapter examines the relationship between Russian domestic politics and policy towards Northeast Asia in the context of the gradual centralization of power that has been observable over the past five years. Under Yeltsin, Russia was buoyed by the ideology of democracy and adopted particular foreign policy positions that were considered compatible with these values. This change included a close identification with the West and the repudiation or down-playing of relations with former Soviet allies. Subsequently, however, economic decline, and alarm over public disorder prompted his successor Vladimir Putin to strengthen the state and to weaken the power bases of the opposition. Putin's centralization of power in Moscow facilitated the elevation of state interest above the ideological concerns of the Yeltsin era, and allowed foreign policy readjustments based on practical calculations of benefit. With a firm control of Russian politics Putin could make decisions relating to Asia Pacific neighbors, which would have been problematic for a weaker leader.

The linkages between domestic politics and foreign policy can be understood in two ways. First, the general parameters of foreign policy may be established by public opinion or political culture and the government in office may be obligated to give expression to widely held expectations of foreign policy. Over the long term the general direction of foreign policy conforms to domestic political values, though short term decisions may be made for instrumental reasons. If foreign policy decisions conflict with domestic political values or depart significantly from expectations, the result may be a change of government, political polarization, or internal conflict. In pluralist political systems competing political parties may represent different value systems in which case foreign policy may be shaped by the ideology of the party in power. Value systems are subject to change and in some cases the sudden shock of regime collapse or defeat may stimulate an agonizing reinterpretation of domestic values. The unanticipated collapse of the Soviet Union precipitated a value reinterpretation and an attempt to realign foreign policy closely with the West. Foreign policy during the Yeltsin period was shaped by the ideology of the group of Western-oriented liberals who had gathered around the presidential administration and who failed to obtain the support of the Russian people at large. Foreign policy cannot, however, challenge domestic values for too long and in this case considerable domestic conflict was created which isolated the liberals and undermined their position.

Secondly, the ruling regime may intervene in domestic politics to shape political values, and to influence political opinion in a way that would support its desired policies. Such a regime would be guided by its understanding of dominant political values or culture which it would claim to represent to invoke legitimacy in its support. With this declared legitimacy it could re-shape political institutions and adjust the political system to facilitate its continuation while marginalizing the opposition and all those identified with alternative values. A highly interventionist regime would restrict the domestic inputs into foreign policy decision-making by controlling the political parties, institutions, the media and public agencies. The result would be considerable freedom of action in foreign policy and the ability to use it in the process of reshaping domestic values. Putin's presidency represents an interventionist government which has taken upon itself the task of consolidating and stabilizing the Russian state after the cataclysmic Soviet collapse. Putin's presidency has attempted to reconstruct the Russian political system through the mechanism of a dominant party and supporting institutions. The intention has been to establish a state-supported framework for political activity within which the business oligarchs and the regional governors would be allocated a role. Putin's task in foreign policy is to maintain good relations with the West while pursuing domestic policies which some in the West regard as a betrayal of Russia's democratic aspirations. To his supporters Putin's policies are based on a recognition of Russian political realities and his foreign policy is a reflection of Russia's geopolitical location.

The Yeltsin period

Under Yeltsin, the democratic transformation of a Russia that had been subjected to centuries of authoritarian rule was attempted. Foreign Minister and prominent Westernizer Andrei Kozyrev identified the relationship between domestic politics and foreign policy stressing the importance of foreign policy as an instrument of domestic reform. For Kozyrev, a strategic relationship with the West was critical as it would stabilize Russia's democracy and provide an anchor for political and economic reform.[1] Yeltsin's pro-West foreign policy entailed the repudiation of Soviet expansionism, support for global and regional security cooperation and the negotiation of nuclear arms control agreements with the US.[2] The pro-Western policy had repercussions for the Asia Pacific region. The Westernizers around Yeltsin intended to resolve the territorial dispute with Japan over the Northern/Kurile islands, and to encourage Japanese investment in Russia's Far East. They regarded Stalin's occupation of the four islands as illegal and were prepared to return them to Japan in return for a border settlement. Yeltsin was swayed by contradictory impulses but by then nationalist opposition within the Supreme Soviet had crystallized; the Foreign Ministry was accused of attempting to sell "Russian" territory to the Japanese. Russians were fearful of the consequences of the loss of further territory after the Soviet collapse and Yeltsin postponed the issue.[3]

Over the Korean Peninsula the Westernizers had a clear vision. They had intended to abandon North Korea, which was expected to collapse, and were willing to allow the 1961 treaty of friendship to lapse. They were most concerned by the North's nuclear program from 1992 to 1994 which threatened the stability of the peninsula. Yeltsin moved to strengthen the relationship with South Korea whose support was regarded as necessary for the development of the Russian Far East. It was hoped that the *Chaebol* could offer the finance and investment that the Japanese were unwilling to provide. Yeltsin visited Seoul in November 1992 in a much-heralded trip to demonstrate Russia's interest in the South but the results were meager. South Korea lost interest in Russia after it had downgraded its relationship with North Korea and turned to China whose role on the Korean Peninsula was enhanced, particularly after diplomatic relations were established with Seoul in August 1992.[4]

China presented a problem for Yeltsin's Westernizers as it was too important for Russia's security to ignore. Russia's liberals were critical of China's human rights record and the Chinese regime's behavior at Tiananmen Square in June 1989. Yeltsin publicly criticized the regime over the Tiananmen incident at a time when, as Russian Republic President, he clashed openly with the Soviet apparatus. For Yeltsin, the ruling Chinese Communist Party was a child of Soviet communism and tainted with the same crimes. Despite this sentiment Yeltsin's government's policy towards China was based on pragmatic realism and accommodation for various reasons. One important reason was border security as Russia shared a 4,300 km border with China and memories of the border clashes of 1969 were still strong. The Soviet Union on 15 May 1991 concluded a border agreement with Beijing to prevent further clashes and to forestall the revival of Chinese territorial claims to Siberia and the Russian Far East. The treaty recognized the current border which ran along the Argun, Amur and Ussuri rivers and adopted the Thalweg principle whereby the many islands in these rivers would be apportioned according to the location of the main channel. Although in most cases the direction of the main channel was clear three river islands were disputed and were left unresolved. The treaty was most significant for Russia since it meant that vast Chinese claims to the Far East which had been expressed during the bitter years of Sino–Soviet conflict were put to rest. This territorial resolution provided a much weakened Russia with the assurance of a stable eastern border at a time when concern for border stability was heightened. Moreover, in Russian thinking China was a counterweight to a North Atlantic Treaty Organization (NATO) which was then preparing to embrace Poland, Hungry and the Czech Republic, an expansion which was considered provocative by Russia's security establishment. China also supported Russia's territorial integrity over Chechnya and became the salvation of Russia's defence industries after the collapse of the Soviet Union deprived them of state support.[5] The significance of China for Russia was demonstrated when Yeltsin visited Beijing on 25 April 1996 when both sides declared a "strategic partnership."[6] On 27 April Yeltsin and Jiang

Zemin joined the presidents of Kazakhstan, Kyrgyzstan and Tajikistan for the conclusion of the Shanghai agreement on border security. This meeting became the basis of what became the Shanghai Cooperation Organization (SCO) which was created in 2001.

Despite the best intentions on the part of the Yeltsin presidency and its close supporters, Russia's turn to the West could not be sustained. Russia's Westernizers were always a minority and their emergence at the helm of power after 1991 placed them in a position of vulnerability. Non liberal parties predominated after the elections of 12 December 1993 for the new Duma that was created by the new constitution promulgated in the same month. Vladimir Zhirinovsky's nationalist and controversial but decidedly non-liberal Liberal Democratic Party emerged as the strongest party in the Duma with 23 percent of the vote. The Communist Party (CP) under Gennadii Zyuganov received 16 percent and its ally the Agrarian Party, headed by Mikhail Lapshin, obtained 8 percent, together they were the strongest force in the Duma. There was no democratic or liberal party of any political weight and those like Yavlinskii's *Yabloko* were confined to the margins of politics. The CP acted to focus resentment and frustration against the market policies pushed by the Westernizers and the privatization promoted by Deputy Prime Minister Anatolii Chubais above all. Russia's nationalists and communists turned against Yeltsin's Westernizers and liberals, pointing to NATO's expansion eastwards as a sign that the West was fundamentally hostile to Russia. This conviction contributed to the Russian Duma's refusal to ratify Strategic Arms Reduction Talks (START-2) in 1996. The impact was noticeable in January 1996 when the much-maligned Westernizer Andrei Kozyrev was forced to resign, deserted by Yeltsin, who then appointed the political realist Yevgennii Primakov as his successor. Russian realists and nationalists who had vigorously criticized the pro Western policy as humiliating demanded greater attention to China, the Korean Peninsula and Asia in general. In their view, geopolitical location prevented Russia from embracing the West and demanded a reassessment of foreign policy that would bring it into line with Russia's geopolitical realities.

The Putin era

Vladimir Putin is no Westernizer, but what Russians have called a *silovik* or a proponent of a strong state. As a former KGB Colonel and admirer of Yuri Andropov, Putin is a realist whose mission is to reconstruct state authority and to bridle the disintegrative tendencies of the Yeltsin era. Putin moved from his native St. Petersburg to Moscow when on 26 March 1997 he was made deputy to the head of the presidential administration. He was appointed by Yeltsin as head of the Federal Security Service (FSS) on 25 July 1998 and secretary of the Security Council on 29 March 1999. On 9 August 1999 he was elevated to the position of prime minister as Yeltsin regretted the disorder of the late 1990s, particularly after the financial crash of August 1998. Yeltsin on 31 December 1999 declared Putin to be acting president and his successor, and then resigned.[7] Elected president on

26 March 2000 Putin acted with caution and deliberation to strengthen the Russian state. He has brought his own *siloviki* supporters, former KGB colleagues and military men, from St. Petersburg into the presidential administration, into the key power ministries, interior, defence, the FSS, the Foreign Ministry and the Prosecutor-General's Office. Putin and his supporters have pursued a consistent policy of centralizing power within a government-sponsored party, eradicating competing centers of power and removing challenges to the state from the business oligarchy and regional administrations.[8] Russian commentators have claimed that Putin seeks to establish a "controlled pluralism," or a managed democracy where political groups would interact within the parameters of the strong state.[9]

The centralization of power

Yeltsin's difficulty was that he faced a hostile Supreme Soviet opposed to his economic and foreign policy, which he could not influence or remove except by non-democratic means. Putin and his supporters have maneuvered to control the Duma and public debate by creating and then strengthening United Russia [*Yedinstvo*] as the government political party.[10] Putin's demonstration of strong leadership encouraged smaller parties to fall in line as he exploited the alarm over the chaos and anarchy of the Yeltsin period. In one notable case Gennadii Raikov, leader of the National Party of Russia and previously a staunch critic of Yeltsin, in January 2002 joined United Russia on the basis of personal loyalty to Putin.[11] With this and other support Putin could destroy Communist influence in the Duma despite the CP's electoral strength. In the Duma elections of 19 December 1999 the CP was the strongest party receiving 24.3 percent of the vote. Despite this show of strength, under Putin's direction the Duma on 3 April 2002 voted to remove Communist and Agrarian Party deputies from 7 out of 29 committee chairmanships, which were then distributed to United Russia and allies. One reason for the coup was the strength of the business lobby in the Duma and the alliances forged between companies and Duma deputies, particularly in the provinces. The Communists were out of touch with social trends and faded away, their message belonged to the past. Above all, Russian society had adapted to business and commerce and the Communists were blamed for obstructing necessary legislation which would promote this trend.

Russia's liberals claim that Putin's intention is the restoration of Soviet Communism. As they see it, Putin threatens Russian democracy while cleverly manipulating democratic appearances to cover his actions and to maintain international support. No doubt, Putin has often revealed nostalgia for the Soviet period and in his address to both houses of parliament on 25 April 2005 lamented the collapse of the Soviet Union as the "greatest geopolitical tragedy of the last century."[12] This comment was widely disseminated in the Western press but the rest of the speech went largely unreported, there Putin stressed that "without freedom and democracy there can be no order or stability, nor can there be the consistent implementation of the selected economic course."[13] His efforts to remove the social benefits and welfare privileges that were characteristic of the Soviet era, at the cost of his own popularity, indicate more complex motives than those attributed to him by Russian liberals. Putin has defined his most immediate aim as political stability and the termination of the social chaos and economic disorder that has plagued Russia over the past decade. In this effort he has tapped strong political support from many Russians whose yearning for order is confused with the stability of Soviet times.[14] Putin's efforts to bring order to society and to browbeat the business oligarchs into submission have boosted his popularity and standing and account for his electoral success. The paradox is that Russia's Westernizers attempted to promote democracy by non-democratic means, by enforcing democratization and imposing the free market upon a confused and disoriented population. Putin, however, came to power democratically in 2000 and received a renewed mandate in 2004. The frustration of Russia's liberals lies in their sense of rejection in that given democracy and free choice the Russians have not voted for them, but have once again elected a strong leader.

Putin also moved to control the business oligarchy to prevent it from challenging state authority. The eight major oligarchs were a group of business leaders who had profited immensely from Chubais's privatization policies over 1992–3, when state assets were sold off to well-connected former party members at ridiculous prices. They scrambled to take control of functions and utilities which had been previously state-owned, including oil and gas, minerals, railways, financial services and the media. Those that ventured into politics seeking to match their economic power with political influence were targeted by Putin. The first was the media oligarch Vladimir Gusinsky who was arrested and then exiled in June 2000; then came Boris Berezovsky who emerged as a powerful figure under Yeltsin and who promoted Putin's rise to the presidency, he fled into exile in November 2000. Perhaps the most troubling challenge was from Mikhail Khodorkovsky whose activities as head of Yukos Oil Company presaged a freedom for business that would ignore the role of the state. Khodorkovsky moved quickly to transform Yukos into an international company involved in production in Kazakhstan and elsewhere, one whose size and global status would supposedly protect him against the Russian government.[15] His decision in May 2003 to favor China in the construction of an oil pipeline from the Siberian fields placed him immediately in conflict with the president who had other ideas. Khodorkovsky's arrest on 25 October 2003 was predictable, as was his continued incarceration and eventual sentencing on 31 May 2005 to 9 years of imprisonment. At issue here is the relationship between state and business as the oligarchs tested their power to create a compliant government which would reflect their business interests and protect their wealth and property from the danger of seizure. Putin has declared a new model of state business relations in which business would accept the primacy of the state and would assume social responsibilities. He called for business investment in education, health and the ecology and insisted that unless business takes care of the social needs of the people there could be no stable business environment.[16] Despite the dire predictions of the liberals Putin's actions have increased his popularity amongst the people who have little affection for the oligarchs and their plundered wealth.[17]

The trend towards domestic consolidation was indicated in the Duma elections of 7 December 2003. The result was success for the government-supported United Russia Party which won 49.3 percent of the vote and 222/350 seats. The Communist Party was second with 11.8 percent of the vote with 53 seats; Zhirinovsky's LDP was third with 8.4 percent and 38 seats. Russian commentators heralded a one-party Duma and expected that another 60 independent deputies would join United Russia as the "party of power." With dominance of the Duma assured, it was anticipated that Putin would introduce constitutional and legal changes to strengthen the role of the state. In the presidential elections of 14 March 2004 he won 71 percent of the vote, in 2000 his vote was 44.8 percent. Russian liberals such as Irina Khakamada castigated Putin for stifling democracy and for reviving authoritarianism but the failure of the liberals to unite in a common platform conceded the ground to the government party. Russian commentators explained Putin's success in terms of his innate appreciation of Russian political culture where voters follow the strongest leader and party.[18] The anarchy and disorder of the post-Soviet period have reinforced the tendency of Russians to seek strong leadership, which would only be countered by the creation of effective political institutions and functioning opposition parties.

After having bridled the oligarchs Putin moved to emasculate the power of Russia's 89 governors of republics, krai and oblasts who controlled local elections to ensure their own power base. Traditionally, governors in Russia were appointed by the center but democratization gave them the means to free themselves from central control. Some governors ruled like feudal lords, excluding opponents in sham elections, while some republics directly challenged the center, Tatarstan for example insisted upon adopting the Latin alphabet. In May 2000 Putin created 7 federal regions, each with a presidential representative, in an effort to reassert central control but their powers over the governors were ill-defined and ineffectual. Putin's solution was to revert to the traditional practice of appointing governors which was announced on 13 September 2004 during a meeting of the regional governors with the cabinet of ministers. Governors would be nominated by the presidential administration and then offered as candidates for election to local legislatures.[19] On 3 December 2004 the law was passed by the Duma; the president was given the power to dissolve the local legislature if it refused the appointed candidate for governor three times; the president could also remove a governor for poor performance or if he failed to retain the trust of the electorate.[20] Russian commentators noted that Putin had effected a constitutional change by decree which further reduced democratic freedoms.[21]

The centralization of political power under Putin has had important consequences for foreign and security policy. While Yeltsin was in conflict with his domestic opponents he depended upon Western support to prop up his weak authority. Without the same need for Western support Putin could develop a foreign policy which would be more closely aligned with Russia's geopolitical interests in Asia, avoiding the contradictions inherent in Yeltsin's pro-Western policy.

Within the intelligentsia there were the Eurasianists and their sympathizers, like Alexander Lukin, who opposed the Western priority in foreign policy and who claimed that Russia was closer to Asia than the West. Lukin expressed a realist's justification for Putin's policy changes and argued that Russia could never become close to the West because it feared rival centers of power. He wrote that Russia should develop closer relations with countervailing Asian centers of power such as China and India.[22] Foreign Minister Igor' Ivanov in July 2000 explained the new foreign policy guidelines of the Putin government, which replaced those promulgated under Yeltsin in 1993. He stressed Russia's great power status as one of the influential centers of power in a multipolar system and identified American unilateralism as a threat.[23] Rather than allying with the West Putin has promoted the idea of a multipolar world which does not exclude cooperation with the West over international terrorism and nuclear arms reductions. Multipolarity demands the development of relations with centers of Asian power and both China and India have been stressed by Putin's foreign policy team.

A second motive for promoting closer ties with the Asia Pacific region was economic and Putin's government has repeatedly stressed that the economic future of Russia's Far East depends upon it. Ivanov stated that Russia's integration into the Asia Pacific was necessary for the economic development of Siberia and the Far East and that Russia would actively participate in all regional groupings, the Asia-Pacific Economic Cooperation, the Association of Southeast Asian Nations and the Shanghai Cooperation Organization.[24] Putin himself wrote that foreign policy had been given an Asian direction and that Russia sought the benefits of Asian economic integration to assist its own economic growth.[25] During the Duma hearings on Asia Pacific policy in December 2001 economic aims were similarly emphasized. Head of the Duma Committee on International Affairs, Dmitrii Rogozin, stressed that policy towards the Asia Pacific region should aim at uplifting the economy of the Russian Far East. Deputy Foreign Minister Alexander Losyukov declared that security demanded that Russia overcome the economic crisis of the Far East, and that more attention to the Asia Pacific region was justified.[26] In his speech to the Foreign Ministry on 12 June 2004 Putin noted that the Asia Pacific region was the most "dynamic" in the world and stressed the need to develop bilateral relations with China and India.[27]

China

China's significance for Russia has been elevated as a result of Putin's search for geopolitical balance within multipolarity. During his first official visit to Beijing in July 2000 Putin stressed the importance of the strategic partnership to "defend the global balance of power."[28] Both Jiang Zemin and Putin expressed a common interest in opposing American hegemony and Ballistic Missile Defence (BMD) which was then being promoted by the Clinton administration. Both leaders once again stressed their opposition to separatism and their defence of sovereignty and territorial integrity in relation to Taiwan and Chechnya.[29] Jiang Zemin met Putin in Moscow in July 2001 and signed a 20 year treaty of friendship which was the product of complex pressures in the relationship. In an interview with the Russian media, Jiang Zemin admitted that the initiative for the treaty was his, and that he had intended to place the relationship with Russia on a secure footing to minimize the impact of shifting preferences within the younger generation of Chinese leaders. Jiang Zemin had studied in Russia from 1955 to 1956 and could still speak Russian and on this occasion sang Russian songs. The new generation of Chinese leaders had no such experience and were oriented to the West. To prevent the lapse of interest in Russia, the Chinese leader pressed for a treaty of friendship with Russia which would bind future generations.[30] Both sides downplayed the significance of the treaty to remove all suspicion that they were allying against America. The Russian side declared that it was no alliance, but a move for "more predictable and balanced relations between the two powers," and that both countries intended to defend their interests against American hegemony.[31] Common geopolitical interest continued to bring Russia and China together after Jiang Zemin left the stage, particularly after the Bush administration's invasion of Iraq in March 2003. Hu Jintao's first visit abroad as head of state and party leader was to Moscow in July 2003, where with Putin he stressed multipolarity and supported the role of the UN.[32] Not surprisingly, neither Putin nor Hu was willing to include specific complaints against America in the joint declaration as both valued their relationships with the US.[33]

A strengthened president could act against the oligarchs and could override their commercial decisions when they conflicted with state policy. On 29 May 2003, Yukos concluded an agreement with the China National Petroleum Corporation for the construction of the 2,400 km oil pipeline from Angarsk in Eastern Siberia to Daqing in China's Northeast, at an estimated cost of $2.9 billion. The agreement indicated broad range targets for Chinese purchases of Russian oil over 2005–2030 up to $150 billion which would turn Yukos into a major supplier for the Chinese market. The decision became entangled with the oligarchs' political challenge to the presidency as Yukos director Mikhail Khodorkovsky had become a notable critic of Putin and had funded liberal political parties in the Duma. Khodorkovsky attempted to use the agreement with China to shield his business operations from political intervention in the hope that the president would respect an agreement with Russia's strategic partner. Working with China would allow him to expand his commercial activities and to turn his company into an international energy corporation, listing on Western stock markets and attracting Western investment. Khodorkovsky's position would become unassailable and he could influence Russian politics to benefit the oligarchs and their commercial interests. The Russian government was divided over the pipeline agreement as the Energy Ministry saw the benefits of attracting extensive Chinese involvement in the development of Russia's energy industries.[34] Putin, however, perceived a direct challenge and saw alternative opportunities in constructing a pipeline to Nakhodka which would allow Russia to export to Japan, Korea, and other markets besides China. For all these reasons Putin had Khodorkovsky arrested and sentenced. [35]

Prime Minister Mikhail Kas'yanov visited Beijing and on 25 September had advised his counterpart Wen Jiabao that a decision on the pipeline had been post-poned for ecological reasons. The Chinese insisted that Russia had an obligation to China based on their oft-proclaimed strategic partnership and also pointed to the problem of "political trust" in the relationship which could affect their future relations.[36] Within the Chinese leadership there was the view that Russia should be punished for its actions, and that China should impose tough conditions for entry into the World Trade Organization which Russia hoped to join by 2006. Nonetheless, the Russian government moved to defuse tensions with China over this issue by promising that a branch oil pipeline to Daqing would be built which would service the Chinese market. Kas'yanov first raised the idea of a branch line in March 2003 and during his visit to Tokyo in December 2003 he declared that one project with two lines was being considered, one to Japan and the other to China.[37] The Russian government also indicated that it would involve Chinese companies in the development of Russian energy resources and in the privatiza-tion of Russian energy companies. In any case the Chinese wanted to secure access to Russian energy and had no intention of shielding Khodorkovsky or con-fronting Putin over the issue. Putin's measures to strengthen the state and to rein in the oligarchs had Chinese approval, despite the benefits that one of those oli-garchs had promised them, as the Chinese Communist Party was wary of similar challenges from its own business community. China appealed to the Russian gov-ernment to ensure that Yukos would deliver its contracted quota of oil; according to a 2002 contract this was 1 million tons until the end of 2004.[38]

When Prime Minister Mikhail Fradkov finally announced the decision on 31 December 2004 in favor of the Japanese route it included provision for the branch line to Daqing to satisfy China. The Russian government, and the Energy Ministry in particular, regarded the Chinese route as more feasible, it was 800 km shorter and less expensive than the initial estimate of $5.8 billion for the Japanese route, in which case the benefits would flow to Russia more rapidly. They were also disturbed by the fact that there were insufficient oil reserves in West Siberia to feed both lines which required 80 million tons annually, and that the invest-ment required to develop new fields in East Siberia could reach $90–100 billion over several decades.[39]

Putin's strengthened domestic position also allowed him to reach a final terri-torial settlement with China without fear of provoking protest and opposition. During his visit to Beijing on 14 October 2004 Putin reached an agreement over the three remaining river islands whose status was undecided.[40] China's geopolit-ical significance for Russia was such that an eventual resolution of the territorial problem had to be negotiated and could not be delayed. The decision followed Putin's new policy of appointing regional governors in the previous month which ensured that public opposition by obstreperous governors would be eliminated. Bolshoi Island in the Argun River was given to China; Tarabov Island in the Amur River near Khabarovsk was also ceded to China while neighboring Bolshoi Ussuriisk was partitioned.[41] Putin accepted the Amur channel, which went by the city of Khabarovsk, as the Thalweg and not the Kazakevicheva channel which was further south. The Khabarovsk governor and local people had been strongly opposed to any concession to the Chinese over this issue and now discovered that their president had disregarded their concerns. Khabarovsk people protested that there were 16,000 dachas and gardens, two villages, and four farms which produce meat and milk for the city in the islands which were to be handed to the Chinese.[42] Some public protests were held but Governor Viktor Ishaev reluctantly accepted the decision.

Ishaev was concerned about his survival as governor and could not let the territorial problem with China divert his attention. He claimed that he was one of the initiators of the new policy of appointing governors, that the unity of Russia was most important in the face of a "colossal threat" posed by the oligarchs and this was the fundamental reason for introducing the new vertical or unitary system of government.[43] Like many governors who feared for their future under the new law, Ishaev moved to ingratiate himself with the President with protestations of loyalty. Protesting voices were heard from Sakhalin oblast deputy Sergei Ponomarev who declared that the return of the islands to China was "illegal" under the constitution and that a referendum was required to decide their fate.[44] In any case, the oblast deputy had no gubernatorial position to protect. In Moscow, the Federal Duma held hearings on the territorial agreement and queried the cost for Russia. Putin stressed that it had removed the most dangerous problem in relations with China and few were disposed to challenge him on this point.[45]

The Korean Peninsula

Putin repudiated Yeltsin's effort to ostracize North Korea. Under Yeltsin an acrimonious debate between the Westernizers and foreign policy realists erupted; realists decried the loss of influence caused by Yeltsin's policy of ignoring the North. While Russia moved behind the South it lost influence over the North and all possibility of playing a role over the Korean Peninsula. The realists criticized Russia's exclusion from the negotiations that resulted in the Agreed Framework of October 1994 that brought a temporary respite to the nuclear crisis. Putin moved rapidly to renew the relationship with the North and to elevate Russia's position with both sides. Without the ideological abhorrence of the North which was characteristic of the Westernizers, Putin could forge closer relations with Pyongyang in order to be taken more seriously by the South, and to claim a position in negotiations relating to the future of the peninsula. Putin understood that a relationship with the North was required for Russia to press for six party talks and to counter the American insistence on four party talks.[46]

The change in relations with the North was effected when Foreign Minister Igor Ivanov visited Pyongyang in February 2000 and signed a new treaty of friendship and cooperation. It replaced the 1961 treaty which expired in 1990, and was extended for five years. Article one of the 1961 treaty committed Russia to the defence of the North and was the cause of much concern for Yeltsin's presidential administration which was willing to allow the treaty to lapse entirely. Under Putin the Foreign Ministry intended to negotiate a new treaty, or to remove article one from the old treaty while the North wanted to include a Russian nuclear guarantee which the Russians naturally resisted.[47] Putin visited Pyongyang in June 2000 which was the first visit ever by a Russian leader to North Korea, an indication of his priorities. Foreign Ministry Deputy Director Georgi Tolopaya explained that the purpose was to establish balanced relations with both North and South on the Korean Peninsula, to place Russia in the position of mediator between them, and to demonstrate Russia as a "great power."[48]

Soon afterwards in July 2000 Putin joined the G-8 summit in Okinawa where he had intended to demonstrate that Russia was the only major power that could claim influence with the North. At the G-8 summit he declared that the North was willing to terminate its ballistic missile program, a misinterpretation of Kim Jong Il's intentions which was quickly repudiated by the North, leaving Putin embarrassed.[49] Putin then visited Seoul in February 2001 where, in a meeting with South Korean parliamentary deputies, he outlined "five principles for regulating the inter-Korean issue," and pledged Russia's support for peaceful reunification.[50] He hosted Kim Jong Il in Moscow in July 2001 and in an interview with *Rossiiskaya Gazeta* Kim stressed that BMD brought the North and Russia together, and that a new relationship had been forged with Russia.[51] *Izvestiya*, however, expressed the liberals' horror at Kim Jong Il referring to him as the "specter of Communism;" his regime was regarded as "the one preserved monument to Stalinism."[52] Within the Russian government there was also the hope that the North would reform its economy and open up to the outside world. In the Russian view economic change in the North could be promoted by the inter-Korean railway project which would connect the Asia Pacific with Europe via the trans Siberian railway. Russia would offer its services as a transport bridge to Europe which could reduce shipping time and costs.[53]

By maintaining regular contact with the North, Putin had hoped to promote dialogue over its nuclear program. To do this he wanted to have Pyongyang removed from the list of the "axis of evil" countries, to which the Bush administration had consigned it in January 2001. The Russian side also maneuvered to prevent the Bush administration from resorting to force over the issue, a concern which was raised when Defence Secretary Donald Rumsfeld declared that America could overcome Iraq and North Korea simultaneously.[54] Foreign Minister Ivanov in January 2003 proposed a "package" plan which would allow Russia to act as an intermediary between the North and the US. The main features of the plan included the strict observance of the non-nuclear status of the Korean Peninsula and the 1994 Framework Agreement, a guarantee of the North's security, and a renewal of humanitarian and economic aid to the North.[55] The Russians claimed that without their involvement the issue would not be resolved, as unlike America they were a "disinterested" mediator with no intention to topple the Northern regime.[56] The Bush administration initially attempted to exclude Russia from negotiations with the North insisting on four party negotiations involving the two Koreas, the US and China. Russian Foreign Minister Sergei Lavrov noted with satisfaction that both Koreas called for Russia's inclusion, the North was particularly motivated by the need for balance against the Bush administration and was reportedly attracted by Russia's "package" plan.[57] Lavrov outlined Russia's intention to develop trilateral collaboration over the Korean Peninsula between Russia, the North and South Korea and claimed that Russia's relationship with the North ensured it of a key role in the negotiations.[58] After a visit to Seoul in July 2004 he declared that the South expected Russia to use its influence with the North to prevent it from developing nuclear weapons. Three rounds of 6 party talks involving Russia and Japan were held in Beijing in August 2003, February and August 2004 but the results were not encouraging. Deputy Foreign Minister Alexander Losyukov claimed that the talks at least agreed upon a working group of experts to examine the issue, he was apprehensive that without dialogue the Korean Peninsula may "blow up."[59] Despite the inconclusive result of the 6 party talks, the Russians could at least take comfort in the achievement of their aim, they had rectified Yeltsin's error in being excluded from the negotiations over the Korean Peninsula. South Korean President Roh Moo-hyun visited Moscow in September 2004 seeking Russia's support for his efforts to improve relations with the North, thereby confirming Russia's role. Commentators averred that Russia was able to assume this role because of its "good relations" with the North, which demonstrated the extent to which policy had changed since Yeltsin.[60]

Japan

Towards the end of his period of office Yeltsin revealed an impulsive disposition to search for a territorial settlement with Japan. When Yeltsin hosted Japanese Prime Minister Keizo Obuchi in Moscow in November 1998 he announced that a peace treaty with Japan would be signed by 2000 which would entail a territorial settlement beforehand.[61] Yeltsin acted impetuously and completely surprised his own government, which raised Russian suspicions that a secret deal was being prepared with Japan. Yeltsin again came under criticism from within the Duma and his Foreign Ministry was again accused of betrayal. The Foreign Ministry was compelled to explain to the irritated Japanese that a peace treaty by the year 2000 was not intended and was out of the question, and that an interim treaty could be signed instead.[62] Putin has been consistent and measured in his behavior seeking a compromise based on the 1956 Soviet–Japanese agreement to break the logjam in relations with Japan. There were several incentives for a resolution of this issue as the territorial problem has hindered Japanese involvement in the development of Russia's Far East, making it more open to Chinese economic influence. To escape the prospect of Russia becoming an economic appendage of China, Putin was compelled to improve relations with Japan and to overcome the obstacle posed by the territorial dispute. Some Russians saw Japan as Russia's "potential" ally in the region which would in the future look to Russia for support against China and a united Korea.[63] Another reason why Putin probed for a compromise was the perception amongst Russians that the Japanese side would be amenable. Over 2000–2001 Liberal Democratic Party politician Muneo Suzuki revealed considerable influence over the Japanese Foreign Ministry arising from his promotion of the ministry's interests in the various Diet committees of which he was a member. In some cases, senior ministry officials ordered their subordinates to obey Suzuki despite the fact that he had no formal authority. Suzuki's constituency was in Nemuro, Hokkaido, and he promoted construction projects in the disputed islands, which were funded by the Japanese government, anticipating that his own constituents would benefit. He tended to be impatient with official policy over the issue and regarded it as an impediment to his plans. A Foreign Ministry document dated 13 June 1995 noted that Suzuki called upon Foreign Ministry officials to drop the claim to the Northern Islands and to promote relations with Russia instead.[64] Suzuki worked with the Russian "school" in the Foreign Ministry, which included European Bureau chief Kazuhiko Togo and non career officer Masaru Sato, to draft the Yoshiro Mori government's position over the issue. They pressed for separate negotiations over the two sets of islands so that two could be returned first, and the other two later.[65] Suzuki was clear about the first two islands but his vagueness or nonchalance about the second step undermined the Japanese insistence on the return of all the islands. Foreign Minister Yoriko Kawaguchi later admitted that Suzuki had "exceptional influence over the Ministry which common sense should not permit."[66] The members of the Russian "school" were removed from their positions for their efforts in distorting official policy and Suzuki was arrested for corruption in June 2002.

Within this context Putin advocated a compromise solution during his visit to Tokyo in October 2000. He affirmed the validity of the 19 October 1956 agreement, according to which the Soviet Union agreed to return two of the four islands to Japan. When Putin and Mori met in Irkutsk in March 2001 they agreed that the 1956 declaration was a "basic legal document" that serves as a starting point for negotiating a peace treaty.[67] Though their joint statement reaffirmed the Tokyo declaration of 1993, there was no specific mention of the two step return of all the islands and the signing of a peace treaty, which up till then had been included in Japanese statements over the issue. The Russian press accordingly reported that Mori was disposed towards a compromise based on the 1956 declaration.[68] The two sides had different interpretations of the 1956 declaration, however, as the Japanese insisted that it was a binding declaration which would lead to a return of all four islands, while the Russians claimed it was only a gesture of goodwill which was later nullified by the signing of Japan's alliance with the US in January 1960. Putin's demarche once again triggered a domestic backlash as it was feared a deal with Japan was in the offing. The Sakhalin administration reacted fiercely to Putin's meeting with Mori in 2001 and declared that the disputed territory was an "inalienable" part of Russia. The Administration's Committee for the Defence of the Kurils proposed that the Federal Duma "renounce" the 1956 declaration and reminded Moscow that changes to Russia's borders require the agreement of local authorities according to Article 66 (2) of the 1993 constitution.[69] The Sakhalin administration publicized the issue as a threat to national security and contacted other local authorities demanding that the Federal Duma conduct special hearings on the issue, which were held in March 2002.

The hearings were organized by the Duma Committees on Security, on International Affairs and on Geopolitics. The result was a repudiation of Japanese claims to the islands and the insistence that they were indisputably Russian territory. During the hearings Yevgennii Nazdratenko, head of the State Fisheries Commission and governor of Primor'ye over 1993–2001 declared that the islands were "absolutely" Russian territory. Chairman of the Duma committee on International Affairs and Rodina faction leader, Dmitrii Rogozin, stressed that income from fishing alone could reach $4 billion annually and that Russia should strengthen its sovereignty over the area.[70] Rogozin noted that the area in question was rich in oil gas reserves and declared that "oil is now more important for civilization" as a reason not to consider the return of any of the islands. Sakhalin governor Igor' Fakhutdinov emphasized the strategic value of the islands and opined that Russian could not allow foreign access to the Sea of Okhotsk, and that Kamchatka was "Russia's shield" against foreign intrusion.[71] The hearings noted the economic importance of the islands in terms of energy and fishing resources and concluded that Russia could make no concessions over the islands. The Foreign Ministry was advised to sign a treaty of good neighborliness with Japan and not a peace treaty.[72]

Putin's sterilization of the regional governors removed a major source of opposition to his compromise proposal, which was announced by Foreign Minister Sergei Lavrov on 15 November 2004. Lavrov declared over NTV television the willingness to transfer two islands to Japan under the 1956 agreement. He declared that the 1956 declaration was legally binding on Russia, and that a peace treaty with Japan could be signed after which there could be a territorial resolution.[73] Sakhalin governor Ivan Malakov's opposition was muted this time, he noted that Russia could develop business and commercial relations with Japan even without a peace treaty, and that there was no need for any transfer of islands to Japan.[74] Sakhalin oblast deputies protested that the declaration created a dangerous precedent for Russia's relations with others, they complained that they were not consulted and that it would result in further territorial concessions to Japan, threatening Russia's national security. They called upon Moscow to listen to the views of local authorities and to abide by the results of the Federal Duma hearings of 18 March 2002.[75] Chairman of the External Economic Relations Committee of Sakhalin oblast Vladislav Rukavets publicly voiced his opposition as did the Mayor of Yuzhno-Sakhalinsk and various protest groups.[76] Dmitri Rogozin declared that Lavrov's declaration had no "legal" basis and that a defeated country such as Japan cannot "dictate peace terms."[77] In comparison with 2002 the opposition was considerably restrained which was indicative of the president's control over politics.

What had Putin expected from the Japanese side? The Japanese had made it clear that they would reject any compromise offer and insisted on the two plus two formula, the quick return of two islands and the later return of the remaining two.[78] To avoid any misunderstanding Japanese Foreign Minister Yoriko Kawaguchi had stressed that all islands must be returned according to the 1993 Tokyo declaration, Prime Minister Junichiro Koizumi told Putin at the G-8 summit in June 2004 that a peace treaty would follow the return of all the islands, and that would be considered "full" normalization of relations.[79] Putin had no illusions about the Japanese view of the 1956 agreement and still he went ahead. Cabinet Secretary Hiroyuki Hosoda on 15 November dismissed the declaration as nothing new, Koizumi himself repeated what he had affirmed earlier. The conspiratorial Russian explanation has it that a solution based on the 1956 declaration alone made no sense and that the real objective was to surrender all the islands to Japan. Head of the Council of Foreign and Defence Policy, Sergei Karaganov, expressed this view of Putin's policy and hoped that the transfer of the islands would be at least be accompanied by massive Japanese investment into the Far East.[80]

Conspiratorial interpretations aside, there were at least three reasons for Putin's demarche. One was that Putin intended to deal with the issue on the basis of legality and was genuinely persuaded that the 1956 agreement represented the extent of Russia's legal obligation over the issue. Putin later explained that the 1956 declaration had been ratified by both the Supreme Soviet and the Japanese Diet, which showed that the Japanese legally only expected the return of two islands. According to Putin, Article 9 of the agreement made the conclusion of a peace treaty a preliminary condition before the return of any islands and not the reverse as demanded by the Japanese side.[81] The second reason was that the Russians continued to perceive Suzuki's influence in the Japanese Foreign Ministry despite the removal of two key members of the Russian "school." Russian commentators noted that there were "influential diplomats" in the Japanese Foreign Ministry who were disposed to accept a compromise based on the two plus two proposal. Implementation of the two plus two proposal would require the immediate transfer of two islands to Japan and Russia would then recognize that the remaining two, Etorofu and Kunashiri would be subject to negotiations.[82] The third reason was Japanese interest in Russian energy which was demonstrated when the Japanese government lobbied for its preferred route for the Siberian oil pipeline. The need for Russian oil could outweigh the need for an immediate resolution of the territorial issue in which case the Japanese may become more amenable to a compromise solution. Energy may have given Putin the confidence to press for a solution to the issue on Russian terms.

Japanese interest in the pipeline was expressed when Prime Minister Junichiro Koizumi visited Moscow in January 2003 and outlined a proposal for the construction of an oil pipeline from Eastern Siberia to Nakhodka on the Pacific coast.[83] The Japanese later offered $7 billion to finance costs, $5 billion in loans and $2 billion to develop new oil fields in East Siberia.[84] Not only did the Japanese route promise large-scale Japanese funding but it would allow the export of Russian oil to other markets in the Western Pacific, Korea, the Western US, as well as Japan. The pipeline deal presented an opportunity to engage Japan in the exploitation of Russia's energy resources in general and to stimulate the development of the Far East. For this reason it was strongly supported by Russian Far Eastern governors; Kharbarovsk Governor Viktor Ishaev demanded that the pipeline go to Sovietskaya Gavan or close by; Primor'ye Governor Sergei

Dar'kin wanted the terminal at Perevoznaya Bay, near Vladivostok.[85] Russian commentators claimed that Japan's need for Russian oil would result in a postponement of the territorial issue.[86] Russia indeed was becoming more deeply embedded in Japanese energy plans which may lend credence to this view; Japanese companies have a 30 percent stake in the Sakhalin one project and 40 percent in Sakhalin two, the idea of an "energy bridge" between Sakhalin and Hokkaido has also been proposed for the transport of Russian gas and electricity.[87] Japanese investment in Russia to date was estimated at $3.5 billion, $2.5 billion of which was invested in the Sakhalin energy projects.[88] Nonetheless, the Japanese have argued that funding for the planned pipeline and for other energy projects would give them leverage over Russia, and that there was no alternative to Japan as a source of funds for these objectives. According to the Japanese side these two issues, energy and territory, would be separated in the way asserted by Koizumi when he met Putin in January 2003. Then he discussed a "plan of action" with Putin which separated the issues so that progress over energy and the territorial issue would take place simultaneously.[89] Since then the Japanese have insisted that Putin initiate progress towards a return of all the islands, which indicates that the territorial issue will not drop out of sight.[90]

Conclusion

The relationship between Russian domestic politics and Asia Pacific policy has been examined in this chapter in terms of the experience of two Russian presidents. Yeltsin and his group of Westernizers sought a clear break with the Soviet past and attempted to situate Russia firmly with the West to provide a foundation for its domestic transformation into a liberal democracy. Russia's experience of liberal democracy was limited and the result was not the anticipated clear break, but rather a complex effort to absorb new norms from the external world while clinging onto the past. In Russia's case the Soviet collapse resulted in an unprecedented exposure to liberal values as well as confusion and disorientation amongst the general public, which stimulated a yearning for the traditional values of order and security. The Yeltsin revolution brought with it chaos and disorder which ironically strengthened the typically Russian craving for strong rule, providing a fertile ground for Putin's interventionist presidency. Putin's efforts to shape the institutions of Russia's political system into a supporting foundation for a strong state have been facilitated by the rudimentary condition of Russia's political institutions, the absence of democratic values and the traditional deference paid to strong rulers. Putin has curtailed the influence of the political parties and the regional governors into foreign policy decision-making which has been concentrated into fewer hands. Greater flexibility for presidential diplomatic maneuver in relation to China and Japan has been the most evident result.

The consequences for foreign policy have been highlighted accordingly. Yeltsin's government declared an alliance with the West and attempted to adopt Western positions over a range of issues including North Korea, which it ignored, but not over China which it could not ignore. While reaffirming the importance of the West, Putin crafted a foreign policy based on Russia's geopolitical location and immediate interests in which case the strategic significance with China was reaffirmed and strengthened, North Korea was treated as an ally and Russia insisted on an intermediary role in the Korean Peninsula. With the recentralization of power in the presidency Putin could override the oligarchs and could decide the direction of the Siberian oil pipeline in favor of Japan, with a branch line to China. He could emasculate the regional governors to negotiate a final territorial settlement with China, and to offer a compromise to Japan with the intention of improving relations with both. As a result of these moves Putin may position Russia more favorably between China and Japan to obtain their balanced involvement in the development of the Russian Far East. The concern for balance to ensure that Russia would not become excessively dependent on any one country has been a marked feature of Putin's policies.

Notes

1   Andrei Kozyrev, *Preobrazhenie,* Moscow, 1995, pp. 48, 49, 210.
2   On Russian foreign policy during the early Yeltsin era see Leszek Buszynski, *Russian Foreign Policy after the Cold War,* Praeger: Westport, Connecticut, 1996.
3   For the Yeltsin period in Russian–Japan relations see Deputy Foreign Minister, Georgi Kunadze, "A Russian View of Russo–Japanese Relations, 1991–1993," also Konstantin Sarkisov, "Russo–Japanese Relations after Yeltsin's Re-election in 1996," in Gilbert Rozman (ed.) *Japan and Russia: The tortuous Path to Normalization,* New York: St. Martin's Press, 2000; Tsuyoshi Hasegawa, "Russo-Japanese Relations and the security of North-East Asia in the 21st Century," in Gennady Chufrin (ed.), *Russia and Asia: The Emerging Security Agenda.* Oxford and New York: Oxford University Press, 1999.
4   See Alexander N. Fedorovsky, "Russian policy and interests on the Korean Peninsula," in Gennady Chufrin (ed.) *Russia and Asia: The Emerging Security Agenda.*
5   In April 1991 China agreed to purchase 26 Su-27s which were delivered over 1991–3. In 1995 Russia allowed China to produce the SU-27 under license in a $2 billion deal. Other equipment purchased by China included SA-10 air defence missile batteries, 400 T-72, 50 T-80 tanks. In November 1994 China concluded a deal for the purchase of 4 Kilo class submarines with an option for the purchase of an additional six. During this period China also demonstrated an interest in a Soviet-built aircraft carrier but negotiations were inconclusive.
6   On Russia–China relations during the Yeltsin period, see Yuri V. Tsyganov, "Russia and China: What is in the pipeline," in Gennady Chufrin (ed.) *Russia and Asia: The Emerging Security Agenda.*
7   On Putin's move to Moscow and his appointments by Yeltsin, see Richard Sakwa, *Putin: Russia's Choice,* Routledge: London, 2004, pp. 12–25; Samuel Charap, "The Petersburg Experience: Putin's Political Career and Russian Foreign Policy," *Problems of Post-Communism,* vol. 51, No. 1, January/February 2004.
8   In his electoral message of February 2000, Putin declared that the greatest problem is "loss of government will" and that "there is the need for strong government, the people are not protected in case of a weak government, the stronger the government, the freer the person, what is required is socially accepted law, and only a strong and effective government can live by the law, and only it can guarantee freedom, social, per-

sonal and business. There has to be order." See "Otkrytoe pis'mo Vladimira Putina k rossiiskim izbiratulyam," *Izvestiya*, 25 February 2000.

9 Natal'ya Lapina, "Rezhim kontroliruemogo plyuralizma," *Nezavisimaya Gazeta*, 16 March 2004.

10 See Vladimir Rekhtin, "V Dume dolzhno byt' prezidentskoe bol'shinstvo", *Nezavisimaya Gazeta*, 18 March 2002.

11 Ivan Rodin, "'V Rossii poyavilas' 'nastoyashchaya partiya'," *Nezavisimaya Gazeta*, 10 November 2001.

12 "Putin nazval tri napravleniya razvitiya rossii," *Izvestiya*, 25 April 2005.

13 Ibid.

14 A survey of Russian public opinion conducted in 2004 noted that order was the most important political value. The survey was conducted by the All-Russian Centre for the Study of Social Opinion, some 60 percent of 1600 people asked over April and May 2004 placed order above justice, democracy or human rights. *Politiki I partiii', No. 93, Vserossiiskii Tsentr Izycheniya Obshchestvennogo Mneniya*, Moscow, 23 June 2004. Online. Available HTTP: <http://www.wciom.ru/?pt=42&article=807> (accessed 30 August 2005).

15 Anna Skornyakova, "Yukos vykhodit za granitsu," *Nezavisimaya Gazeta*, 29 September 2003.

16 Natal'ya Melikova, "Putin prizval biznes zabotit'sya o narode," *Nezavisimaya Gazeta*, 24 December 2003.

17 On the oligarchs and their role, see David E. Hoffman, *The Oligarchs; Wealth and Power in the New Russia*, New York: Public Affairs, 2002.

18 Anatolii Kostyukov, "Putin upustil svoi shans," *Nezavisimaya Gazeta*, 12 March 2004.

19 "Vystuplenie prezidenta Rossii Vladimira Putina na rashirennom zasedanii pravitel'stva s uchasteim glav sub'ektov RF 13 Sentyabra 2004 goda," *Nezavisimaya Gazeta*, 14 September 2004.

20 Denis Larikov, "Duma podderzhala zakon o gubernatorakh," *Utro.ru*, 3 December 2004. Online. Available HTTP: <http://www.utro.ru/articles/print/2004/12/03/382458.shtml> (accessed 4 December 2004).

21 "Stroitsya unitarnoe gosudarstvo s voennoi byurokratiei," *Nezavisimaya Gazeta*, 14 September 2004.

22 Alexander Lukin, "Osobyi put' Kitaya," *Nezavisimaya Gazeta*, 17 July 2001.

23 Kontseptsya vneshnei politiki rossiiskoi federatsii," *Nezavisimaya Gazeta*, 11 July 2000.

24 Ibid.

25 "Vladimir Putin: Rossiya: Novye vostochnye perspektivy," *Nezavisimaya Gazeta*, 14 November 2000.

26 "Otnoshenie Rossii so stranami Aziatsko-Tikhookeanskogo regiona," *Press Sluzhba Gosduma RF*, 9 December 2000.

27 *Vystuplenie Prezidenta Rossii V. V. Putina na plenarnom zasedanii soveshchaniya posolov I postoyannykh predstavitelei Rossii*, Moscow: Ministry of Foreign Affairs, 12 June 2004.

28 Svetlana Babaeva, "Kogda soseda lushche rodstvennika," *Izvestiya*, 19 July 2000.

29 Dmitrii Gornostaev, "Rossiya I Kitai ob'edinnilis' po voprosu PRO," *Nezavisimaya Gazeta*, 19 July 2000.

30 Sergei Luzyanin, "Kitai I Rossiya podpishut novyi dogovor," *Nezavisimaya Gazeta*, 14 July 2001.

31 Svetlana Babaeva, Yekaterina Grigor'eva, "Drugaya geometriya," *Izvestiya*, 17 July 2001.

32 Mikhail Petrov, "Sotrudnichestvo – prioritetnyi kyrs RF I KNR," *Itar Tass*, 27 May 2003.

33 Yevgennii Verlin, "Nefteprovod "Rossiya-Kitai" zavis v vozdukhe," *Nezavisimaya Gazeta*, 26 May 2003.

34 Marina Borisova, Pyotr Orekhin, "Kitai Prirastaet rossiiskoi neft'yu," *Nezavisimaya Gazeta*, 29 May 2003.
35 On the Khodorkovsky affair see, Andrew Jack, *Inside Putin's Russia,* Oxford: Oxford University Press, 2004, pp. 306–313.
36 Sergei Luzyanin, "Pekin pytaetsya 'vospityvat' Moskvu," *Nezavisimaya Gazeta,* 24 November 2003.
37 Yevgeniya Obukhova, Anna Skornyakova, "Mikhail Kas'yanov poobeshchal nefteprovod I Yaponii I Kitayu," *Nezavisimaya Gazeta*, 16 December 2003.
38 Anna Skornyakova, Pyotr Orekhin, Artur Blinov, "Kitai prizivaet nadavit na YUKOS," *Nezavisimaya Gazeta,* 22 September 2004.
39 Yevgennii Bogomol'nyi, "Osvoenie ugelobodorodykh zapasov Vostochnoi Sibiri neobkhodimo I neizbezhno," *Nezavisimaya Gazeta,* 22 March 2005.
40 "Rossiya I Kitai podelili progranichnye ostrova porovinu-istochnik v MID RF," *Interfax,* 21 October 2004.
41 See *Izvestiya*, 19 November 2004.
42 "Kharabovsk vystupaet protiv predachi rossiiskikh zemel' Kitaiyu ...," *Regnum*, 5 November 2004. Online. Available HTTP: <http://www.regnum.ru/news/355340.html> (accessed 3 December 2004).
43 Andrei Skobot, "Viktor Ishaev: Prezidentu khotelos' soblyusti demokratiyu I edinonachalie no poluchalos' ne vse," *Nezavisimaya Gazeta*, 16 September 2004.
44 Dmitrii Ivolga, "Rossiyane gotovy voevat' za Kurili," *Utro.ru,* 25 November 2004. Online. Available HTTP: <http://www.utro.ru/articles/print/2004/11/25/378523.shtml> (accessed 4 December 2004).
45 "Gosduma Khochet vyyasnit za chto Putin podaril Kitayu poltora ostrova," *NEWSru.com,* 20 October 2004. Online. Available HTTP: <http://newsru.com/arch/russia/20oct2004> (accessed 4 December 2005).
46 See Seung Ham Yang, Woosang Kim and Yongho Kim, "Russo–North Korean Relations in the 2000s", *Asian Survey,* vol. 44, No. 6, November/December 2004.
47 Yuri Golotyuk, "Koreiskim raketchikam poverili na slovo," *Izvestiya,* 17 February 2000.
48 Gennadii Charodeev, Maxim Yusin, "Putin letil v Pkhen'yan," *Izvestiya,* 10 June 2000.
49 Dmitrii Gornostaev, "Kogda Kim Chen Ir shutil?" *Nezavisimaya Gazeta,* 15 August 2000.
50 The first principle was no external interference, the second was all issues should be resolved peacefully according the joint Korean declaration of 15 June 2000, the third was peaceful reunification, the fourth was the non-nuclear status of the Korean Peninsula, the fifth was Russian economic support in bring about reunification. "Putin vydvinil printsipov mezhkoreiskogo uregulirovaniya," *Nezavisimaya Gazeta,* 28 February 2001.
51 "My dorozhim Koreisko-rossiiskoi dryzhboi," *Rossiiskaya Gazeta,* 27 July 2001.
52 Gayz Alimov, "Prizrak Kommunizma," *Izvestiya,* 4 August 2001.
53 Andrei Fedorov, "KNDR-na starte protsessa peremen," *Nezavisimaya Gazeta,* 22 August 2002.
54 Ivan Yesin, "KNDR gotova unichtozhit' ves' mir," *Utro.ru,* 24 December 2002. Online. Available HTTP: <http:www.utro.ru/articles/20021224183334118508.shtml> (accessed 30 August 2005).
55 Andrei Napkin, "Rossiya nomirut SshA I KNDR," *Utro.ru,* 12 January 2003. Online. Available HTTP: <http://www.utro.ru/articles/20030112170036121359.shtml> (accessed 30 August 2005).
56 Georgii Bulygev, Alexander Vorontsov, "Koreiskaya problema na pereput'e," *Nezavisimaya Gazeta,* 18 June 2003.
57 Vitalii Dymarskii, "Sergei Lavrov; My v posredniki ne rvalis," *Rossiiskaya Gazeta,* 6 June 2004.

58 "Koreiskii duplet Sergei Lavrova," *Olo.ru*, 5 July 2004. Online. Available HTTP: <http://7-04.olo.ru/news/politic/39296.html> (accessed 4 December 2004).
59 Dmitrii Suslov, "Koreya mozhet vzorvat'sya," *Nezavisimaya Gazeta*, 5 March 2004.
60 Maxim Novikov, Oleg Kir'yanov, "Seul nadeesya na Moskvu," *Rossiiskaya Gazeta*, 21 September 2004.
61 "Moscow Declaration targets Treaty in 2000," *Japan Times,* 15 November 2000.
62 *Japan Times,* 4 August 2000.
63 Vitalii Tretiakov, "Putin's Pragmatic Foreign Policy," *International Affairs*, vol. 48, issue 3, 2002.
64 "Suzuki Says Drop Claim to Hoppo Ryodo," *Japan Times*, 13 March 2002.
65 *Asahi*, 3 April 2002.
66 *Japan Times,* 5 March 2002.
67 "Mori, Putin reaffirm 1956 pact," *Japan Times,* 27 March 2001; Dmitrii Kosyrev, "Kholodnoe voskresen'e v Irkutske," *Nezavisimaya Gazeta*, 27 March 2001.
68 Vasilii Golovin, "Sensatsiya ot Mori," *Nezavisimaya Gazeta*, 15 May 2001.
69 "Samyi zhguchii vopros dlya Rossii," *Region*, [Yuzhno- Sakhalinsk] no 24 [186] 15 June 2001. Online. Available HTTP: <http://vff-s.narod.ru/kur/k_sk06a.html> (accessed 4 December 2004).
70 "Rossiya ne otdast Kurily: Gosduma rekomduet prekatit' peregovory," *Lenta.ru*, 18 March 2002. Online. Available HTTP: <http://lenta.ru/Russia/2002/03/18/kuriles1/> (accessed 3 December 2004).
71 Valerii Dabydov, "Dmitrii Rogozin soglasen prodat' Yuzhnye Kurily," *Pravda*, 20 May 2004.
72 "Parliamentskie slushaniya," *Gosudarsvennoi Dumy Federal'nogo Sobraniya Rossiiskoi Federatsii*, 19 March 2002. Online. Available HTTP: <http://www.akdi.ru/gd/pl_sl/K07/190302.html> (accessed 3 January 2003).
73 "Nachalo kontsa; Rossiya otdaet samurayam Kuril'skie ostrova," *Pravda*, 15 November 2004.
74 *Sakhalin.info*, 2 December 2004. Online. Available HTTP: <http://www.sakhalin.info/news/26640> (accessed 3 December 2004).
75 "Sakhalinskaya Duma protiv peredachi ostrova Yaponii," *Sakhalin.info*, 16 November 2004. Online. Available HTTP: <http://www.sakhalin.info/news/26376> (accessed 3 December 2004).
76 *Sakhalin.info*, 17 November 2004. Online. Available HTTP: <http://www.sakhalin.info/news/26413> (accessed 3 December 2004).
77 Yuliya Petrovskaya, "'krem' poka ne otdaet yapontsam ostrova'," *Nezavisimaya Gazeta*, 16 November 2004.
78 "MID Yaponii obvinil Igorya Ivanova v dvulichii," *Lenta.ru*, 5 February 2002 Online. Available HTTP: <http://lenta.ru/Russia/2002/02/05/putin_mori> (accessed 6 February 2002).
79 "Yaponiya soglasna tol'ko na chetyre ostrova," *Izvestiya*, 26 June 2004,
80 Sergei Belukhin, "Rossiyu gotovyat k potere," *Utro.ru*, 15 November 2004. Online. Available HTTP: <http://www.utro.ru.articles/print/2004/11/15/373895.shtml> (accessed 3 December 2004); "Zayavlenie Lavrova po Kurilam…," *NEWSru.com*, 14 November 2004.
81 Vitalii Ivashov, "Yaponiya zabyla pro Kurili…," *Utro.ru*, 14 January 2005. Online. Available HTTP: <http://www.utro.ru/articles/print/2005/01/14/396377.shtml> (accessed 15 January 2005).
82 Vasilii Golovnin, "Yapontsy reshili pomolchat," *Izvestiya*, 15 November 2004.
83 Yevgenii Verlin, "Yaponiya poluchit ostrova, no tol'ko esli stanet dprygom Rossii," *Nezavisimaya Gazeta*, 13 January 2003.
84 *International Herald Tribune*, 14 October 2003.
85 Vasilii Avchenko, "A u nas truboprovod," *Vladivostok Novosti*, 27 July 2004.
86 Yevgenni Verlin, "Yaponiya poluchit ostrova."

87 Anton Zherbolin, "Rossiyu I Yaponiyu soedinit nefteprovod," *Utro.ru*, 29 June 2003. Online. Available HTTP: <http://www.utro.ru/articles/2003/06/29/209852.shtml> (accessed 3 December 2004).
88 From *Utro.ru*, 1 February 2005.
89 Andrei Sorokin, "Rossiya I Yaponiya: Ostrova Ch'i?" *Utro.ru*, 11 January 2003. Online. Available HTTP: <http://www.utro.ru/articles/20030111123017121201.shtml> (accessed 3 December 2004).
90 "Japan pushes for Progress with Russia on Territorial Dispute," *Nikkei*, 8 February 2005.

8 Mediating geopolitics, markets and regionalism: domestic politics in Japan's post-Cold War relations with China

Peng Er Lam

Transforming East Asia's political economy and impacting on Sino–Japanese relations are at least three factors: the Cold War's end, the demise of the flying geese pattern of development and the rise of regional Free Trade Agreements (FTAs). During the halcyon days of the Cold War, Washington, Beijing and Tokyo were de facto allies against Moscow.[1] The two Asian neighbors, driven by geopolitical imperatives against the Soviet Union, expediently downplayed their differences over Japan's past invasion of the Chinese mainland and an appropriate apology from Tokyo. However, with the end of the Cold War and the absence of a common threat, Japan and China are no longer strategic partners and lack the geopolitical incentive to sweep their burden of history under the carpet. Indeed, the past has become a thorn in the flesh of Sino–Japanese relations even in the twenty-first century.

The rapid economic rise of China since the 1990s has, according to Japan's Ministry of Economics, Trade and Industry 2001 White Paper, rendered the flying geese model of development obsolete.[2] Hitherto, post-war Japan was the leading goose, which according to the economic principle of comparative advantage, moved up the technological ladder as its labor wages became more expensive, and shed less technologically advanced industries to the next echelon of geese: the Newly Industrializing Economies (NIEs) of Hong Kong, Singapore, South Korea and Taiwan. These NIEs, in turn, moved up the ladder of production and sophistication and shed their more labor-intensive industries to the next wave: Indonesia, Malaysia, the Philippines and Thailand. Simply put, Japan was at the very heart of East Asia's network of industrial production.[3] However, Japan's "bubble" economy burst in 1991. Its subsequent decade-long economic stagnation, coupled with the phenomenal economic rise of China, not only ended the flying geese pattern of economic development but also led to anxiety within Japan that China poses a threat, at least in the economic dimension.

The phenomenon of a power in relative decline facing a rising power which challenges the status quo is a common theme in international relations.[4] The prickly relations between Tokyo and Beijing are, in part, due to this phenomenon of "rising China, stagnating Japan." If Japan had continued to enjoy high economic growth since the early 1990s coupled with a China mired in low growth and dependent on Japanese investments and Official Development Assistance, then Tokyo is likely to be more confident and Beijing less so in their bilateral relations. There would have been less angst about the Chinese mainland among the Japanese elite and public if China had remained economically weak and Japan strong.

Ironically, the economic rise of China has also provided an engine of growth for Japanese exports which helped to pull Japan out of its economic stagnation by 2003. By the end of 2004, the total value of Japan's trade with China had overtaken its trade with the US. While deeper economic interdependence between China and Japan does not necessarily mitigate Sino–Japanese political tension, both countries have greater economic incentives to keep their relations on an even keel.

The third major transformation in post-Cold War East Asia is the rise of FTAs and the tentative quest in the region for a nascent East Asian Community (EAC). Such a regional grouping would have been impossible during the Cold War when East Asian countries were polarized around the contending US and Soviet superpowers. China and Japan today are competing to forge closer bilateral and regional ties with Southeast Asian countries. Nevertheless, despite uneasy Sino–Japanese political relations, Beijing and Tokyo appear to have accepted the fact that they are both key players in East Asian regionalism. Symbolizing regional aspirations for an EAC is the December 2005 East Asian Summit in Kuala Lumpur. While neither Beijing nor Tokyo is willing to yield leadership to the other in an emerging EAC, both sides can conceivably benefit from a multilateral framework which can help to diffuse and mitigate bilateral tension.

Central argument

Undoubtedly, structural changes in the international system from Cold War bipolarity to post-Cold War unipolarity, the uneven development of power in East Asia (rising China, stagnating Japan), increasing economic interdependence, and emerging regionalism have profoundly impacted on Sino–Japanese relations. But the external nexus of geopolitics, markets and regionalism must be filtered and mediated by the domestic politics of both countries. International relations are not made by a single rational actor called the state. Moreover, the "black box" of policy making must be unpacked by looking at the domestic political system. Indeed, domestic actors, institutions and processes would contest, negotiate and shape Tokyo's relations with Beijing. These domestic players include: the Japanese Prime Minister, the ruling Liberal Democratic Party (LDP) and its factions, opposition parties, the national bureaucracy, local governments, interest groups including Big Business, the mass media and public opinion.[5]

The unipolar structure of the international system (in which the US is the sole superpower in the post-Cold War era) does not predetermine Sino–Japanese relations per se. While Tokyo's alliance with Washington is the cornerstone of its foreign policy, it does not mean that Tokyo's relations towards Beijing are made in Washington.[6] Moreover, rising economic interdependence and forging regional FTAs are no guarantee that Sino–Japanese relations will remain cordial and sound. Though both countries have different regime-types, political leaders cannot ignore or easily manipulate mass sentiments towards their neighbors.

Armed by information technology including the Internet, emails and mobile phones, public opinion and nationalistic sentiments could well be a destabilizing factor in Sino–Japanese relations. Carrying their burden of history, China and Japan have yet to play the role of France and Germany which acted as the lynchpin of post-war West European regionalism. Even though Beijing and Tokyo are engaged in competitive and separate FTAs to woo the Association of Southeast Asian Nations (ASEAN) states, it is conceivable that Southeast Asia might become a bridge between the two Northeast Asian giants. However, a web of FTAs and multilateral activities in East Asia does not necessarily guarantee better Sino–Japanese relations. In the last resort, messy domestic politics will filter, digest and rank the external "inputs;" domestic political competition and compromises made will mean that policy outcomes will not necessarily be consistent or ideal for bilateral ties and East Asian regionalism. There is more than a grain of truth to the adage: "All politics is local."

This chapter seeks to examine the domestic sources of Japan's relations with China and how they intersect and internalize the external factors impinging on this bilateral relationship against the backdrop of a nascent East Asian regionalism. First is an analysis of China's rise which has sparked fear of a China "threat" among politicians, the mass media and public opinion. Next is a discussion of Sino–Japanese economic interdependence and the views of Japan's business community on bilateral ties. Following that is a study of Sino–Japanese relations against the backdrop of FTAs and a nascent East Asian regionalism, and the roles of policy networks and think-tanks in regional community building, sub-regional governments, NGOs, and the agricultural lobby as a force of resistance to FTAs. The chapter will then examine the pivotal role of Prime Minister Koizumi Junichiro in bilateral relations. Finally is an assessment of the future of Sino–Japanese relations anchored within a multilateral East Asian framework and the role of domestic actors who can facilitate or undermine the regional project of an EAC.

China's rise: domestic perceptions of "threat"

The fear that Japan is trading places with China as the top country in East Asia fuels anxiety among many Japanese towards Beijing.[7] The Chinese mainland is enjoying inexorable economic growth and emerging as the factory of the world with its seemingly endless supply of cheap and skilled labor. Nevertheless, Japan remains the second largest economy in the world with a GDP more than three times larger than China today while having less than 10 percent of the Chinese mainland population.[8] Although China's phenomenal economic growth is impressive, it is still a poor country on a per capita basis. But if the Chinese economy continues to grow unabatedly for the next two decades, the country is likely to reach middle-income status and able to translate its economic resources into political influence and military power.

Presumably, many Japanese are nervous that Beijing will supersede Tokyo both economically and politically within two to three decades. Reinforcing the US–Japan Alliance with the 1997 New Defense Guidelines and again the 2005 US–Japan Consultative Talks (2 + 2 Talks in which Taiwan is mentioned explicitly for the first time as falling within the ambit of the alliance) does not assuage Japanese anxiety that China might emerge as a great, assertive and arrogant power. Moreover, Tokyo's decision to proceed with joint research in ballistic missile defense with Washington suggests that this missile system can conceivably be deployed against Beijing even though the ostensible reason is the North Korean nuclear threat.

The souring of Japanese elite and mass opinion towards Beijing cannot be attributed solely to the phenomenon of " a rising China and a stagnating Japan." The 1989 Tiananmen crackdown, Beijing's missile tests in Taiwan Strait to intimidate Taipei in 1995 and 1996, Chinese nuclear testing in 1995 and 1996, President Jiang Zemin's disastrous 1998 Japan visit (where he boorishly harped on the historical issue at almost every stop), the appalling behavior of Chinese hooligans against the Japanese national team in the 2004 Asia soccer cup competition held in China, anti-Japanese demonstrations in various Chinese cities in April 2005 and Vice Premier Wu Yi's abrupt cancellation of her meeting with Prime Minister Koizumi in May the same year have cumulatively turned public opinion against Beijing. Accordingly to a 2004 survey conducted by the Prime Minister's Office, only 36.7 percent of the Japanese were friendly towards China —a historical low in Japanese public opinion (Figure 8.1). This mutual dislike between the public of both Asian nations begs the question: Can there be genuine East Asian cooperation when Sino–Japanese relations, especially mass sentiments are at rock-bottom—the worst in over three decades?

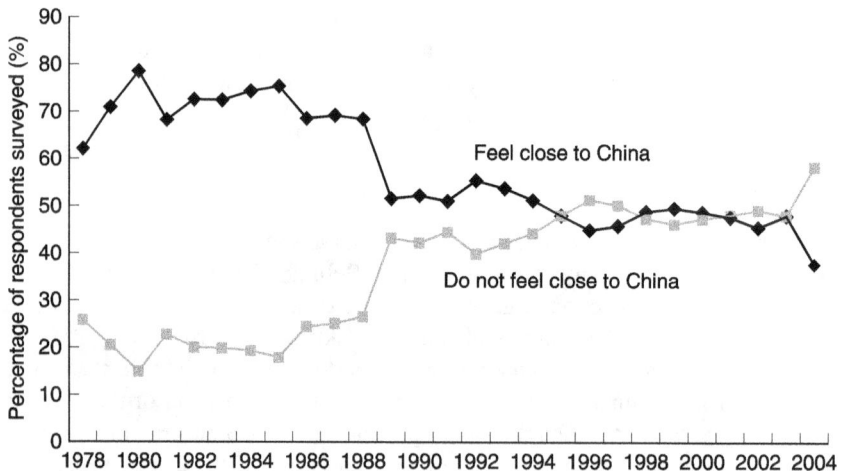

Source: Cabinet Office, Government of Japan.

Figure 8.1 Indicator of sentiments in Japan towards China, 1978–2004.

Despite this trend of deteriorating sentiments towards Beijing, there is a wide spectrum of views held by different opinion shapers in Japanese domestic politics. While there is disquiet about Chinese attitudes and behavior towards Japan, there is no consensus on whether China constitutes a real threat or an opportunity. Even among those who consider the China threat question seriously, they emphasize different types of threats: military, political, economic and environmental.[9] Ironically, some worry that China would become too strong; others fear that a weakened and ungovernable China would also be problematic. Paradoxically, a weak China unable to address serious domestic social, economic and political problems may also destabilize the region with mass unrest, anarchy and refugee flows. Although there is a diversity of views within Japan towards the Chinese mainland, the correlation of forces within the domestic arena has become more critical of China.

Political leaders, bureaucrats and opinion shapers: more assertive towards China

At one end of the political spectrum are the rightwing politicians and media who would harp on the so-called China threat regardless of what Beijing does or does not do. The most prominent right wing critic of Beijing is Ishihara Shintaro, Governor of Tokyo and one of the most popular politicians in the country. The rightwing media includes the *Sankei Shimbun,* a daily newspaper, and *Shokun* and *Sapio* monthly magazines. These rightwing media often lamblast China for its threat to use force to prevent *de jure* Taiwan independence, making territorial claims in the disputed East China Sea, and harping on the history issue including textbooks and Yasukuni Shrine visits by the Japanese Prime Minister. The *Sankei Shimbun* is also skeptical about an EAC and places emphasis on the US–Japan Alliance to deal with Beijing.

The centrist *Yomiuri Shimbun* is rather critical of Beijing even though it does not label it a menace in an outright way. Prestigious monthly magazines such as *Chuo Koron* and *Bungei Shunju* also tend to adopt this centrist perspective towards the mainland. Thus far, the mainstream view, as represented by Prime Minister Koizumi, is that China is an opportunity and not a threat to Japan. In December 2004, Tokyo's National Security Council and the Cabinet approved the *National Defense Program Guideline (NDPG) for Financial Year 2005 and After*. Reviewing the security environment surrounding Japan, the NDPG noted: "China, which has a strong influence on the security in this region, has been modernizing its nuclear and missile capabilities as well as naval air forces, and expanding its area of operation at sea. We will have to remain attentive to its future course." [10] Thus, the centrist view is that Tokyo will carefully watch what Beijing does while not considering it a threat yet. Moreover, if the Japanese government is hostile to the mainland or truly believes that it is a threat, then Tokyo's defense budget would have increased accordingly. However, Tokyo's 2005 defense budget has been reduced compared to the year before.[11]

On the left is the *Asahi Shimbun* which advocates the joint development of energy resources in the East China Sea and anchoring Sino–Japanese relations within an EAC. *Sekai*, the monthly magazine, also adopts the idealistic, liberal and pacifistic line towards China. Interestingly, it was the *Asahi Shimbun* which blew the whistle that the souls of 14 Class A war criminals were secretly interred in Yasukuni Shrine, much to the chagrin of the right wingers. Many right wingers believe that if the *Asahi Shimbun* has not earlier played up the reposition of Class A war criminals' souls in Yasukuni and the revision of history textbook issue, Beijing would not have been alerted and Sino–Japanese relations would not have been so acrimonious. However, the influence of the political left, including the *Asahi Shimbun*, is on the wane.

A key reason for the decline of leftist influence is the demise of the Social Democratic Party of Japan (SDPJ), the main and perennial opposition party between 1955 and 1993. Traditionally, the SDPJ has been friendly towards Beijing and had an informal line of communication with it even before official relations were established between the two countries in 1972. However, the SDPJ lost its reason for existence and went into rapid decline after its leader Murayama Tomiichi expediently abandoned its hallmark of unarmed neutrality and recognized the status of the Self Defense Forces as constitutional in 1994 to become the Prime Minister and junior partner within a coalition government with its erstwhile enemy, the conservative LDP.

Another reason for a less friendly Japan towards China is the demise of the ex-Tanaka faction (ex-Hashimoto) which dominated the ruling LDP since the early 1970s. Until the tenure of Prime Minister Koizumi who relies on mass populism for his political support, almost all LDP Prime Ministers had to secure the consent of the Tanaka faction and its offspring to stay in office. Prime Minister Tanaka Kakuei established diplomatic relations with Beijing in 1972 and the Tanaka faction has always taken pride for its pivotal role in normalizing ties with its neighbor. Since the firing of Tanaka Makiko, the daughter of Kakuei, as the foreign minister by Koizumi in 2002, no cabinet members in the Koizumi Administration are reputed to be sympathetic to China.

Koizumi Cabinet members with a hawkish reputation include Foreign Minister Machimura Nobutaka and Minister of Economics, Trade and Industry Nakagawa Shoichi. In the midst of anti-Japanese protests in the Chinese mainland in April 2005, Nakagawa derogatorily remarked that China is a "scary" country and also announced the awarding of exploratory rights to Japanese companies for natural gas fields on the Japanese side of the median line Tokyo has established in an Exclusive Economic Zone in the disputed East China Sea. That the Koizumi Administration reversed a nearly four-decade old policy of not awarding exploratory rights in the East China Sea can be interpreted as a new assertiveness towards Beijing. Minister Nakagawa and Internal Affairs and Communications Minister Aso Taro are supporters of the right-wing Association to "Write New History Textbooks" (*Tsukurukai*), a purveyor of whitewashed textbooks about Japanese colonization of Korea and invasion of China.[12]

Generational change has led to a new breed of politicians born after World War II who are more assertive towards Beijing. Generally, they do not feel personally responsible for Japanese atrocities which took place in Asia more than half a century ago and the need for endless apologies to Beijing. Powerful and senior LDP politicians who had remembrances of the War, and were apologetic and friendly towards Beijing, such as former Secretary General Nonaka Hiromu (ex-Tanaka faction), have also retired from the political arena. Many younger politicians from both the ruling LDP and opposition Democratic Party of Japan (DPJ) who are assertive towards Beijing and Pyongyang also subscribe to the thesis that Japan should become a "normal state" (one which actively participates in collective security within the framework of the United Nations and the US–Japan Alliance) and also jettison Article Nine, the famous no-war clause of the Japanese constitution.

Neo-nationalism on the part of some younger LDP Diet members can be interpreted as more than just a reflection of their conservative values: it is also a political strategy for voter mobilization. For example, Abe Shinzo, former LDP secretary general who became very popular after taking a hard line stance towards North Korea over the issue of Japanese nationals being abducted by Pyongyang, is also critical of China and a staunch supporter of Prime Minister Koizumi's visit to Yasukuni Shrine. In an era when the bubble economy has burst and the state suffering from huge fiscal deficits, the LDP traditional mode of governance and resource distribution to construction companies and rural communities based on massive public works spending and job creation to stimulate the local economies and obtain votes are no longer sustainable. Hoisting the flag of nationalism is relatively cost-free (in terms of money) to a politician unlike pork-barrel politics. Besides appealing to non-party affiliated voters who may dislike China, neo-nationalist LDP politicians can also seek support from the War Bereaved Family Association (*Izokukai*) with a one-million membership and the Association of Shinto Shrines (*Jinja Honcho*), which controls and administers more than 80,000 shrines.[13]

Unlike some of the younger DPJ politicians who are also neo-nationalists and critical of Beijing, then DPJ President Okada Katsuya has criticized the Koizumi Administration for the deterioration in Sino–Japanese relations and also advocated an emphasis on Asia.[14] The DPJ has reconstituted itself as a serious opposition party which is hungry for power, unlike the SDPJ which was satisfied to remain merely as the perennial opposition party during the Cold War. In the 2003 Lower House Elections and the 2004 Upper House Elections, the DPJ made impressive gains including inroads into rural Japan, the bastion of the LDP. In contrast, the LDP is a deeply fragmented party torn between those who support or oppose the structural reforms advocated by Koizumi. It is not inconceivable that a divided LDP suffering from the hollowing out of its traditional social bases of electoral support (farmers, construction companies and postal masters), a lack of charismatic leaders after Koizumi and Abe Shinzo, and abandonment by its coalition partner, the New Komeito, would lead to the collapse of LDP one-party dominance. The flip side of the coin is that the DPJ must appear credible to voters before it can displace the LDP.

However, a hypothetical DPJ–Komeito coalition government is no guarantee that Sino–Japanese relations would necessarily improve. It will also depend on how reconciliatory China is as much as a friendly DPJ government. Conceivably, relations with Beijing are likely to improve because a DPJ Prime Minister will probably abandon visits to Yasukuni and build a new secular war memorial to commemorate the victims of war. Not beholden to agricultural interests, a DPJ government is likely to clinch more FTAs in East Asia, paving the way in the long run to an EAC which encompasses both neighbors. The prospects of Sino–Japanese relations are probably better off with a non-LDP Prime Minister. There were at least two precedents: Hosokawa Morihiro and Murayama were non-LDP Prime Ministers who were more reconciliatory and forthcoming on the issue of an apology to China. Until the advent of a DPJ-led coalition government, Sino–Japanese relations are likely to remain prickly.

Negative sentiments towards China have also crept into the Ministry of Foreign Affairs (MOFA). Hitherto, the China School within MOFA was very influential in the formulation of Tokyo's policies towards Beijing. This school comprises of around one hundred career diplomats who have invested many years learning the Chinese language and culture.[15] The China School generally believes that Tokyo should adopt a friendly and cooperative approach to Beijing. Despite the China School's considerable knowledge of the mainland, other MOFA diplomats and LDP politicians have criticized the School for being too sympathetic to Beijing and not adequately defending Tokyo's interest. In 2005, the Koizumi Administration replaced Anami Koreshige, a leader of the China School, as ambassador to Beijing with Iimura Yutaka, an economics expert who is not reputed to be knowledgeable on Sino–Japanese affairs.

Markets: the economic ties that binds?

The appointment of an economics expert as the new ambassador may not be a bad thing especially when bilateral trade is a bright spot in Sino–Japanese relations. In 2004, total trade between Japan and China (including HK) reached US$213 billion, accounting for 20.1 percent of Japan's total trade while trade between Japan and the US was valued at US$197 billion or 19 percent of Japan's total trade.[16] Rising economic interdependence, especially trade between the two neighbors will create incentives for them not to rupture their political ties (Figure 8.2).

However, the reality check is that close economic ties between China and Japan in the 1930s did not prevent them from going to war. A Japanese scholar noted: "Modern history had also made the economies of the two countries quite interdependent. According to the average statistics of the 1930s, China was the largest destination for Japan's exports, with a share of the total amounting to 26 percent, and the third largest source of imports with a share of 12 percent. According to the statistics of 1938, Japan was the second largest market for China's exports, with a share of 14 percent, and its number one source of imports with a share of 24 percent."[17]

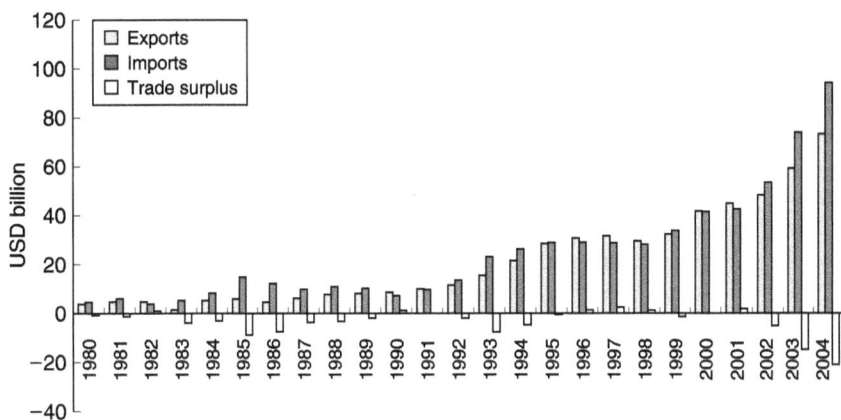

Source: *China Foreign Economics Statistics* (1979–91); *China Statistical Yearbook* (various issues).

Figure 8.2 Sino–Japan bilateral trade, 1980–2004.

Japan's deepening economic ties with the mainland have created winners and losers in the domestic arena. There is the fear that relentless Chinese competition will eclipse Japan's sunset industries and force Japanese factories to relocate to the mainland to take advantage of its lower cost of production, skilled labor and huge domestic market leading to the economic hollowing out of Japan. Trade frictions have also arisen over Chinese exports of leeks, mushrooms and straws for tatami mats to Japan. Despite negative public sentiments towards Beijing, Japanese business continues to invest in the mainland because there is money to be made.[18] Representing the sentiments of many Japanese business leaders concerned about the deterioration in Sino–Japanese political ties were IBM Japan Chairman Kitashiro Kakutaro and Chairman of Fuji Xerox and *Keizai Doyukai* (Japan Association of Corporate Executives) Kobayashi Yotaro, who urged Prime Minister Koizumi not to visit Yasukuni Shrine. Kobayashi's appeal triggered a rightwing backlash which included the dispatch of sound trucks to harass him and the hurling of Molotov cocktail against his home.[19]

While the national government in Tokyo has political friction with Beijing, many local governments and regions have sought better economic and cultural ties with their counterparts in the Chinese mainland. Since the bursting of the bubble economy, many local governments have to grapple with the problems of no growth, unemployment and fiscal deficits. Faced with such problems, some of these local governments have sought to seize economic opportunities by establishing ties with various localities in a rising China. Reflecting the importance and interest in the Chinese market, many Japanese local governments have established representative offices in the mainland. Indeed, with the exception of the US, Japanese local governments have the highest number of representative offices and sister-to-sister city relationships in China than any country in the world.[20]

Interestingly, local governments in Japan have conducted their own versions of friendly relations with China despite the more assertive tone of the central government in Tokyo towards Beijing. In this regard, local governments in a Japanese democratic system do enjoy relative autonomy and certain latitude to pursue their own approaches to international relations. Generally, local governments focus on economic and cultural ties and not on acrimonious issues like history, territorial disputes and the Taiwan problem which enwrap the national government.

Despite the trend of negative sentiments among the public towards China, Japanese Non-Governmental Organizations (NGOs) have proliferated in the Chinese mainland. There are now more than a thousand Japanese NGOs active in China engaged in cultural interaction and environmental protection. Take, for example, Green Earth Network (GEN), an Osaka-based NGO committed to greening the loess plateau in Datong, Shanxi province.[21] By 2003, GEN has planted more than 13 million trees in that province in partnership with the locals in Shanxi. Japanese NGOs such as GEN help to enhance people-to-people relationship between the two Asian neighbors despite their historical problems. Their frame of reference often transcends the national state and focuses on common cross-border problems especially environmental degradation. Indeed, the ethos of Japanese NGOs in China is often based on voluntarism, altruism and a sense of regional community. Conceivably, the activities of NGOs and the sister-to-sister city relationships of local governments are part of the integrative forces for an East Asian regionalism along with the economic ties that bind.

Anchoring China–Japan relations within East Asian regionalism?

In 2000 and 2001, then Prime Minister Zhu Rongji stole a march on Tokyo when he proposed an FTA with Southeast Asia, a region considered to be Japan's economic backyard. There was consternation in the Japanese media that Beijing is strategically trumping Tokyo for regional influence. In actuality, Tokyo and Singapore already began talks for an FTA in December 1999. Presumably, Beijing was unlikely to be oblivious to Japanese overtures to establish an FTA with Singapore and this was probably a consideration in Zhu's FTA proposal.[22] In the wake of Zhu's FTA offer to Southeast Asia, Prime Minister Koizumi offered a comprehensive economic partnership with Southeast Asia in January 2002. By August 2005, Tokyo had succeeded in clinching bilateral FTAs with Singapore, Malaysia, the Philippines and Thailand. If not for the Chinese overtures to Southeast Asia and pressure on Japan, Tokyo is less likely to have a sense of urgency to clinch FTAs with the region especially when market opening has been a politically contentious issue in Japanese domestic politics.

Supporting FTAs are the big economic federations (especially Keidanren which represent the interests of big businesses in the export sector), the Ministry of Economy, Trade and Industry and the Ministry of Foreign Affairs. Opposing FTAs are certain sunset industries which sought domestic protection, high tariffs and other import restrictions, the agricultural lobby and the Ministry of Agriculture, Forestries and Fisheries. Japan's very first FTA was with Singapore, a city-state without an agricultural sector, to preclude opposition especially from the agricultural lobby.[23] However, the Japan–Singapore FTA was merely the thin end of the wedge for Tokyo to set a precedent for subsequent FTAs with Mexico and various ASEAN states, countries with a significant agricultural sector. There are at least two reasons why a wave of bilateral FTAs has finally taken place. First is the decline in the demography and political clout of the agricultural lobby (hitherto, the most loyal supporters of the LDP) and second is the fear of being superseded in Southeast Asia by Beijing if Tokyo were to delay its FTAs with the region.

Rising economic interdependence is necessary but not sufficient for regional cooperation and an EAC. Nevertheless, the forthcoming China–Southeast Asia FTA, the Japan–Southeast Asia economic partnership and Tokyo's bilateral FTAs with various ASEAN countries are the building blocks of greater East Asian cooperation (see Appendices 8 and 9). An analogy is that East Asian regionalism is similar to Lego blocks. Southeast Asia, with separate FTAs with China and Japan, is the Lego block that helps to further interlock the two Northeast Asian giants together even though a bilateral Sino–Japanese FTA is not on the horizon. In contrast to the European experience of regionalism, it is not the cooperative spirit of Beijing and Tokyo *a la* Paris and Bonn but the sense of competition between the two Northeast Asian giants that drives East Asian regionalism.

The long-term trend is that intra-East Asian trade will increase. While economic interdependence does not automatically improve Sino–Japanese ties and construct an EAC, it will create incentives for Tokyo and Beijing to keep their relations on an even keel. Is nascent East Asian regionalism driven by ideas or necessity? The probable answer is: both. Then Malaysian Prime Minister Mahathir's proposal of an East Asian Economic Group that was subsequently downgraded to a caucus (EAEC) in the early 1990s was still-born after Washington raised its opposition and Tokyo heeded the preference of its ally. The Keidanren then was interested in the economic prospects of an EAEC but to no avail when the Japanese government did not extend its support to Mahathir's scheme.

The Asian Financial Crisis of 1997–8 was a momentous and turbulent period for East Asia. The crisis led to regime change in South Korea, Thailand and Indonesia and also paved the way for the Chiangmai Initiative, a regional effort to prevent a recurrence of currency exchange instability, and the formation of ASEAN Plus Three (APT) which comprises China, Japan and South Korea too. Earlier, not wanting to undermine the American-led International Monetary Fund or see the emergence of a yen-bloc at the expense of the US dollar as the de facto global currency, Washington vetoed Tokyo's proposal for an Asian Monetary Fund to aid the region in financial crisis.

The 6th APT Summit in Phnom Penh in November 2002 endorsed the Final Report of the East Asian Study Group and requested that 17 short-term measures in the report be implemented as soon as possible. Out of 17, China picked Network of East Asian Think tanks (NEAT), a second-track to APT, to spearhead the initiative. Annual Neat meetings were held in 2003 (Beijing), 2004 (Bangkok) and August 2005 (Tokyo). Ito Kenichi's Japan Forum on International Relations is the point institution to coordinate with other Japanese think-tanks to represent their nation in the NEAT second track process. Initially, many Japanese opinion shapers and academics were alarmed that the Chinese appeared to be in the driver's seat of the NEAT process. But Japan NEAT, led by Ito and supported by the nation's Ministry of Foreign Affairs, has dynamically participated and jointly led the NEAT process because it has the brainpower and financial resources to do so.

Stimulated by the launching of NEAT in 2003, The Council on East Asian Community (CEAC) was inaugurated in Japan in May 2004. By mid 2005, the CEAC comprised 12 think tank members, 63 individual members (including many academics) and 14 corporate members. Ex-Prime Minister Nakasone Yasuhiro is the CEAC Chairman while Ito Kenichi is its President. Corporate members include Nippon Steel Corporation and Toyota Motor Corporation while representatives come from the Ministry of Foreign Affairs, Ministry of Finance and the Ministry of Economy, Trade and Industry.[24]

Thus far, several NEAT Working Groups have focused on and hosted meetings on different areas of regional cooperation in 2005: energy security cooperation (Singapore NEAT); East Asian financial cooperation (China NEAT), overall architecture of community building in East Asia (Japan NEAT) and guiding principles to East Asian Community (Malaysia NEAT and Japan NEAT as co-sponsors). The proposals of these various NEAT Working Groups were then presented at the 3rd NEAT Annual Conference in Tokyo with the view of forwarding them to the December 2005 First East Asian Summit in Kuala Lumpur.

In these various working groups and annual conferences, the Chinese and Japanese delegates have maintained a cordial interaction within a multilateral setting. Interestingly, despite the rise of negative sentiments in Japan towards China, many Japanese scholars and associates of NEAT Japan and its supportive think-tanks appear to be very keen to join in the regional endeavor to build an EAC in the long term.[25] The Japanese NEAT participants are generally neither naïve nor cynical about the prospects of an EAC as a long term regional project fraught with many challenges, both seen and unseen. Nevertheless, there are some differences between China and Japan especially on the issue of regional membership. The Chinese prefer membership to be limited to the APT (deepen rather than to broaden) while the Japanese wish to bring in the Australians and the Americans to balance the Chinese. Another reason for the active commitment of Beijing and Tokyo in East Asian regionalism is the desire not to yield leadership of nascent process and institution building to each other.

Japanese Prime Minister as a pivotal player

Positive domestic sentiments about integrative markets and a nascent EAC do not preclude the Prime Minister from playing a decisive yet negative role in Tokyo's relations with Beijing. Indeed, the deterioration of ties between the two central governments can be attributed, in part, to the personality of Prime Minister Koizumi and the policies pursued by his administration. His insistence of making annual visits to Yasukuni Shrine and a one-dimensional emphasis on the US–Japan Alliance has worsened political relations between the two Asian neighbors.

The Japanese Prime Minister is often not considered to be a pivotal figure in policy making including the formulation of foreign relations.[26] The key institutions in policymaking are the powerful ministries and the LDP's policy-making divisions (which run parallel to the ministries), Public Affairs Research Council and the Executive Council.[27] These state and party institutions maintain close ties with their respective interest groups and clientele. The Japanese Prime Minister is often weak, especially if he is not a powerful LDP faction leader. In certain cases, the Prime Minister might be just a titular leader dependent on the support of more powerful faction leaders and their coalitions. But there are exceptions.

Tanaka Kakuei was a powerful faction leader in his own right. After President Nixon decided to open relations with China, Tanaka decided to move rapidly to normalize relations with Beijing. This upset the LDP's Taiwan lobby, which argued that Tokyo has a moral obligation not to abandon Taipei, particularly since its leader Chiang Kai-shek has magnanimously not demanded reparations from Japan.[28] According to Gerald Curtis, "Kosaka (Zentaro), who was head of a special LDP committee on China policy at that time, asked Tanaka how he could contemplate deserting Taiwan and Chiang when Japanese attached such importance to values of *giri ninjo*, of obligation and human feeling. Tanaka replied instantly to Kosaka that *giri ninjo* is important in relations among people, but the government has to consider what is in the best interests of the nation. We need to have relations with China. I'm going to recognize China." [29] Another LDP Prime Minister with a weaker character and factional support might have been less decisive in establishing ties with China.

Koizumi is another exceptional Prime Minister. Unlike Tanaka, he is not the leader of a powerful faction but his power base was an unprecedented public opinion support especially in the early years of his premiership. The public, exasperated by the political and economic malaise in the nation, responded warmly to Koizumi's charisma and promises of structural reform and to "destroy" the LDP if necessary to revitalize the country and its economy. Besides a reliance on populism, Koizumi also sought to secure the support of the right wing within and outside the LDP by promising that he will visit Yasukuni Shrine once he is elected party president.[30] His chief rival then was Hashimoto Ryutaro, leader of the most powerful faction (ex-Tanaka faction) and former head of the War Bereaved Family Association.

Previously, Nakasone and Hashimoto have visited Yasukuni Shrine but stopped doing so during their tenure as Prime Minister after vehement protests from China. However, Koizumi has insisted on visiting Yasukuni Shrine every year despite its negative impact on Sino–Japanese relations. Arguably, the burden of history in Sino–Japanese ties can be lightened by half if Koizumi has not adamantly visited Yasukuni. The consequence of Koizumi's annual visits to Yasukuni Shrine is Beijing's suspension of official visits between the two Asian neighbors. That the top leaders of the two most powerful Asian countries with common interests cannot even meet in either nation is an unfortunate development.

Why did Koizumi insist on visiting Yasukuni even though it antagonizes the Chinese leaders and masses? Besides the electoral promise made to clinch the party presidency as a prerequisite to become the Prime Minister, it appears that Koizumi has an intense personal and emotional attachment to kamikaze pilots who are honored at the Shrine. According to the media, his father Junya established a civilian airport near Kagoshima to stimulate the regional economy.[31] Unfortunately, World War II broke out and the military acquired the airport, and towards the war's end used the airport as a kamikaze base. Subsequently, 201 kamikaze pilots flew from the base which Junya built and never returned. Apparently, the Koizumi family felt a deep responsibility and remorse for the deaths of the young kamikaze pilots even though that was not their intention when the airport was built. To Koizumi, visiting Yasukuni is a reflection of his own personal credo to honor the victims of war including the kamikaze pilots and not a glorification of war.

That the domestic political arena is deeply divided over Koizumi's annual visits to Yasukuni can be seen by the unprecedented appeal by Kono Yohei, the speaker of the Lower House, and five former Prime Ministers in June 2005 for Koizumi not to visit Yasukuni again for the sake of the national interest to not worsen ties with an important neighbor.[32] In the wake of anti-Japanese protests in China in April 2005, Japanese public opinion was split down the center concerning the appropriateness of Koizumi's Yasukuni visit.[33] However, some 300 Diet members, mostly from the LDP, urged Koizumi not to bow to Chinese pressure and to go ahead with his Yasukuni Shrine visit on the 60th Anniversary of World War II's end. Opposing this move, a smaller and older group of LDP Diet members said that Koizumi should steer clear of Yasukuni. They blamed the visits for undermining Chinese support for Tokyo's bid for a permanent seat on the United Nations Security Council and warned that future visits could damage trade between the two neighbors.[34]

According to the Japanese media, the Yasukuni issue became intertwined with political maneuvers in anticipation of Koizumi's planned retirement as Prime Minister in September 2006. Former LDP Secretary General Abe Shinzo heads the pro-Yasukuni group comprising more than 110 junior LDP Diet members when it was launched in June 2005. In the following month, Noda Takeshi led around 40 LDP Diet members who are critical of Koizumi's Yasukuni visits to form a countervailing group. Noda's group included senior Diet members such as former Chief Cabinet Secretary Gotoda Masaharu, former LDP Secretary General Kato Koichi, former Foreign Minister Komura Masahiko and former Agriculture, Forestry and Fisheries Minister Oshima Tadamori.[35]

Koizumi's departure as Prime Minister does not guarantee that bilateral ties will necessarily improve. It depends on the attitude of the next Prime Minister towards Beijing and Yasukuni Shrine visits. Abe Shinzo, widely tipped to be a future Prime Minister, has strongly supported Koizumi's Yasukuni visits, much to the chagrin of China. Indeed, future LDP Prime Ministers might even adopt a more assertive stance towards the mainland. However, a Prime Minister from the DPJ is likely to be more conciliatory towards Beijing over the Yasukuni Shrine visit and other historical issues like textbook revisions. The Japanese political system is developing into a "two party plus system": two big parties, the LDP and DPJ, and a pivotal party, the New Komeito. If LDP one-party-dominance were to collapse leading to a system where the two main parties rotate in power, the role of the Prime Minister towards China would, in part, be influenced by the ideological hue of his party.

However, regardless of who emerges as a successor to Koizumi, the new Prime Minister must deal with a rising China. Hitherto, there is a tacit understanding within the LDP leadership that the Prime Minister designate should be someone who is able to deal with the US. There is the likelihood that in the years ahead, future Prime Ministers of Japan are expected to be politicians who can deal with China and keep relations on an even keel. In summary, the role of the Japanese Prime Minister shows that he can aggravate Sino–Japanese relations (in the case of Koizumi), despite favorable trends in the regional political economy such as deeper economic interdependence and regional aspirations for an EAC.

Prospects for Sino–Japanese relations and East Asian cooperation

An old Arab proverb says: "Those who claim to forecast the future are all lying, even if, by chance, they are later proved right." With this caveat in mind, two scenarios—optimistic and pessimistic—are considered. The sanguine view is that economic interdependence will strengthen inexorably in East Asia and will underpin an EAC. Regional cooperation within a multilateral framework can also help to mitigate the sharp edges of bilateral tension between China and Japan. East Asian summits, the governmental level APT and its second track NEAT activities, cultural exchanges (such as Japanese and Korean cultural exports to Southeast Asia) can provide the institutional and cultural underpinnings, in the long term, for an EAC. However, better Sino–Japanese relations within the ambit of East Asian regionalism are dependent on the domestic politics of these nations.

The pessimistic view would be unfavorable trends in the international system coinciding with the rise of virulent nationalism in both countries. In the worst scenario, the US considers a rising China to be a strategic threat and pressures Japan to further strengthen its military and dovetail into US global war fighting strategy. Taipei increasingly flirts with *de jure* independence and increases the danger that Tokyo will be dragged into a conflict with Beijing over Taiwan as a result of its alliance with Washington if the latter chooses to intervene in the Taiwan Strait. Meanwhile, the parties in power in both China and Japan seek to bolster their mass popularity and regime legitimacy by appealing to nationalism against each other. Friction over the history issue and territorial dispute in the East China Sea continues unabated. Bilateral and regional cooperation then are held hostage to domestic politics in both nations.

However, there are some grounds for guarded optimism. Within a decade or two, the political clout of the agricultural lobby, construction industry and postal masters in Japan will be significantly weaker and the LDP might well be out of power. Moreover, the region would enjoy greater economic interdependence. Such an outcome will facilitate an economic community between China, Japan and the region in the long run. Nevertheless, much depends on the wisdom of top political leaders as they maneuver the potential pitfalls of party, bureaucratic and interest group politics to promote regional cooperation. Since regional cooperation is too important to be left to just Prime Ministers, Presidents and their representatives, it is also important for local governments, think-tanks, scholars and NGOs to fight for the hearts and minds of the general public to construct an EAC even though the road will be a long and arduous one.

Notes

1 See Ezra Vogel, Yuan Ming and Tanaka Akihiko (eds), *The Golden Age of the US–China–Japan Triangle: 1972–1989*, Cambridge: Harvard University Asia Center, 2002.
2 Ministry of Economy, Trade and Industry, *White Paper on International Trade 2001: External Economic Policies Challenges in the 21st Century*, Tokyo: Ministry of Economy, Trade and Industry, 2001, p.15. The White Paper noted: "Asia is said to have echoed Japan's development path in a flying geese pattern.... However, this flying-geese pattern of development in East Asia has also begun to change with the emergence of China. China is not only pushing up its production and export volume, but has also increased its international competitiveness from the comparative labor-intensive textile industry through to the comparatively technological-intensive machinery industry."
3 Walter Hatch and Kozo Yamamura, *Asia in Japan's Embrace: Building a Regional Production Alliance*, Cambridge: Cambridge University Press, 1996.
4 More than two millennia ago, Thucydides identified the fundamental cause of the Peloponnesian War: "What made war inevitable was the growth of Athenian power and the fear which this caused in Sparta." See Thucydides, *The Peloponnesian War*, Harmondsworth, Middlesex: Penguin, 1983, p.23. See also Robert Glipin, *War and Change in World Politics*, Cambridge: Cambridge University Press, 1981; and Paul Kennedy, *The Rise and Fall of Great Powers: Economic Change and Military Conflict from 1500 to 2000*, New York: Random House, 1987.
5 The classic account of the domestic sources of Japanese foreign policy is Donald C. Hellmann, *Japanese Foreign Policy and Domestic Politics: The Peace Agreement with the Soviet Union*, Berkeley and Los Angeles, University of California Press, 1969. On the domestic sources of Tokyo's relations with Beijing, see Quansheng Zhao, *Japanese Policymaking: The Politics Behind Politics; Informal Mechanisms and the Making of China Policy*, Westport, Connecticut: Praeger, 1993.
6 Undeniably, the US-Japan security relationship compelled Tokyo not to recognize Beijing before Washington's diplomatic overtures with the Chinese mainland in 1971. However, Prime Minister Tanaka Kakuei decided to recognize Beijing in 1972 before the US did in 1979. Tanaka's decision was hotly disputed by many LDP politicians who were sympathetic to Taipei. In this regard, changes in the international system may present favorable opportunities for policy change but these are not necessarily done deals. Shifts in foreign policy are often contested in the domestic arena. The timing and extent of change or non-change are often dependent on a constellation of domestic factors including the personality and influence of the Prime Minister at the time, the factional balance, the strength and policy orientation of the opposition parties and the national mood.

7   On the rise of China and its impact on the region and Japan, see Kokubun Ryosei and Wang Jisi (eds), *The Rise of China and a Changing East Asian Order*, Tokyo: Japan Center for International Exchange, 2004; and Lam Peng Er (ed.), *Japan's Relations with China: Facing a Rising Power*, London and New York: Routledge, 2006.

8   In 2002, Japan's GDP was US$3.98 trillion (12.3 percent of world's total GDP) while China's was US$1.24 trillion (3.8 percent of world's total). See Asahi Shimbun, *Japan Almanac 2004*, Tokyo: Asahi Shimbun, 2003, p. 56.

9   For the best academic book on various Japanese conceptions of the so-called China Threat, see Amako Satoshi (ed.), *Chugoku wa kyoi ka* (Is China a Threat?), Tokyo: Keiso shoten, 1997.

10 *National Defense Program Guideline for Financial Year 2005 and After*, 10 December 2004, p. 3.

11 The media reported: "Defense spending for fiscal 2005 will fall by 1.0 percent, according to the draft budget approved Monday. The figure is down for the third straight year, thanks to sharp cuts in costs for personnel and existing equipment to pave the way for increased spending for missile defense and other new measures under a revised defense policy outline. The draft defense budget for the fiscal year beginning April 1 amounts to 4.856 trillion yen, down 46.7 billion yen from the initial budget for the current fiscal year.... The draft budget is in line with the December 10 New National Defense Program Outline and five-year defense buildup plan. It emphasizes the importance of streamlining personnel and mainstay equipment while improving capabilities to deal with ballistic missiles and new threats, including terrorism and commando attacks." See *Japan Times*, 21 December 2004.

12 Hebert Bix, "Hirohito and History: Japanese and American Perspectives on the Emperor and World War II in Asia," *Japan Focus*, 24 July 2005.

13 See the Association of Shinto Shrine's website online. Available HTTP: <http://www.jinjahoncho.or.jp/en/> (accessed 7 August 2005). For *Izokukai's* website, see online. Available HTTP: <http://www.nippon-izolukai.jp/topic.html> (accessed 7 August 2005).

14 "Nichu dakai mezashi shichi gatsu hochu he: Okada shi Ajia Jushi o hyomei" (To visit China in July and seek a breakthrough in Japan–China relations: Okabe announces his emphasis on Asia), *Sankei Shimbun*, 21 June 2005.

15 " 'China School' gets caned over North Korean fiasco," *Mainichi Interactive*, 21 May 2002.

16 See "China Passes U.S. in trade with Japan: 2004 Figures show Asian Giant's Muscle," *Washington Post*, 27 January 2005.

17 Statistics by Maruyama Nobuo quoted in Seiichiro Takagi, "In Search of a Sustainable Equal Partnership: Japan–China Relations in the Post-Cold War Era," *Japan Review of International Affairs*, Spring 1999, p.18.

18 For a classic account on the business community in China, see Sadako Ogata, "The Business Community and Japanese Foreign Policy: Normalization of Relations with the People's Republic of China," in Robert A. Scalapino (ed.) *The Foreign Policy of Modern Japan*, Berkeley: University of California Press, 1977.

19 Philip J. Cunningham, "Jumping to the Right," *Japan Focus*, No. 210, 2004.

20 According to Purnendra Jain, by April 2001, there were 276 cases of sister-city relations between China and Japan. See Purnendra Jain, "Forging New Bilateral Relations: Japan's Sub-national Governments in China," Conference on Contemporary China–Japan Relations: Conflict and Cooperation, East Asian Institute, Singapore, 1–2 August 2002. See also Glenn D. Hook, "Building Yellow Sea Bridges: Kyushu's Role in Sino–Japanese Relations," Conference on Contemporary China–Japan Relations: Conflict and Cooperation, East Asian Institute, Singapore, 1–2 August 2002.

21 This account on Japanese NGOs in China and GEN in Shanxi is based on Takahara Akio, "Japanese NGOs in China," Conference on Contemporary China–Japan

Relations: Conflict and Cooperation, East Asian Institute, Singapore, 1–2 August 2002.

22 Apparently, Beijing has two other considerations. First, Beijing wants to establish cordial relations with Southeast Asia to dissuade them from joining any future American scheme to contain China. Second, by opening up China's huge domestic market to the Southeast Asian countries and offering them a stake in its growing economy, Beijing hopes to allay the fears of certain Southeast Asian countries that the mainland will become a threat and a bully when it becomes a great economic power.

23 Even then Singapore accepted tariffs on ornamental fishes and orchids as a concession to the Japanese agricultural lobby.

24 See the website of the Japan Forum on International Relations on The Council on East Asian Community. Online. Available HTTP: <http://www.ceac.jp/e/e1-introduction. html> (accessed 7 August 2005).

25 A key participant from NEAT Japan in various working groups and annual conference is Professor Tanaka Akihiko, a scholar who is very knowledgeable about China.

26 On the role of the Japanese Prime Minister, see Kenji Hayao, *The Japanese Prime Minister and Pubic Policy*, Pittsburgh and London: University of Pittsburgh Press, 1993; and Tomohito Shinoda, *Leading Japan: The Role of the Prime Minister*, Westport, Connecticut: Praeger, 2000.

27 Koizumi has benefited from various reforms to party and state which have strengthened the hands of the Prime Minister. A major set of reforms adopted in the 1990s consisted of the administrative reforms undertaken by the Hashimoto administration in 1996–97. According to Machidori Satoshi, these reforms included setting up the Cabinet Office as an executive staff body, specially designated ministers of state, advisors, and a number of policy councils, such as the newly created Council on Economic and Fiscal Policy. Machidori noted: "These changes have created a base allowing the prime minister to make policy decisions free of the restraints that were formerly imposed by the ruling party and the ministries." Machidori also argued that while former Prime Minister Mori Yoshiro lacked the will to use these resources made available by administrative reforms, the Koizumi Administration has taken advantage of these reforms to transform the policymaking process. See Machidori Satoshi, "The 1990s Reforms have transformed Japanese Politics," *Japan Echo*, June 2005, p. 40.

28 On the domestic sources of Japan's normalization with China, especially on the roles of factions and the pro-Beijing and pro-Taiwan lobby within the LDP, see *Haruhiro Fukui, Party in Power: The Japanese Liberal-Democrats and Policy-making*, Canberra: Australian National University Press, 1970, pp. 240–62.

29 Gerald L. Curtis, *The Logic of Japanese Politics: Leaders, Institutions and the Limits of Change*, New York: Columbia University Press, 1999, p. 13.

30 For an excellent account on the rightwing groups and the Yasukuni issue, see Daiki Shibuichi, "The Yasukuni Shrine Dispute and the Politics of Identity in Japan," *Asian Survey*, Vol. 45, No. 2, March/April 2005.

31 The following account is from "Ties that tempt fate: Koizumi and Yasukuni Shrine," *Mainichi Shimbun*, 13 August 2001.

32 "Ex-Prime Ministers hit Yasukuni visits," *Japan Times*, 2 June 2005.

33 According to a Mainichi Shimbun survey, 50 percent of Japanese public opinion disapproved of Koizumi's Yasukuni visit while 41 percent approved it. See "More Japanese against visit to shrine: poll," *Today on-line*, 20 June 2005.

34 "War Shrine Visit: 300 lawmakers tell Koizumi: Go ahead," *Straits Times*, Singapore, 3 August 2005.

35 "LDP members worried about shrine row form up," *Japan Times*, 13 July 2005; and "Yasukuni sanpai shinchoha ga benkyokai o hassoku posuto koizumi gutaika ka" (Post-Koizumi concretization with the inauguration of an anti-Yasukuni Shrine Visit Study Group), *Asahi Shimbun*, 12 July 2005.

Part III

Non-governmental sources of regional cooperation

9 Transnational cooperation among NGOs in Northeast Asia: from re-thinking development towards re-thinking security

Daehoon Lee

Introduction

Unprecedented trends are now taking place in Northeast Asia, particularly in the field of peace and security. Taken together, these trends may have potential to change the frame of cooperation and contention in the region. First and foremost, the gravity of potential conflict in the region is increasingly recognized. Some certainty in the stalemate-like situation of the Cold War has been put aside for more conflictual dynamism to take the dominant status. Security concerns on the posture of North Korea run high. Despite the frequent description of the US–North Korean conflict as of a recent origin, citing the Pyongyang's nuclear program as a cause for example, this conflict stems from the period of modern state formation in Korea and un-concluded war of 1950–3. Concurrently, an unprecedented social transition is occurring in South Korea along with democratization and rapid expansion of civil society since the late 1980s. Interestingly many social changes are often expressed in the language of security—"degradation of security awareness" and "rise of anti-war/anti-US sentiment" among young generations and "rise/internationalization of peace movement." It is also interesting to note that many of the key social actors involved in this transition question legitimacy of the regional structure born from the 1950–3 conflict, for example, raise the issue of the legitimacy of the ROK—US alliance.

In order to understand regional-domestic linkages in the development of non-governmental activities in Northeast Asia, this chapter asks how *regionalization* of non-governmental organizations (NGOs) has shaped development of NGO cooperation in the region in the 1990s and examines interactions taking place among international, regional, and local non-governmental groups in three prominent areas where such interactions have been taken actively, development/environment, war crimes, and peace/security. Recognizing many critiques towards and reflections on limitations of romantic or urban imaginations for transnational[1] cooperation among civil society actors,[2] this chapter chose three areas of non-governmental cooperation that seek to go beyond such limitations and exert impact on the essential political environment that is democracy.[3] Although the normative aspect of transnational non-governmental activities has been often elaborated,[4] its implication to particular historical development of democracy in Asia is not easily found. The non-governmental interactions will be examined, in this light, for its regional–domestic linkages and, on the third topic of peace and security, for their impact on local NGOs in South Korea. Meaningful regional interactions began to occur in the 1990s and this has to do with democratization in South Korea, rendering liberal space to wider NGO activities. Before this change, the only civil society worth mentioning in the region was in Japan.

In this chapter, I use the concept of "regionalization" of NGOs to refer to the intentional reach-out to transnational activities by non-governmental groups with regards to Asia in general or to Northeast Asia. The practices of regionalization of NGOs are envisaged as both transnational cooperation among local NGOs and interactions between local NGOs with international and regional organizations.

NGO cooperation for re-thinking development

The sustained outbreak of Minamata disease of mercury contamination since 1956 in Japan was a result of one of the world's biggest and worst cases of industrial pollution, and as such has affected Japanese civil society in many ways. One of the effects was a process of re-thinking "developmentalism" in civil society. This is particularly well illustrated by the "Minamata Declaration" initiated by Japanese civic groups, signed by three hundred and sixty NGO representatives from Asia and the Pacific and adopted by thousands of NGO activists gathered in the city of Minamata in 1989. This was the first significant call to re-thinking "developmentalism" in the region initiated by Japanese social action groups, which have echoed in the following networks among NGOs in the region.

The Declaration[5] takes note of the lessons of the Minamata disease and the cases of Bhopal and Chernobyl as benchmarks of the time, and raises various questions on the democratic rights of the affected peoples. It questions the role of dominant enterprises, the nature of values in the modern knowledge system, internal colonization in the developmental process, and the role of states in protecting vulnerable people. Reflecting dominant thoughts among participating NGOs responding to these questions, it concludes:

> We recognize that the struggles of subjugated peoples for self-determination, independence, and to establish their own governments, or of people to change or improve their governments, are crucial. At the same time, we believe that, in the long run, it is the *transborder political actions of the people*, marginalizing states and countering the power of international capital that will produce the 21st century that we hope for.... All people, especially the oppressed people, have a natural and universal right to criticize, oppose, or prevent the implementation of decisions affecting their lives, no matter where those decisions are made.... Transborder political action, support and solidarity campaigns across borders will gradually develop a new 'people,' that transcends existing divisions, especially between people living in the North and the South.
>
> (*Minamata declaration*, author's emphasis added)

This synthesis was the finalization of a process known as People's Plan 21 (PP21) hosted in August 1989 in various provinces in Japan by a coalition of Japanese NGOs. PP21 process was perhaps the earliest regionalization initiatives by civil groups in Asia outside religious and political communities. The whole PP21 process comprised of nineteen international workshops, conferences, and festivals, most of which were held in different local communities under the aspiration of *transborder democracy*. Taking three months altogether, it was one of the most comprehensive and intensive processes by civic groups in Asia at the time. The deliberations were on the regional–local linkages of "development" in Asia that was modeled after the post-War development in Japan—poverty and development, women's situation and development, human rights and development, national security and development, environment and development, etc.

Many participating NGOs in Asia held two follow-up conferences and eventually identified "transborder participatory democracy" as the core value and aspiration of NGOs working towards some sort of regional cooperation. One of the key initiators of PP21 explains the notion as follows:

> The transborder participatory democracy we posited is a dynamic process as well as a goal. It is a permanent democratization process based in "democracy on the spot"—emancipatory transformation of everyday relationships in the family, community, workplace, and other institutions of life—extending beyond social, cultural, and state barriers, and reaching, influencing, and ultimately controlling the global decision making mechanisms wherever they are located.
>
> (Muto Ichio, *Alliance of Hope and Challenges of Global Democracy*)[6]

The impact of the PP21 process is readily recognized in many NGOs from Asia that participated in it. The process left a lasting mark among the participants as it "provided a forum linking immediate problems with global ones" and "bringing in global perspective" to local actions.[7] In Asia, PP21 was widely conceived as having generated a regional momentum for NGOs in several aspects, namely, making visible an Asia–Pacific regional voice of the people and bringing together their aspirations for alternative models of development, trans-border democracy and self-empowerment. For local groups that did not have comparable experiences, PP21 brought in the idea of regional inter-connectedness of their issues and realities in a unique way.

However, it is interesting to note that there were very few participants in this process from Northeast Asia except from Japan. Civic groups in South Korea were in general pre-occupied with political democratization, and there was little to mention of civil society in China in the late 1980s. Therefore, the process of PP21 was hardly known or had little impact to NGOs on the sub-regional level in Northeast Asia.

An interesting contrast to the process of PP21 has appeared in the case of cooperation among non-governmental environmental organizations in Northeast Asia. Interaction among civic environment groups in the region is often cited as one of the most active among the general NGO community. What makes the difference is rather clear from the nature of the issues themselves. First, the issues are clearly regional in nature: migration of pollutants, migratory birds, dusty wind from inland China, acid rain, air pollution and oceanic pollution. Second, the development of international environmental regimes in the 1990s has created a favorable environment for regional NGO interactions. NGOs, along with governments, were strongly compelled to cope with global and regional environmental changes through the institutionalization of, notably, the Climate Change Convention and Biodiversity Convention concluded in the United Nations Conference on Environment and Development in 1992, and Kyoto Protocol, one of the strongest environmental regimes that impose binding duties to the concerned parties.

Along with the development of global environmental regimes, inter-governmental cooperation progressed in the region. Bilateral agreements for environmental cooperation have been concluded among Korea, Japan, China and Russia from 1991 to 1994. It went parallel to the formation of the first multilateral cooperation among Northeast Asian countries in 1991, the Northeast Asian Conference on Environmental Cooperation, the agenda of which in the past years have included concerted approaches to solve national and local environmental problems, such as migratory pollution, acid rain, international transshipment of toxic waste, and climate change. In 1992, the Meeting of Senior Officials on Environmental Cooperation on Northeast Asia was organized by the United Nations Economic and Social Commission for Asia and the Pacific (UNESCAP). There are also the meetings of three environmental ministers of South Korea, Japan and China (the Tripartite Environmental Ministers Meeting: TEMM) and regional cooperation on Tumen River Area Development Program. Many of these meetings invited NGO representatives, even though the latter often play the role of raising questions on the substance of inter-governmental cooperation.

Regional environmental cooperation among non-governmental groups has its roots in humble exchange programs for environmental activists and scholars between South Korea and Japan in the early 1970s. The initiatives came from common understanding that export of Japan's pollution-causing industries to South Korea had to be monitored and the business–government collusion under authoritarian regime in South Korea was a factor aggravating the situation.

With a serious case of heavy-metal pollution in the mid 1980s in Onsan in South Korea which accommodated Japanese chemical companies, exchange between environmental groups in the two countries increased rapidly, forming the basis for wider networks and networks on other related agenda. For example, an Anti-Nuke Asia Forum was organized in 1993 in Japan with active participation from Korean partners, and conversely, Atmosphere Action Network East Asia was formed in 1995 in Seoul. Environmental groups from South Korea and Japan played a leading role in establishing Asian Pacific NGO Environmental Conference in 1993 in Kyoto, which later hosted an NGO Forum in parallel with the Conference of Parties of the Climate Change Convention, in Kyoto in 1997. Various other fora were organized where non-governmental groups from the two countries took initiatives on other environmental issues in Northeast Asia.[8]

There are several factors explaining how and why active and relatively successful regional cooperation experienced by environmental NGOs have come about in Northeast Asia. Common interest was created as the effects of rapid industrialization were socially recognized in Japan, South Korea and China. The progress in global institutionalization created favorable conditions for public awareness of the problems and, therefore, support for NGO activities. Bilateral and multilateral cooperation among the countries in the region was concurrently developing and often involved NGOs in the process.

Environmental groups in Japan often took regional initiatives and were supported by newly formed and rapidly expanding environmental groups in South Korea under a shared view that environmental degradation in China was a major regional concern. The domestic cooperation experienced among national and local governments, business and NGOs in Japan creates a source of push for regional cooperation along with Official Development Assistance (ODA) funding. The expansion of civil society and middle class in South Korea in the 1980s and after helped to create momentum for environmental NGOs.

NGO cooperation for re-visiting war crimes: sexual slavery

Beginning in 1931 and throughout the period of the invasion of Asia and the Pacific, the Japanese government enslaved approximately 200,000 girls from Korea, China, Taiwan, Indonesia, Malaysia, Burma, the Philippines and Holland for sexual purposes, and established their brothels over the territories occupied by the Japanese imperial army. During that time, women were enslaved by force, abduction and deception into sexual slavery. The issue, however, has been long kept in silence owing to continued denial of the fact by the Japanese government and existence of social taboo that placed false shame on the victimized women. It only began to draw public attention since the 1980s in South Korea and Japan. The initial breakthrough owes to a few women victims and the work done by women's rights groups.[9]

In the late 1980s, NGOs, particularly women's groups, began to raise this issue as a major agenda in their movement in South Korea. In 1990, the Korea Council for the Women Drafted for Military Slavery by Japan (*JungDaeHyup* hereinafter)[10] was established as a coalition for this issue with participation of 22 leading women's movement groups in the country. A nation-wide women's rights umbrella organization, the Korea Women's Associations United (KWAU)[11] played a crucial role in this development, and signified the importance of this agenda, KWAU being a major player in setting the agenda for civil society and promoting solidarity within the larger community of NGOs. The coalition succeeded in acquiring wider support and cooperation among other civic groups including professional groups and trade unions, which helped gain public recognition of the issue.

In this light, the rise of the issue of wartime sexual slavery was seen as an expected outcome of the development of the women's movement in South Korea, which started with the problems of women worker's rights, sex trade in and around the US bases, and sex tourism in the 1970s. As Korean and Japanese women's groups had already established a network of cooperation since the 1970s on issues related to sex tourism in Asia, this has contributed to close collaboration between the two sides on the issues of former military sexual slavery.

Since its establishment, *JungDaeHyup* has hosted public testimonies of the former victims and to date is holding weekly demonstrations in front of the Japanese Embassy in Seoul. The weekly demonstration, the Wednesday Demonstration as it is called, drew wide attention over the years, becoming a symbolic venue of women's solidarity in Asia on the issue of violence against women.[12] *JungDaeHyup*'s official demand to the government of Japan includes recognition of the former sexual slavery as a crime, full acknowledgement, official apology by the government of Japan based on a Diet resolution, legal reparation to all victims, truthful recording in history textbooks, construction of a memorial and resource centre, and punishment of the responsible persons.

Since 1992, *JungDaeHyup* also held six sessions of Asian Solidarity Conference until 2003, which served as a space of networking and strategizing for all concerned groups and individuals on the issue. It was in the first conference that concerned groups agreed, among others, to use the designation *military sexual slavery by Japan* instead of the commonly used, derogatory "comfort women." In the 1998 conference, the participants agreed to hold the aforementioned Tribunal in Tokyo. Since the Tokyo Tribunal, the conference later developed into a wider consultation for international solidarity.

From 8th to 12th December 2000, NGOs jointly held the first International Tribunal on War Crimes on Sexual Slavery by the Japanese Military in Tokyo. The Tribunal was first proposed by Matsui Yayori of the Violence against Women in War–Network Japan during the annual Asian Solidarity Conference of 1998, with reference to the Bertrand Russell Tribunal of 1967 that investigated war crimes committed by the United States during the Vietnam War. With the objectives "to restore justice and dignity to victims and to pressure the Japanese government to take responsibility for crimes committed during World War Two and the post-war era; to promote women's human rights...; and to cultivate the ground for a shared future in Asia based on reconciliation,"[13] it was organized by civic groups of Japan and six countries in Asia of the victims, South Korea, North Korea, China, the Philippines, Malaysia and Indonesia.[14] The proposal was also influenced by the newly established International Criminal Court, whose jurisdiction included sexual violence against women during conflict, but not retrospectively, therefore excluding the cases by the former Japanese military during World War Two.

The charter of the Tribunal has been drafted in such a way that the rules and procedures parallel those of a legal court. Its aim was to clarify not only crimes committed before and during World War Two but also negligence in not prosecuting war criminals and compensating victims during the post-war era.[15]

The Tribunal, presided over by Gabrielle Kirk McDonald as the chief judge, former president of the International Criminal Tribunal for the former Yugoslavia, found the Japanese government and Emperor guilty of crimes related to the practice and negligence of sexual slavery in the former Imperial Army of Japan.[16] Though legally non-binding, this civic tribunal signified internationalization of the issue, with initiatives coming from South Korea and close collaboration with a number of women's and professional groups in Northeast Asia, including North Korea and China. The Tribunal is seen as having "remarkable educational effects for the public, and in particular for women, on issues of human rights, violence against women, war crimes, international law, the role of documentation, the problematic perspectives of dominant histories, etc" with women "becoming more confident that they can rewrite history and effect a more just society."[17]

Similarly, Korean and Japanese women's groups worked together since 1992 in the Commission on Human Rights and other human rights fora of the United Nations. In 1993, the Vienna World Conference on Human Rights included the issue of "comfort women" in its declaration. In 1996, with the support of inter-national NGOs such as the International Commission of Jurists and the World Council of Churches, women's groups from Korea and Japan worked with the Special Rapporteur on violence against women in the Commission on Human Rights, Rahdika Coomaraswamy, whose report was accepted in the Commission in 1996, identifying for the first time the criminal practice of sexual slavery by the former Imperial Army of Japan. In 1998, the Special Rapporteur to the Sub-Commission on Human Rights, Gay McDougall, presented her report on system-atic rape and sexual slavery stating, "The constitution of military sexual slavery, the 'comfort women,' was planned systematically and carefully, ordered and car-ried out by the government of Japan."[18]

The International Labour Organization (ILO), on the other hand, responded to the complaint of uncompensated forced labor filed by the Korean Federation of Trade Unions in 1995, and then adopted a recommendation for appropriate remuneration for the victims of "comfort women" cases by the Japanese govern-ment in 1999, 2001, and 2002. The series of deliberations in the international human rights bodies led the Japan Federation of Bar Associations to conclude in 1995 that the "Comfort Women system was created and administered by the Japanese State and Imperial Army and implemented by related authorities" and that "immediately after the war the Japanese government issued orders to destroy or burn all evidence…on Comfort Women." The Bar Association recom-mends that Japanese government pay individual compensation and take other measures.[19]

Though yet to reach a conclusion, the regional NGO cooperation on the issue of sexual slavery reflects social progress of the 1990s in the region, especially in South Korea and other democratizing societies such as Taiwan and partly China. Unprecedented cooperation developed between North and South Koreas on the issue also coincides with thawing relationship between two Koreas during the same decade. At the initial stage, the cooperation benefited from regional solidar-ity already promoted by women's groups in Asia since the 1970s on regional issues such as sex tourism. It seems reasonable to deduce that the social mood created with democratization and empowerment of women's rights groups allowed the former victims to do "coming-out" and voice their ignored lives.

Along with democratization, the nature of the issue demonstrated to the public the fact that colonialism in South Korea and war responsibilities in Japan remained partly but significantly unresolved. The new agenda-setting global conferences hosted by the UN and other existing human rights fora also provided valuable space in internationalizing and regionalizing the issue.

NGO cooperation for re-thinking security in South Korea

Conflict, threat, security and non-state actors [20]

During the time of the authoritarian regimes in South Korea, NGOs focused mainly on political democratization and peaceful reunification. While unable to engage with any North Korean partners due to forbidding constraints such as the National Security Law, they advocated instead alternative principles and a roadmap to unification to the Cold-War-style official policies. For the government, such discourse was regarded dangerous to national unity. Civic leaders of such initiatives were often put under severe control, because the contention directly involved how to interpret the North Korean threat.

The state's control over security issues was vital in the legitimization of the authoritarian governments. Civil society groups trying to redefine security issues and the perception of threats were in fact working to ease the state's monopoly control over national security, which in turn prompted de-legitimization of the authoritarian rule and consequently a democratization process.

With a political process towards democracy on track since the late 1980s, NGOs and religious groups began illegal communication with and visits to the North in order to hold direct talks with the North Korean authorities despite severe legal consequences. Such visits were regarded as sensational as much as it was regarded impossible, but also as it demonstrated the possibility of friendly talks and of reaching common understanding across the ideological division in Korea. An outlawed visit to North Korea in 1989 by a young student, Lim Soo-Kyong, for example, caused such public sensation and celebration at the same time within the two Korean societies that deeply controversial debates ensued over the legitimacy of hostility in Korea. As a trend, prospect and legitimacy of "peaceful" unification gained wider reception in the civil society in South Korea when contrasted to the justification of the ongoing confrontational stalemate situation. Such a prospect was to accompany more public debates on other security issues involving the role of the US forces in Korea, disarmament, and political agenda for national unification.

With democratization, public pressure to depoliticize the military gained momentum, along with successful campaigns to bring to justice two former presidents who were responsible for illegal coups in 1979 and 1980, and by the mid 1990s politics was conducted free from Korean military influence. At the same time, NGOs began to raise issues of human rights violations during the compulsory military service, out of which a conscientious objectors movement was born. The revival of parliamentarian politics and civil society campaigns to depoliticize the military have helped to shape an initial form of civilian control over the military, which is vital in conflict management in Korea.

After 1993, as the world became aware of the serious economic failure in North Korea, new civic groups began to emerge in order to enhance humanitarian aid to the north and raise such concerns in the south. Legal constraints on non-governmental groups sending aid to North Korea began to ease in the late 1990s. Noted for their initiatives and success in mobilizing public donations and sending food and aid to the north are the South–North Sharing Campaign, Good Friends: Center for Peace, Human Rights and Refugees, and the Korean Sharing Movement. Such non-governmental humanitarian aid focuses, in addition to food aid, on health care, the modernization of hospitals, agricultural infrastructure and forestation. The total amount reached US$ 51 million in 2002 in comparison to US$ 8,375 of governmental humanitarian aid.

With the introduction of the Sunshine Policy of Kim Dae-Jung in 1998, social and cultural exchanges between the two Koreas expanded rapidly. Civic groups actively supported the human exchange aspect of the new policy and began to organize regular sports events, joint academic meetings, cultural exchange visits and joint commemoration events, such as sending a delegation to the May Day ceremony in Pyongyang. At the same time, the sheer number of civilians visiting the other side for various civilian purposes rose dramatically. Compared to the single case of a civilian visit to North Korea in 1989, more than twelve thousand South Koreans visited the North and one thousand North Koreans visited the south in 2002. The humanitarian impact of these visits and their effect on boosting mutual understanding are enormous and are slowly but surely affecting each society.

In the meantime, the US issue began to surface as the institutional and cultural pressure for silencing it waned with democratization. Various groups representing the victims of offences arising from the daily activities of the US military bases led to this trend, stimulating many civic and religious groups to question the legitimacy of the US forces while North–South relations were thawing. Anti-landmine campaigns also highlighted the long-hidden reality of the unfair treatment of the victims and arrogant stance of the US forces on this matter. Scholars and religious groups in the two Koreas began to hold joint meetings on such agendas. In general, South Korea in the 1990s saw a great surge of NGO peace initiatives in humanitarian, academic, religious, sports and political fields, greatly diminishing the militarist-confrontational stance towards the north and actively inviting North Koreans to enter a new space of engagement.

As tension grew between Seoul and Washington along with the Bush administration's new approach to North Korea, there was deep disappointment among the Korean public. Some of it was expressed in large-scale anti-American demonstrations in South Korea in 2002–03. NGOs continue to advocate for a peaceful settlement of the tension between North Korea and the US, and hope to build a "peace buffer" by further expanding North–South exchange and cooperation. The large scale demonstrations against the Korean troops being dispatched to Iraq in 2003 also shows the nature of the growing public sentiment concerning US arrogance over Korean affairs. There is a concern over the implications for Korea of the US pre-emptive strike doctrine applied to Iraq. Another concern is the unequal nature of decision making between South Korea and the US, especially in military affairs. The rapid rise and expansion of the peace movement reflects this change in the public mind, centered on rationalizing the ROK–US relations beyond the Cold War tradition.

A new NGO initiative was mooted in summer 2003: Peace groups in the US and in South Korea have developed closer cooperation in advocating peaceful resolution of the tension. Along with advocacy work, they organized a "lobby" tour of a delegation[21] from South Korea to the US—a delegation which was composed of members of the National Assembly, scholars and peace advocates—to have alternative discussions on North Korean issues with key policy makers, civil society leaders and parliamentarians. After the visit, an awareness-raising campaign is jointly planned, to introduce a broader perspective of the North Korean issue to the wider public in the US.

NGO initiatives for peaceful settlement of Korean affairs reflect a continuing interest in shifting security politics[22] towards normal politics. NGO initiatives for inter-Korean conflict resolution centered on political democratization (de-securitization[23] of the national security state) and independence from the US influence (de-securitization of foreign policies). Political democratization since 1987 has close connections with the social pressure towards de-securitizing the DPRK–US tension over nuclear and missile issues. In the longer perspective, this has invited and will invite transnational civil society groups to work for new international relations in Northeast Asia, including the ROK–US military alliance.

Deep changes

Since the division of Korea in 1948, the mutual interaction of pretentiously non-interacting two Koreas has deeply penetrated in the way whereby politics and economics functioned and how each state defined itself and its people vis-à-vis the other. In South Korea, the purpose of the state, growth, and ideology was defined as what North Korea is not, and vice versa in North Korea. The two Koreas held each other together at distance to become an integral part of each other. So when there is a deep change in one side, it affects the other, inevitably displaying reciprocity of the bipolar interaction.

Coming into the 1990s, however, what we see in Korea is the fundamental shake-up of this overarching, mutually defining system that has governed every facet of life for so long. The global structure that sustained the Korean division and the Cold War was dismantled with the fall of the Berlin Wall. Manifesting the dynamics of deep-level bottom-up transformation, the gradual democratization in South Korea since 1987 opened up large social, political and cultural spaces in the south where the psychological ice wall dividing the two Koreas began to melt down, flushing away a large portion of hatred and bias. This is effective in melting down a large portion of world-view subjugated to the purpose of division. A new perspective was bound to come, especially among the younger generations who are rather free from the Cold War thinking, going beyond the boundary of national politics and reaching global politics. It began to emerge in the South, asking a potentially explosive question to oneself: what and who are we if we are not everything that is not North Korea and not everything partial to the US interest? A new, critical perception of self-identity[24] in the South is a key to understanding what is happening in Korea today.

Voluntary social energy in South Korea's civil society has been usually known with the notion of "democratization" and "reunification" during the past decades. The peace movement has not been widely known or familiarized as an independent grouping of non-governmental organizations or social movements until very recently. During the first US–Iraq War ("Gulf War"), only a few NGOs issued anti-war statements, for example. Even during the nuclear crisis in 1994, a coherent anti-war movement did not exist in South Korea.

But since 2001, where key civil society actors such as labor unions and popular social movement groups began to voice together in a firm anti-war stance, the notion of a peace movement surfaced quickly and it began to represent what "democratic movement" used to represent in the 1970s and 1980s—the "reason" of the society vis-à-vis the "logic" of national interest. Notably, the way that "peace movement" became the central notion describing the civil society of South Korea today emerged from what we witnessed in 2002, a massive participation of people in voicing the arrogance of the US over the deaths of two girls.[25] This was considered to have direct impact to the presidential campaign that led Roh Moo-hyun to presidency. "Peace movement" itself cannot be said to have a political influence, but its influence is indirectly felt by the rapid change of public opinions on "peace and security" issues in South Korea's politics today. The hugely changed public perception of threat was revealing to some and alarming to others in this respect.[26]

This was partly possible because the state "reason" has been preventing proper public debates over the US issues, including the ROK–US alliance, joint military exercises, crimes committed by American servicemen towards Korean civilians, the US bases issues, etc. When civil society actors successfully broke this taboo with a high degree of popular support and participation, it represented a new "reason" emerging, not just as a new logical critique, but with an ethical supremacy as shown in the case of the nationwide mourning for the two dead girls. This mourning represented a non-state-dictated mourning for all victims of the unfair relationship between the two countries, a very deeply ethical act that few could openly challenge.

NGO-initiated regionalization of security agenda

Along with major convergence of NGOs on peace and security issues, South Korean NGOs began to seek regionalization of peace initiatives in many ways. One good example was to get actively connected to a regional civic group that works on alternative thinking on security, Asia Regional Exchange for New Alternatives (ARENA).[27] Another example is the participation to a global process called Global Partnership for the Prevention of Armed Conflict (GPPAC). This was initiated by the European Centre for Conflict Prevention[28] in 2003 in response to the UN Secretary-General's Recommendation of May 2002 calling for partnership between governments and non-governmental groups in global conflict prevention. More contentious example is given by NGO interactions concerning human rights situation in North Korea.

ARENA is an interesting case of transborder cooperation among non-governmental groups on security, for two reasons: first, it has been vital in connecting local peace groups to regional and global issues of peace and security, and second, it has been conducting a strong program in challenging statist approach to security issues in the region. One incidence of its program in "challenge security approach" was the 2003 ARENA Regional School titled "*Pyunghwa* (meaning peace in Korean): Alternatives to the American War." It was held in South Korea with participants from across Asia.[29] The 2003 Regional School[30] aimed, in particular, for alternative conceptualizations of security, such as those proposed by the "human security" and "people's security" frameworks, and a return to more comprehensive political analyses on the major global–local agenda facing Asian peace movements.

A reading of the motivations of this forum, expressed in "The Challenges Ahead"[31] of the plan, gives an insight into the basic problematic of the peace groups involved. They were concerned in demystifying the current dominant security discourses from the perspective of non-state groups, especially victims of conflict, and engaging into the politics surrounding peace and security issues with a belief that transborder activities of non-state groups might have some impact on inter-state politics in the region.

The program included, as main topics, inputs from experts on analysis of the language of the war on terrorism and the economic, political and military strategies behind the US–Iraq war, Bush administration's global roll-back strategy and its implications to Northeast Asia, rise of militarism and prospects of conflict management, examples of successful conflict prevention initiatives of civil society groups. Participants responded to the inputs with their own "ground stories" and suggestions.

The Regional School was received by the participants as highly relevant and successful, with evaluations such as "the relevance of the topics on peace and security (national and regional levels), deconstruction of terms and the opportunity to learn more about the workings of the anti-US bases movements in the region" and "the democratic space made available for the youth to take the leading role in the process." It seemed that the participants found this a very enriching process that has effectively developed a stronger sense of confidence in their own work and their own capabilities.

The Regional School is just one example of the works carried out by regional non-governmental groups like ARENA. Being a forum of critically engaged scholars, ARENA provides a space for sharing and developing joint intellectual and practical endeavors on topics deemed important to the region. Security has become one of the central topics. ARENA's wing for security issues have been conducting public fora on the war on Iraq and on linkages between impact of economic globalization and conflicts, research and publications on militarization and compilation of local, traditional visions of peace, fact-finding on women's situation in Afghanistan, etc.

At the same time, ARENA has connected many of the critical intellectuals active in questioning the culture of militarism along with peace movement groups in respective societies, to promote exchange of views and joint publication. This networking was aimed at showing the extent of militarization in state, government and civil society; explaining how militarization is interlinked with militarist nationalism, patriarchy, stereotyping etc.; establishing how militarized notions of security add to the insecurity of the peoples and the state; communicating the need for de-construction and the discussion of militarization; and presenting an alternative by showing peace and peoples security as alternatives.[32] It has brought ten country chapters in the Asian region: India, Indonesia, Japan, Malaysia, Nepal, Pakistan, Philippines, South Korea, Sri Lanka, and Thailand.

One of the immediate impacts of the 2003 Regional School was the effect of networking on the US bases issues. With its theme focused on the question of the US security policies in the region, the Regional School drew attention among the "US bases groups" in the region—non-governmental groups dealing with issues of the US military bases. The consultation held immediately after the school was attended by activists from Okinawa, Japan, Indonesia, Korea, the Philippines, Thailand, and the US. Participants shared their analysis of the situation of US bases and military presence in the region and discussed possible joint campaigns to raise public awareness of the rapidly increasing militarization in the region. Some of the agreements they reached included; to hold a forum on the issue during the World Social Forum 2004 to be held in Mumbai, India, to produce a publication, "An Asian Report on US Military Bases and Presence in the Region," to strongly include feminist perspective in the campaigns, and to promote more exchanges among young concerned people.

Meanwhile, the GPPAC networks were initiated by the European Centre for Conflict Prevention in 2003, as mentioned before. Regional networking has developed in different regions of the world. In Asia, it was ARENA and other groups who promoted it, and the Asian regional networking is participated in by groups such as Initiative for International Dialogue (Philippines), South East Asian Conflict Studies Network, SUARAM (Voice of the Malaysian Peoples), World Vision Asia-Pacific Disaster Management Office, Asian Regional Exchange for New Alternatives, Women Making Peace (Korea), Peace Boat (Japan), Women's League of Burma, Ortigas Peace Institute (Philippines), Sisters in Islam (Malaysia), and FORUM Asia. Northeast sub-regional networking is also in development.[33]

The objective of regional and sub-regional networks, called GPPAC networks, is to formulate a consensus on the role and capacity-building process of civil society groups in the area of conflict prevention and cooperation with international and governmental agencies. The global conference of all GPPAC networks in 2005 is viewed as a forum to reach common, global action plans.

The Northeast Asian network is trying to invite relevant groups from China, Taiwan and North Korea into the forum, and have raised as key agenda issues such as international justice to the victims of sexual slavery by the military, development of regional historical textbooks, reconciliation between North and South Korea, prevention of militarization, information and publication for non-violence and peace culture. By 2005, it is expected that this networking will synthesize a region-wide civil society consensus on conflict resolution agenda and proposals for management/resolution of the conflicts. In regard to the conflict in Northeast Asia, the network is serving as a platform for common agenda setting for South Korean and Japanese peace groups, with groups from China and Taiwan yet to join.

The GPPAC process had its sub-regional process in Northeast Asia culminating at the Northeast Asian Conference on the Role of Civil Society in the Prevention of Violent Conflict held in Tokyo, Japan on 1–4 February 2005. The participants representing over fifty NGOs from nine cities in the region adopted the Northeast Asia Regional Action Agenda.[34] The adopted agenda included the following areas as recommendations for action: building a regional system for peaceful coexistence through disarmament and demilitarization; promoting humanitarian assistance and development assistance; building a society that recognizes justice, human rights and diversity; and realizing a sustainable economy and economic justice. The goal of the adopted agenda is well reflected in the following statement by one of the key organizers of this meeting, Peace Boat of Japan:[35]

> Adoption of the Action Agenda is testament to the common spirit of Northeast Asian civil society to work together for peace and security. Moreover, the conference provided stimulus for everyone involved to deepen their commitment to building a culture of prevention and work together in the future at a regional level. The GPPAC Northeast Asia network is now turning its attention to promoting the ideas set out in the Action Agenda at the local level as well as at the international level...
>
> (Peace Boat, *Civil Society*)

Other key players were GPPAC Northeast Asia regional steering group (consisting of leading peace NGOs in the region), and supported by the United Nations University, the United Nations Information Center, the United Nations Development Program and the European Centre for Conflict Prevention.

The motivation for these groups to come together to develop a regional and international agenda setting on peace and security issues were, as noted by the organizers, the fragile security situation in Northeast Asia, namely, the nuclear crisis in the Korean peninsula, moves to revise Japan's war-renouncing constitution, the Taiwan Strait issue, numerous territorial disputes, and a generalized lack of confidence and cooperation within the region.[36] Another motivation was that these issues were to be resolved through political and social changes, and therefore could not be exclusively left to governments.

The following "Ten Guiding Principles for the Prevention of Violent Conflict in Northeast Asia"[37] have been agreed to by GPPAC Northeast Asia: respect for the peaceful resolution of conflict; creating a cooperative security system through denuclearization and demilitarization of the region; ensuring local ownership and human security in creating a regional mechanism for peace; promoting peaceful engagement to areas of conflict and potential danger; importance of gender justice in conflict prevention; establishing institutions for conflict prevention based on recognition of justice, human rights and diversity; promoting a culture of peace and culture of prevention; building sustainable regional economies; promoting new partnerships among civil society, governments, regional organizations and the UN for conflict prevention; and capacity building of civil society for conflict prevention.

Observations

The activities of NGOs described above illustrate some aspects of how domestic and regional factors mutually affect each other in developing regional non-governmental cooperation. In the field of what may be called the "critique of developmentalism," at the initial stage, major local environmental disasters prompted local NGOs to seek regionalization of the agenda and relevant activities. This was due to the difficulty of resolving the issue locally. At the same time, the development of international norms and standards such as in the Rio Conference on Environment and Development in 1992 contributed to the development of regional cooperation among the governments in Northeast Asia, which in turn contributed to the closer consultative relationship between governments and non-governmental groups. The active phase of exchanges and cooperation among environmental NGOs in Northeast Asia also owes to the expanded space of freedom and positive public reaction in democratizing societies such as South Korea and Taiwan since the early 1990s. This is a reasonable turn-out as developmentalism has been associated with growth-oriented authoritarianism in these societies until the 1980s.

The case of regionalization and internationalization of the issue of wartime sexual slavery, led by women's NGOs in South Korea and Japan, also illustrates that local momentum plays a vital role at the initial stage. Growth of women's movement is one such momentum. However, it was the maturity of some sections of civil society in Japan and South Korea to look at and counter together the impact of sex tourism in Asia. The basis of regional cooperation in this matter, it can be argued, had its origin in the regional nature of the common issues such as sex tourism. Women's NGOs were, however, effective and successful in revealing the long-covered-up human rights violations of the wartime sexual slavery in connection with a sensitive regional issue, and the unresolved wartime responsibility of the Japanese government. Again, the factor of democratization was a key in the civil society dynamics of South Korea, for the coming-out of the victims and creation of more favorable social movements in support of them. At the same time, international human rights norms and procedures explored in the UN human rights bodies provided very important space for internationalizing the issue. Introduction of internationally recognized universal language of human rights was a key in expanding the issue from local to regional and to global arenas. The Tokyo Tribunal demonstrates this point.

The field of security shows less clear picture for the role of NGOs as there is so far very little room for cooperation with governments or for the use of universally recognized norms or languages in the region. The region is still too state-security oriented to accommodate non-governmental interactions in spite of recent efforts to de-securitize the state in many societies in Asia.[38] Compared to the two other subject areas, the regional cooperation among NGOs in this field remain at the initial stage of exchanges and agenda-setting, but not with much interaction with decision-makers. One exceptional change is occurring in South Korea, again due to the bottom-up process of democratization. It is in this society that the linkage of domestic and regional factors can be grasped, in terms of change of perception of threat and questions raised as to the role of traditional security actors such as the stationing of the US forces. Domestic factors such as freedom of speech, democratic aspirations, democratically educated young generations, and the past records of state security agencies play a role in shaping the new agenda pushed by civil society actors. The process is not confined to security issues per se, but by the nature of security affairs, extends to the identity of the state and its regional role as well. This is a highly significant area of inquiry for the future—to what extent democratization of a society influences the hierarchical security arrangement of a region such as Northeast Asia. Regional-network NGOs such as ARENA and global government-NGO consultation process such as GPPAC do provide a certain level of "universal" or "beyond-local" norm and language to the agenda, as seen in the outcome of the Northeast Asian GPPAC process. To what extent these developments will impact on traditionally tightly state-controlled agenda of security, for example in Association of Southeast Asian Nations (ASEAN) or Asia–Pacific Economic Cooperation (APEC) fora remains to be seen.

A common feature of essential importance among "critique of developmentalism," "bringing justice to the past war crimes", and "de-securitization" is the efforts of non-governmental groups to elaborate international-domestic normative linkages such as sustainability, human rights and ethics in international relations. The normative frame itself shows the linkage in all the cases, and this leads to political space in which voluntary organizations and civil society groups work together towards a new form of democratic governance.[39] Be it environmental sustainability, reparation for victims of war crimes, or re-assessment of human security situation, ethics always form a common normative ground for these interactions. Ethical consideration for neglected sections of the society is always there. The fact that this ethical motivation comes from neglect, that is, neglect from the past non-democratic national governance, strongly suggests its linkage with democratization. This leaves us with an important implication that for non-governmental transnational cooperation, development of democratic-normative ground is both the starting point and moving dynamics: starting point in the sense that it envisages the formation of civil society that makes liberal, normative deliberation possible, and moving dynamics in that it envisages transnational solidarity based on internationalized norms.

Notes

1 In this chapter, the term "transnational" is used exchangeably with the term "trans-border."
2 For examples, see André C. Drainvill, "The Fetishism of Global Civil Society: Global Governance, Transnational Urbanism and Sustainable Capitalism in the World Economy," in Michael Peter Smith and Luis Eduardo Guarnizo (eds) *Transnationalism from Below*, New Jersey: Transaction Publishers, 1998; and indirectly, Fahimul Quadir and, Jayant Lele (eds) *Democracy and Civil Society in Asia*, Volumes 1 and 2, London: Palgrave Macmillan, 2004.
3 A well-illustrated approach of this kind on environmental justice and democracy is found in Surendra Lawrence, "Environmental Degradation and Social Justice: Implications for Democracy in Asia," in Fahimul Quadir and Jayant Lele, *Democracy and Civil Society in Asia*, Volumes 1 and 2, London: Palgrave Macmillan, 2004.
4 For examples, see Margaret E. Keck and Kathryn Kikkink, *Activists beyond Borders*, Ithaca, Cornell University Press, 1998; Smith and Guarnizo, *Transnationalism from Below*; and Edwin Amenta and Michael P. Young, "Making an Impact: Conceptual and Methodological Implications of the Collective Goods Criterion," in Sidney Tarrow (ed.) *How Social Movements Matter*, Minnesota: University of Minnesota Press, 1999.
5 *Minamata Declaration*, 24 August 1989. Online. English text available HTTP: <http://www.parc-jp.org/parc_e/About_PARC/Minamata.html> (accessed 1 September 2005).
6 Muto Ichio, "Alliance of Hope and Challenges of Global Democracy," paper presented at the conference on Alliance of Hope: Encounter of 1993 Networks, 18-22 June 1993, Geneva.
7 Author's interviews with key participants who led the process of PP21, in "Imagining by Retrospect: Evaluating PP21 in View of a New Process," unpublished paper, 2002.
8 For examples, the International Dam Conference organized by the Korean Federation of Environmental Movements in 1999, the Eco-Peace Network for Northeast Asia formed in 2000, the Korea–Japan Wetland Network formed in 2000, the Women's Conference on Environment in Northeast Asia active since 2001. Also to be noted are the joint research conducted by environmental groups of Japan, South Korea, China and Indonesia on the public awareness of environmental problems, the Movement for Forest for Peace of 1998 that successfully drew cooperation from North Korea in rebuilding forest in the country, and the cooperation between Korean NGOs and the Taiwan Environmental Protection Union in 1997 opposing the shipment of nuclear waste from Taiwan to North Korea.
9 Three representatives of Korea Church Women United went for a research tour in Japan in 1988 to excavate stories of "comfort women," and in 1991 the first Korean comfort woman Kim Hak-Sun came out to tell her story publicly.
10 Korea Council for the Women Drafted for Military Slavery by Japan (*JungDaeHyup*). Online. Available HTTP: <http://www.womenandwar.net/> (accessed 1 September 2005).
11 *Korea Women's Associations United*. Online. Available HTTP: <http://www.women 21.or.kr/news/default.asp> (accessed 1 September 2005).
12 On the history of the Korea Council for the Women Drafted for Military Slavery by Japan (*JungDaeHyup*). Online. Available HTTP: <http://www.womenandwar.net> (accessed 1 September 2005).
13 Matsui Yayori, "Women's International War Crimes Tribunal on Japan's Military Sexual Slavery," Asian Human Rights Commission — Human Rights Solidarity section. Online.

Available HTTP: <http://www.ahrchk.net/hrsolid/mainfile.php/2000vol10no12/771/> (accessed 23 March 2005).

14 The NGOs that played key role in the Tribunal were *JungDaeHyup* (South Korea), Violence against Women in War—Network Japan (Japan), Asian Center for Women's Human Rights (the Philippines), Taipei Women's Rescue Foundation (Taiwan), Shanghai Research Center for Comfort Women (China), and International Commission of Jurists, among others. Chung Chin-Sung, "Cooperation and Conflict among NGOs in South Korea, Japan and in the West: value orientations of NGOs working on military sexual slavery issue," *International and Regional Studies* (국제.지역연구), Vol. 11. No. 1, Spring 2002, pp. 21–40.

15 Matsui Yayori, "Women's International War Crimes Tribunal on Japan's Military Sexual Slavery."

16 Online. Available HTTP: <http://www1.jca.apc.org/vaww-net-japan/english/womens tribunal2000/whatstribunal.html> and <http://www.womenandwar.net/> (accessed 1 September 2005).

17 Korea Council for the Women Drafted for Military Slavery by Japan (*JungDaeHyup*). Online. Available HTTP: <http://www.womenandwar.net/> and Matsui Yayori, "Women's International War Crimes Tribunal on Japan's Military Sexual Slavery."

18 "Systematic rape, sexual slavery and slavery-like practices during armed conflict," Final report submitted by Gay J. McDougall, Special Rapporteur to the Commission on Human Rights of the United Nations, *Document E/CN.4/Sub.2/1998/13*.

19 Korea Council for the Women Drafted for Military Slavery by Japan (*JungDaeHyup*). Online. Available HTTP: <http://www.womenandwar.net/> (accessed 1 September 2005).

20 This section is partly based on my early work, "Korea: Perilous Crossing and New Dangers," *Conflicts in Asia*, European Centre for Conflict Prevention, 2004.

21 The delegation was composed of three representatives of peace NGOs, two National Assembly members from two opposition parties, and two scholars of international relations.

22 The notion of "security politics" is derived from "politics of security discourse" of Simon Dalby in "Contesting an Essential Concept: Reading the Dilemmas in Contemporary Security Discourse," in Keith Krause and Michael C. Williams (eds) *Critical Security Studies*, Chapel Hill, NC: University of North Carolina Press, 1997; and "securitization-desecuritization tension" of Ole Waever, "Security Analysis: Conceptual Apparatus," in Barry Buzan, et al. *Security: A New Framework for Analysis*, Boulder, CO: Lynne Rienner, 1998.

23 "Securitization" is a move that takes politics beyond the established rules of the game such as democratic procedures and frames the issue either as a special kind of politics or as above politics such as an emergency decree or national security laws. "Desecuritization" refers to a move that restores securitized issue. Refer to Ole Waever, "Security Analysis: Conceptual Apparatus," in Barry Buzan, et al. *Security: A New Framework for Analysis*, Boulder, CO: Lynne Rienner, 1998; and Ole Waever, *Concept of Security*, Institute of Political Science: University of Copenhagen, 1997.

24 The understanding of identity-security relationship here is based on Bill McSweeney, *Security, Identity and Interests: A Sociology of International Relations*, Cambridge: Cambridge University Press, 1999.

25 Two girls aged 14 were crushed to death on 13 June 2002 by a heavy-armored US military vehicle in training. The accident occurred on a local road where military vehicles entered from both sides while the two girls were walking. The driver claimed no proper warning order and visibility difficulty as the causes of the accident, and were acquitted in the US military court. A large part of the Korean public viewed this as a sham trial allowed by an unequal treaty signed by the two governments.

26 The daily newspaper *Dong-a Ilbo* found that 59 percent considered war impossible in October 2000. In 2003, the Korea Institute of National Unification (KINU) found 55

percent of respondents positive when asked how North Korea should be viewed (either as "an object for aid" or as "an object for cooperation"). Some 16 percent cited aid as the main aspect of inter-Korean relations, while only 13 percent cited hostility. When asked which country poses the greatest threat to South Korea, as many people in their twenties answered the U.S. as North Korea (38 percent). A poll conducted by *Joongang Ilbo* and the Washington-based Center for Strategic and International Studies in September 2003 found that only 36 percent considered a North Korean invasion possible within the next three years. In 2002, Pew Global Attitudes Projects found that young generations (under 25 years of age) in South Korea ranked top with those in Canada, the Czech Republic, and Bangladesh in their critical attitude towards the USA. In August 2005, a survey by an ultra-conservative newspaper *Chosun Ilbo* found that 65.9 percent of young generations (under 25 years of age) would side with North Korea in case of a war between North Korea and the USA, whereas 28.1 percent responded to siding with the USA.

27 Asia Regional Exchange for New Alternatives (ARENA) is an NPO with its office in Hong Kong and with its members across Asia. As of 2004, it has 78 fellows in 18 countries. It works as a regional network and community of critical activists and researchers aimed at contributing to a process of people-oriented social change. It was found in 1984 with a perspective to searching for alternative paradigms and discourses. One of its key programs is "Regional School," held almost biannually from 1996, providing a forum for sharing experiences, reflections, analyses, viewpoints and perspectives of Asian scholars and activists on the emerging challenges in Asian societies and the praxis of alternatives. It also serves for strengthening partnerships and cooperation among non-governmental groups in the region.

28 The European Centre for Conflict Prevention is an independent non-governmental organization based in the Netherlands. Its mission is to contribute to prevention and resolution of violent conflicts in the world. It also works as the secretariat of the European Platform for Conflict Prevention and Transformation. The Platform is an open network of some 150 key European organizations working in the field of the prevention and/or resolution of violent conflicts in the international arena. Its mission is to facilitate the exchange of information and experience among participating organizations, as well as to stimulate co-operation. Online. Available HTTP: <http://www.euconflict.org/> (accessed 1 September 2005).

29 The participants included: Korean peace groups such as Women Making Peace, and Centre for Peace and Democracy of People's Solidarity for Participatory Democracy; international relations and sociology scholars from India, Japan, the US, and South Korea; peace groups such as AMAN—Philippines (Muslim group for inter-ethnic conflict resolution), Asian Peace Alliance Japan, Human Rights Center of Ateneo de Manila University School of Law, Applied Socio Economic Research Center—Pakistan, Indonesia Student Christian Movement—Indonesia, and Peace & Culture Foundation—Thailand.

30 The content of the 2003 ARENA Regional School is based on ARENA's document, "Regional School Narrative Report 2003."

31 The challenges are (1) To distinguish the real from the bluff in the politics of security/peace issues and utilize the "security/peace" discourse in the analysis of the very core dynamics of global and regional politics by asking the questions: (a) Who securitizes and deforms issues into "security issues" and (b) What and why, and who wants to deactivate or de-securitize these issues and for what; (2) To analyze what is aimed at behind the language of terrorism; (3) To go beyond the politics of nation-states and "othering"; (4) To articulate "transborder politics" towards an alternative world involving a wide range of social actors beyond those working on normal security issues and devise better ways of forming trans-border alliances (including inter-linking/interconnecting peace and anti-globalization movements); (5) To strengthen

regional cooperation as more and more national governments in Asia embrace Washington's notion of peace and security. See AREANA, "Regional School Narrative Report 2003."

32 ARENA, "War, Militarism and Peace: 1st Year Narrative Report July 2003–June 2004," 2004.

33 The Korea Committee of GPPAC was constituted by ten non-governmental organizations including Women Making Peace, *JungDaeHyup*, People's Solidarity for Participatory Democracy and Lawyers for a Democratic Society.

34 Peace Boat, *Global Partnership for the Prevention of Armed Conflict Northeast Asia Regional Action Agenda*. Online. Available HTTP: <http://www.peaceboat.org/english/nwps/cn/arc/050204/naraan_gppac.pdf> (accessed 18 March 2005).

35 Peace Boat, "Civil Society—the 'other superpower' on the rise in Northeast Asia," Peace Boat News Archive. Online. Available HTTP: <http://www.peaceboat.org/english/nwps/cn/arc/050204/index.html> (accessed 30 August 2005).

36 Ibid.

37 Peace Boat, "Global Partnership for the Prevention of Armed Conflict Northeast Asia Regional Action Agenda."

38 For recent case studies of militarization and efforts to de-securitize the state in Asia, refer to Jayadeva Uyangoda and Anjani Abella (eds), *Militarising State, Society and Culture in Asia*, Asian Regional Exchange for New Alternatives, 2005.

39 See Fahimul Quadir and Jayant Lele, "Introduction: Globalization, Democracy and Civil Society after Financial Crisis of the 1990s," in Fahimul Quadir and Jayant Lele, *Democracy and Civil Society in Asia*, Volumes 1 and 2, London: Palgrave Macmillan, 2004.

Conclusion

Edward Friedman and Sung Chull Kim

In the post-Cold War world, new thinking and new policies are needed in Northeast Asia to preserve peace and prosperity in the region and beyond. Challenging cooperation are the North Korean nuclear crisis and Taiwan Strait tensions. The North Korean nuclear crisis may provoke others in the region to go nuclear, heightening explosive tensions that could destabilize the region, a problem illuminated in Haruki Wada's chapter. The tension in the Taiwan Strait keeps open the possibility that a PRC attack on Taiwan could bring the US, supported by the Japan–US alliance, to oppose China's armed irredentism, leading to a larger war in the region, thereby undermining the sources of regional, perhaps, global prosperity, as explored in Edward Friedman's chapter. More important, as most contributors in this volume note, no government can avoid being influenced and moved by particular domestic political forces that at times trump the potential for peace and prosperity embedded in regional cooperation. It is therefore crucial to comprehend and to counter these internal interests, institutions and ideologies that are the enemies of cooperation in Northeast Asia.

Enemies entrenched in domestic politics

Domestic politics, for particular reasons in individual countries, play a major role in limiting regional cooperation. Nationalist agendas in China and the two Koreas are informed by political entrepreneurs mobilizing historical issues imprinted on lingering memories of Japanese wartime invasion, cruelty and colonial rule. These passionate patriotisms, along with the two contentious security issues mentioned above, often counter the cooperation facilitated by deepening economic interdependence and cultural exchanges. With China, Japan and South Korea are members of the APT and the East Asian summit which are pursuing a regional community in East Asia; yet broader cooperation among the Northeast Asian countries is imperative for achieving the larger goals of an Asian regional community. The big question is, given the politics of Pyongyang, Taipei, Seoul, Tokyo and Beijing, whether or not the governments of Northeast Asia can cooperate on issues other than economic ones, a key topic explored by Kim in the opening chapter. Meanwhile, Moscow and Washington, however many miles they are from North Korea's nuclear facilities and Chinese missile sites in Fujian, across from Taiwan, are deeply involved in the destiny of this region because of their geopolitical strategies and economic linkages. In contrast to China, the two Koreas, and Japan, where patriotic passions infuse historical memories and policy options, policy choices in Russia and the US depend mainly on the top national leader.

China has a central role to play if regional cooperation is to work. Since cooperation facilitating mutual benefit is clearly in the interest of each and all, virtually every nation in the region wishes to participate in China's dynamic economic growth. However, the authoritarian CCP has repressed the robust development of a civil society in China. The CCP presents itself as keeping down chauvinistic elements opposed to cooperation.

As Friedman explains in his chapter, CCP leaders have utilized patriotism to court legitimation by targeting Taiwan to help stabilize a very unequal Chinese society full of anger. For CCP leaders, the spread of democracies in Asia threatens the entrenchment of their power. Consequently, democratic Taiwan—which China insists on incorporating—no longer appears as a leftover issue of a Chinese civil war that ended in 1949 but as a threat to regime survival and to the dignity of the Chinese people. The CCP has revved up so much Chinese emotion about democratic Taiwan that peaceful regional cooperation could lose out to attempted "solutions" imposed by Chinese military force. The patriotism that the CCP believes it needs for stable regime survival constrains regional cooperation while also obscuring somewhat how much peoples on both sides of the Taiwan Strait benefit from cooperative exchanges. A potential win-win game is made to seem zero-sum because of domestic political forces in China.

In South Korea, the engagement policy toward North Korea—both Kim Dae-Jung's Sunshine Policy and also his successor's, Roh Moo-hyun's, Peace and Prosperity Policy—has been facilitated by the shared interests and beliefs among government, business, and NGOs that engagement with the North would decrease tensions and make peaceful coexistence between the two Koreas more likely. The engagement policy toward the North has survived because of a broad coalition. This switch in Seoul's approach to Pyongyang made Washington's more military approach to Pyongyang seem in Korea not to be in the interest of a peaceful and united Korea. A rising nationalism in the period of Roh's presidency targeted the United States. When a second nuclear crisis erupted in 2002, Roh mobilized that widespread anti-American sentiment to be elected president. As president, Roh has continued to utilize, from time to time, this nationalism card for the purpose of domestic politics,[1] trying to make the opposition party seem tied to Japan, America, and a humiliating past.

In general, Roh's domestic political concerns have hampered his presidential capacity to cope with the North Korean nuclear crisis, as Hong explains in his chapter. Unlike what Kim Dae-Jung could do with Bill Clinton, Roh could not at first persuade George W. Bush to actively engage with Pyongyang. Instead tensions worsened, until Bush, bogged down in Iraq, moved toward engagement.

While Roh originally intended for South Korea to play a mediating role between North Korea and the US, Roh was powerless to block North Korea's attempt to drive a wedge between Seoul and Washington. South Korea's role was further constrained by North Korea's declaration of itself as a nuclear state in February 2005. Inter-Korean cooperation is challenged by domestic priorities of leaders in both Seoul and Pyongyang.

In Japan, too, a generational shift carries an enormous impact on regional dynamics. The anti-nuclear, pacifist generation, which promoted a foreign policy opposed to armaments in general and nuclear weapons in particular after World War Two, is passing into history.[2] In addition, with a decline of socialists and communists in the Diet since the early 1990s, there is no large left opposition to conservative political groups. Prime Minister Koizumi's Yasukuni Shrine visits and the approval of conservative history textbooks, while not supported by the majority of Japanese, are also not energetically opposed. These domestic changes in Japan allow governments in China and South Korea to mobilize anti-Japanese nationalism. With Japan moving in a more conservative direction, the megaphone voice of the pacifist movements by *hibakusha* (survivors of atomic bombing) is challenged by amplifiers of ultra-conservative groups for patriotic policies toward the neighboring countries.

Yet, the deepening of economic interdependence among Japan, China and South Korea has created interests opposed to interstate confrontation. Japan's business sector, as with *Nippon Keidanren* (the Japan Business Federation), does not want regional economic relations disrupted. Also, cultural exchanges between South Korea and Japan since 1998 have made the younger generation and TV watchers more appreciative of and empathetic to the other's culture. Korean TV dramas and their stars are popular in Japan, and Japanese fashion designs and pop songs affect Korean youths. In short, economic and cultural factors somewhat counter the tensions unleashed at the interstate level by the new nationalisms in China, Japan and South Korea.

A similar nationalism is rising in Russia. But Russia is outside of this regional cultural *cum* economic integration. President Putin has re-involved Russia in North Korean affairs[3] and been active in energy politics involving China and Japan. As Buszynski's chapter shows, Putin has tried to re-centralize power in Moscow and make Moscow a major player in the region. Putin benefited from a moment of high energy prices and a Chinese quest for Soviet weapons to help the PRC coerce democratic Taiwan to surrender to the CCP as have Hong Kong and Tibet. But it is not yet clear how Putin can manage relations with Northeast Asia to serve his domestic purposes and also advance regional cooperation, as indicated by Moscow's continuing military deliveries to a destabilizing North Korea.[4]

Although America stations one hundred thousand or so servicemen and women in Northeast Asia and has security treaties with South Korea and Japan, it is the China–Taiwan relationship which is most influenced by political clashes in Washington, with US business more sympathetic to Beijing perspectives and an active human rights and Taiwan–American lobby sympathetic to Taipei perspectives.[5] As Cheng notes in his chapter, the partisan American difference on North Korean issues is distinctive, owing to the impact of the ideology of the president, the top decision-maker on security affairs. George W. Bush, in his first term in office, took a hard-line policy on North Korea, treating it as a member of an axis of evil that should perhaps be targeted for attack, a policy that most analysts in the region believe worsened the situation. Bush's policy seemed a hostage to his partisan interest in discrediting anything associated with his Democratic predecessor, Bill Clinton, whose policy to engage North Korea was seen in the region as largely successful. Not until Bush's second term in office, when he was constrained by persistent difficulties in Iraq, did Bush heed the more cooperative concerns of Seoul and Tokyo to engage North Korea. That, however, is not enough to win over South Korea, where the new nationalism and a president who identified with that nationalism were too infused with anti-American sentiment, even while the government in Seoul wanted American troops in South Korea to continue to serve as a trip-wire and hostage to keep North Korea from attacking the South.

Enemies embedded in nationalism

Nationalist passions, especially in Japan, China, and the two Koreas, but also in Russia and Taiwan drive domestic politics and foreign policies in directions that counter the forces of cooperation in Northeast Asia. But not all challenges to cooperation are war-prone.

Anger among Koreans in April 2005 over Japanese insensitivities to and lies about Japan's colonial rule were used by the Roh administration to target pre-1945 Korean collaborators with imperial Japan in order to discredit opposition parties and to entrench its own party's hold on power. The CCP, as the chapter by Dittmer points out, backed Japan-bashing, hate-filled demonstration in Chinese cities in April 2005 in order to legitimate preventing Japan from having a seat on the United Nations Security Council so China would seem the leader of Asia. Discrediting Japan for the CCP is part of a policy to make China the pre-eminent power in the region, something that worries the Japanese government far more than the nationalistic politics of party competition in South Korea.

Still, challenges to cooperation dynamize domestic politics throughout the region. Cooperation is best served when domestic politics fosters political leaders who can check backlash groups that complicate peace-prone cooperation.

Among issues impeding regional cooperation in Northeast Asia are territorial disputes that have been heightened by a clash over either Japan's militarist past or energy resources, what might be called "energy nationalism." Japan's imperial legacy includes claims to the Kurile Islands/Northern Territories, disputed by Russia, and Dokdo/Takeshima disputed by Korea, indeed, effectively controlled by Korea since 1954. Rising Russian nationalism has led Putin to reconsider a 1956 declaration on the return of two out of the four islands to Japan as a starting point for further discussion. While Japan regards the four islands as having been unfairly occupied by Stalin's Red Army just before the end of World War Two, Japan very much wants friendly relations with an oil rich Russia, which is courted by both Japan and China over the Eastern Pipeline. When a local council in Japan in 2005 designated 22 February as "Takeshima Day" in a bid to exert

Japan's sovereignty over the island, Koreans were outraged because the decision reminded them of the humiliation one hundred years ago, that is, Japanese deprivation of Korean sovereignty in 1905.

Some island disputes are not rooted in long historical controversies but are contemporary creations to serve particular interests. The Senkaku Islands have been the target of irredentist challenges from the PRC ever since oil and energy emerged as major political issues at the end of the 1960s. China's oil demand surpassed domestic production in the mid-1990s. Its oil imports doubled between 1999 and 2004.[6] By 2003, China surpassed Japan to become the world's second largest oil consumer.[7] Accordingly, China has sought oil throughout the world — from Sudan, Burma, Kazakhstan, Russia, Nigeria, Venezuela, Iran, Peru, Azerbaijan, the South China Sea, and the East China Sea. In 2005 the China National Offshore Oil Corporation, a large state-owned enterprise, made an abortive $18.5 billion unsolicited bid for an American oil company, Unocal.[8] China's quest to control sources of oil clashed with searches by India and Japan.

Cooperation would be enhanced between the PRC and ASEAN in the South China Sea, as well as with the PRC and Japan in the East China Sea, if the PRC would abandon its rigid and uncompromising irredentist claims to waters and islands and instead negotiates deals, compromises, and understandings with neighbors to get the energy flowing. China, the Koreas, and Japan have been talking for years without result about contested seabed claims in the Yellow Sea and the East China Sea.[9] The onus is on the CCP to stop preventing a peaceful resolution of conflicts it has created. Mutually beneficial arrangements can defeat the enemies of cooperation in Northeast Asia. A cooperative and peaceful future, above all, needs China to move away from a nationalism informed by a notion of restoring China's rightful place in the region, a future project which is interpreted as the maximal conquests of pre-modern empires.[10] China is a great power; therefore, how China acts on its great power ambitions is decisive for the future of cooperation in Northeast Asia. Cooperation requires that the CCP replace a narrow nationalism with an enlightened nationalism more open to win-win games.

Enemies embodied in Sino–Japanese rivalry

What is amazing is how much cooperation there actually has been despite the entrenched enemies of cooperation in Northeast Asia sketched above and throughout this volume. All the countries of the region patently benefit from already existing regional cooperation. Peoples in these countries cannot help but see that their peace and prosperity would be further enhanced by far more regional cooperation. Since it is so much in each country's interest to foster new structures of cooperation, it is worth focusing on and challenging the enemies of cooperation in Northeast Asia. "Sino–Japanese acrimony… presents a real check on the development of an Asian regionalism…"[11]

While conflicts of interest, as with China's and Japan's competition for an oil pipeline from Russia, are inevitable, these conflicts can be resolved to the benefit of all if each could assume that multilateral cooperation is the better way ahead. As the chapter by Lam shows, conflicts of material interests can be resolved so as to avoid confrontation if the political will for regional cooperation can trump narrow nationalisms and very parochial political interests. This, however, is not an easy task.

Political leaders in power in each and every capital city in the region do not readily take-on and try to defeat domestic forces and interests that seem crucial to the various regime's bases of power. Defeating the enemies of cooperation, therefore, is quite a struggle, with many and complex battles. The enemies of cooperation in Northeast Asia are rooted in the domestic politics of each major actor. Despite China's hugely enhanced multilateral cooperation, ruling groups in Beijing fear being portrayed in domestic politics as soft on Japan.

Chinese analysts who understand the importance of Beijing–Tokyo cooperation for sustaining a peaceful and prosperous region have pointed out that "we need the generosity of a great and victorious nation, and do not need to be excessively harsh with Japan."[12] China and Japan should learn from the reconciliation between both Poland and France and the democratic successor to Nazi Germany. France, despite its vivid memory of the cruel military aggression of Nazi Germany, quickly reconciled with the democratic post-war Germany. Poland did the same as soon as it democratized. Reconciliation continues despite the rise of German forces stressing the country's suffering as a victim of Allied bombing during World War Two, and elements bent on revising the post-war constitution, and on promoting a proud nationalism in place of endless apologies and acknowledgments of guilt. That is, cooperation offers blessings to both sides even when the World War Two aggressor is not as apologetic for its atrocious past as previously-invaded neighbors, who suffered atrociously, might wish.

Likewise, regional cooperation in Northeast Asia requires that China build its policies on the imperative of cooperation with a now democratic Japan. But China and Japan have learned little from the better aspects of the European experience. What would it take for Japan tomorrow, as Germany yesterday, to be invited to participate in an honorable way in commemorations of a monstrous world war it initiated? How much can Japan's ruling conservatives and the post-pacifist generation acknowledge that history? Can China, which suffered monstrous crimes against humanity in the age of imperial Japan, stop silencing Chinese voices of moderation and reconciliation instead of facilitating racist Japan-bashing, as in 2005? Inside of China's domestic politics, the CCP well understands that building a better future for the Chinese people requires more looking ahead and less recriminations about the CCP's past of imposing murderous disasters on the Chinese people. The same logic, however, should apply in China's international relations, that is, if peaceful cooperation is to be privileged.

In addition, regional cooperation requires that great power China offer little Taiwan a viable alternative that will appeal to the Taiwanese citizens of a *de facto* independent Taiwanese democracy. But, since 1989 to 1991, from the June 4 crushing of China's democracy movement, which had been headquartered in Tiananmen Square, to the democratization of much of the Soviet affiliated empire from Berlin to Ulan Bator, the CCP has treated the spread of democracy as a direct threat to its own survival in power. Because it prioritizes stabilizing its own authoritarian power, the unaccountable CCP has opposed regional human rights initiatives. It imagines democracy in Taiwan as a threat to stable CCP power in China. It interprets democratization in East Europe and the Baltic States as having undermined the Soviet Union and reduced Russia from a super-power to a weak nation. Given the CCP's self-protective domestic priorities and ambitions for great power predominance in Asia, it is not obvious whether the CCP can continue on a path of substantive regional political cooperation that gets further than economic cooperation. Much of the future of regional cooperation therefore will be decided by political contestation in China.

Chaos or cooperation?

Northeast Asia lacks any overarching multilateral institution for facilitating postwar political cooperation. In the wake of the defeat of Nazi Germany and militaristic Japan in World War Two, the US became the hub of Atlantic and Pacific blocs opposed to Soviet bloc expansionism. In Europe, America became the hub of a multilateral alliance. In Asia, however, a newly democratic Japan would not join an anti-communist alliance with the military dictatorships of the region. Each nation in the region, worried about Beijing's support for insurgents, made separate bilateral security arrangements with America, an architecture described as spokes and hub. This bilateralism allowed a multilateral ASEAN to begin to fill a multilateral void in the 1960s.

ASEAN provides Northeast Asia with an important force for cooperation, as Solingen finds in her chapter. Southeast Asian countries have sought international cooperation premised on consensus and non-interference in order to sustain further peace with prosperity. Previously Asia was plagued by irredentist conflicts. ASEAN and its multilateral cooperation which negated war-prone irredentism became possible only when Sukarno fell in Indonesia and his successor abandoned an irredentist agenda.[13] A similar cooperative order in Northeast Asia may have to await a similar abandonment of irredentist claims, primarily by governments in Beijing and Pyongyang, but also by Tokyo and Moscow. The key to regional cooperation is proper policies by the governments of crucial states. The authoritarian ruling groups in Beijing and Pyongyang, fearful of autonomous societal forces, also block the ability of international NGOs to promote robust civil societies facilitating cooperation to solve new order issues such as environmental degradation, drug trafficking, and the violation of human rights of women and minorities. Efforts at such regional cooperation on these new order issues are defined by the narrow nationalisms of authoritarian parties in Beijing and Pyongyang as subversive interference. As long as key governments in the region treat the region's democracies and NGOs as enemies, there is a strict and damaging limit on regional cooperation in Northeast Asia.

The big question then is cooperation or chaos? If the region's governments act singularly as competing and mistrustful nation states that experience a zero-sum struggle in response to rapidly rising energy demand along with energy depletion, then who has access to energy can all too readily be decided by coercion. Wars and destruction of incalculable proportions would become more likely. Since Asia has been the most rapidly rising—i.e., energy destroying—part of the planet since the end of World War Two, its peoples have a special opportunity to lead the world away from crisis and potential chaos. This requires cooperation and self-discipline at hitherto unknown levels. There are no indications of major progress toward this life enhancing cooperation in Northeast Asia, yet.

Our hope is that, faced by crisis and war-prone competition which portend conflict and chaos and undermine stability and prosperity, the governments of the region will see that regional cooperation and mutual restraint are the only policies which will preserve the region's precious achievements of peace and rising living standards. Cooperation is in the real interest of each and all. The species need not act in a suicidal way. Cooperation is the path to a humane life. But can the diverse peoples and governments of Northeast Asia, given all the domestic obstacles to cooperation detailed by the contributors to this book, actually choose to institutionalize a politics of cooperation? The answer offered by these contributors lies in changes in the domestic politics of each and every government in the region.

Notes

1 For a discussion on the domestic usage of the historical issue, see Gilbert Rozman, *Northeast Asia's Stunted Regionalism: Bilateral Distrust in the Shadow of Globalization*, Cambridge: Cambridge University Press, 2004.

2 One exemplary indicator of the generational shift is that the average age of the survivors of atomic bombing in Hiroshima and Nagasaki, called *hibakusha* in Japan, was 73 years old in 2005. Considering that the *hibakusha* and their generation have remained the core civil activists advocating the maintenance of Article 9 of Japan's constitution and anti-war and anti-nuclear movements, the generational shift opens space for younger people who want Japan to be a normal nation and not one defined by an expansionist empire's witnessing of the horrors of the 1945 atomic bombs.

3 Elizabeth Wishnick, "Russian-North Korean Relations: A New Era?" in Samuel S. Kim and Tai Hwan Lee (eds) *North Korea and Northeast Asia*, Lanham: Rowman & Littlefield, 2002, p. 150.

4 Under Putin, the transfer of Russian missile technology to North Korea continued. In 2000, special aluminum alloy, laser gyroscopes, and connectors and relays used in missile electronics were reportedly transferred to North Korea by cooperative efforts made by Russia and Uzbekistan, and it is said that in 2001 a possible ICBM data was delivered on the occasion of Kim Jong-Il's visit to Khrunichev Space Centre on the outskirts of Moscow. See NEI, *North Korea Profile: Missile*. Online. Available HTTP: <http://www.nti.org/e_research/profiles/NK/Missile/66.html> (accessed on 27 June 2005).

5 Compare Richard Bush, *At Cross Purposes*, Armonk, N.Y.: M. E. Sharpe, 2004 with John Tkacik Jr. (ed.), *Rethinking One China*, Washington, D.C.: The Heritage Foundation, 2004.

6 Matthew Forney, "China's Quest for Oil," *Time*, 18 October 2004.

7 Seth R. DeLong, "Will Washington Tolerate A Chinese–Venezuelan Petrol Pact?" *Energy Bulletin*, 20 January 2005.

8   In China, energy is considered a security sector in which foreign ownership is forbidden.
9   Selig Harrison, ed., *Seabed Petroleum in Northeast Asia: Conflict or Cooperation*, Washington, DC: Woodrow Wilson International Center for Scholars Asia Program, 2005.
10 Edward Friedman, "China's Rise, Asia's Future," *Journal of East Asian Studies*, 6 (2006), pp. 289–303.
11 Peter Gries, "China Eyes the Hegemon," *Orbis*, 2005.
12 Ibid.
13 Amitar Acharya, "Regional Institutions and Asian Security Order," in Muthiah Alagappa (ed.) *Asian Security Order*, Stanford: Stanford University Press, 2003, Chapter 6.

Index

Abe Shinzo 171, 178
Acharya, Amitav 213n.13
Agreed Framework (AF) 47, 70, 71, 72, 92–3, 153, 154
Alagappa, Muthiah 125, 139, 213n.13
Albright, Madeleine 72, 94
Allison, Graham 12n.6, 62, 81n.3
Anami Koreshige 172
anti-American demonstration 193
anti-Americanism 91, 92, 195
anti-Japanese demonstration 7, 23, 122, 168, 170, 178, 208, 210
Anti-Nuke Asia Forum 188
Anti-Secession Law, China 27, 117; see also Taiwan Strait
anti-war/anti-US sentiment see anti-Americanism
ASEAN Plus Three (APT) 9, 31, 32, 46, 116, 175, 176, 179
Asian Development Bank (ADB) 127, 130
Asian financial crisis 19, 175
Asian Monetary Fund (AMF) 9–10
Asian Solidarity Conference 190
Asian Women's Fund 51
Asia-Pacific Economic Cooperation (APEC) 9, 150
Asia Regional Exchange for New Alternatives (ARENA) 195–7
Aso Taro 170
Association of Shinto Shrines (Jinja Honcho) 171
Association of Southeast Asian Nations (ASEAN) 1, 9, 20, 110, 150, 200, 211; anti-terrorism 20; ASEAN Free Trade Area 20; ASEAN Regional Forum (ARF) 6, 30–2; ASEAN Security Community 20; ASEAN way 18, 125, 133, 139; evolution of cooperation in 18; military expenditures in 19;

relations with China 110, 116; relations with China and Japan 29, 167, 174–6; relations with Japan 45–6; role for regional cooperation 1, 211; Vision 2020 20
Atmosphere Action Network East Asia 188
Aung San Suu Kyi 128

Ballistic Missile Defense (BMD) 150, 154
Berezovsky, Boris 148
Bertrand Russell Tribunal 190
Bhopal 186
Biodiversity Convention 188
Biological Weapons Convention 111
border fever 3
Bush, George H. W.: North Korea issue and 69–70; Taiwan Strait issue and 74, 131
Bush, George W.: North Korea issue and 47, 72–3, 95, 193–4; Taiwan Strait issue and 74, 76, 119; US–South Korea relations and 206
Buszynski, Leszek 160n.2
Buzan, Barry 202n.22

Cabestan, Jean-Pierre 140n.3
Carter, Jimmy 74, 76
centralization of power, Russia 147–50; see also Putin
Central Military Commission (CMC), China 104–6
Cha, Victor 82n.17
Chechnya 145
Chemical Weapons Convention 111
Chen Shui-bian 26, 27, 74, 114, 119
Chen Yun 103
Chernobyl 186

China–Japan relations 110, 114, 134, 136; economic interdependence 166, 167, 172–4; exchanges at local level 173–4; FTA issue 175; history issue in 170–1; Japanese NGOs and 174; Koizumi Junichiro on 176–9; ODA and 165; political tension in 166, 173; post-Cold War period 165; regional cooperation and 179–80; rivalry in 209–11; Taiwan Strait issue and 179; Tanaka Kakuei on 177; territorial dispute in 179
China National Petroleum Corporation 151; *see also* energy, Yukos Oil Company
China-Russia relations 110, 145, 150–3; energy issue in 148, 151, 152; multipolarity 150–1; partnership 112; territorial issue and 145, 152–3
China threat 114, 167
China-US relations 114; EP-3 incident 77, 105, 114; normalization 25; partnership 112; permanent normal trade relations 76; Taiwan Strait issue 73–7, 119
Chinese Communist Party (CCP): anti-democratic stance 127–9, 138–9; foreign policy and 103–4; Hong Kong issue 115; Japan's past history and 210; patriotism and 206; regional cooperation and 126–7, 210–11; Taiwan's democracy and 210; Taiwan Strait issue and 114, 129–34, 139; Tibet and Xinjiang and 133; *see also* Chinese foreign policy
Chinese foreign policy: ARF and 31; Mao Zedong and 101; multilateralism in 116, 126, 127; national identity and 118–19, 130, 137; new security concept 113; One China principle 3, 133; organization of 103–9; partnerships 112, 118, 121; peaceful rising (or peaceful evolution) 102, 113–15, 119, 121; soft power 113, 117, 128; state's role on 104–5; transformation of 109–15
Chubais, Anatolii 146
Chuch'e, North Korea 28, 90
Chufrin, Gennady 160n.3
Climate Change Convention 188
Clinton, Bill (William Jefferson): China–US relations 109–10; North Korea issue 69–72, 94; Taiwan Strait issue 74–6
comfort women 51–2, 189–91; *see also* NGOs on war crimes

Common House of Northeast Asia 40–1; obstacles to 47–53
complete, verifiable, and irreversible dismantlement 96
Comprehensive National Power 113; *see also* Chinese foreign policy
Comprehensive Test Ban Treaty 111
Council on East Asian Community (CEAC) 46, 53, 176
Crane, Keith 123n.22
Cross-Strait *see* Taiwan Strait
Curtis, Gerald L. 182n.29

Darfur 128
Democratic Party of Japan 171
democratization 192, 193, 194, 195, 199
Deng Xiaoping 103, 105, 111, 118, 120, 130, 131, 137; internationalization and 26, 102
de-securitization 200
Dokdo/Takeshima 49, 208
Dole, Robert 71
domestic politics: China and 26–7; inter-Korean relations and 86, 92–7; international relations and 2, 4; Japan and 167–72; regional contention and cooperation in Northeast Asia and 21–29, 205–8; regional cooperation in Southeast Asia and 17–21; Russian foreign policy and 143–4, 159; second layer 6–7; US foreign policy and 62–4
domestic-regional linkages 4, 185–6, 199; multilayered perspective 1, 5–8
domestic ruling coalition *see* ruling coalition
Duma 146, 147, 149, 153, 156, 157

East Asian community (EAC) 1, 10, 42, 43, 49, 166, 175, 176, 179; discussions on 45–7; Japan's strategy toward 32; Japan's wartime use of 39; linkage to Northeast Asian community 53–4; skepticism on 169
East Asian Economic Caucus 175
East Asian Study Group 175
East Asian summit 5, 46, 166, 179
East Asian Vision Group (EAVG) 42–3
East China Sea 129, 169, 170, 179, 209
Economic Research Institute of Northeast Asia, Japan 40
Edwards, John 73
energy: competition between China and Japan 10, 208; demand in China 119–20, 151–2, 209; energy

nationalism 10; energy bridge between Sakhalin and Hokkaido 159
Evans, Peter B. 98n.2
Exclusive Economic Zone 170
export-led model: South Korean case 23; Taiwan case 25

Federal Security Service (FSS), Russia 146, 147
flying geese 165
Foot, Rosemary 33n.4
foreign direct investment (FDI) 20, 111
Fradkov, Mikhail 152
Free Trade Agreement (FTA): bilateral negotiations among China, Japan, South Korea 9; China-ASEAN 116; China–ASEAN-Japan 29-30, 167; China–Japan 175; Japan–Singapore partnership 29, 174, 175
Friedman, Edward 141n.21
Fukai, Shigeko N. 34n.19
Fukuyama, Francis 57n.37

Gilley, Bruce 123n.11
Global Partnership for the Prevention of Armed Conflict (GPPAC) 196-9
Good Friends 193
Gorbachev, Mikhail 3, 4
government-organized non-governmental organizations, China 126
Graham, Thomas 63
Greater East Asia Co-prosperity Sphere: Japan's wartime slogan of 38-9
Green Earth Network 174
Gulf War 195
Gusinsky, Vladimir 148

Haass, Richard N. 82n.21
Harrison, Selig 77
Hatch, Walter 180n.3
hawk engagement *see* George W. Bush
Hayao, Kenji 182n.26
Hellmann, Donald C. 180n.5
history issue: Japan's apology 51-2; textbook controversy 23, 167, 170, 171, 179, 207
Holsti, Ole R. 82n.7
Hosokawa Morihiro 50
Hu Jintao 27, 103, 107, 108, 139, 151
Hu Yaobang 103, 108

inter-Korean relations: Joint Declaration of the Denuclearization of the Korean Peninsula 91; North-South Basic Agreement 28, 91; North-South summit 89, 91; nuclear crisis and 93-4; perceptions in 88-9, 91-2, 194-5; railway project 154
internal-external linkages *see* domestic-regional linkages
International Atomic Energy Agency (IAEA) 70
International Criminal Court 190
international non-governmental organizations: humanitarian engagement 8
Iraq War 72, 95, 151, 196
Ishaev, Viktor 153, 158
Ishihara Shintaro 22, 169
Ito Kenichi 175, 176
Ivanov, Igor 150, 153, 154

Jacobson, Harold K. 98n.2
Japan bashing *see* anti-Japanese demonstration
Japanese foreign policy: China School (Tanaka faction) and 170, 172; China threat perception and 167-72; domestic politics and 166, 167; EAC and 174-6; FTA with ASEAN 175; National Defense Program Guideline 169; normal state 171; prime minister's role in 176-9; Russian school and 158
Japan–North Korea relations: Pyongyang Declaration 43, 52
Japan–Russia relations: energy issue 152, 158-9; peace treaty issue 155, 157, 158; Soviet–Japanese agreement in 1956 155-6, 158; territory issue 144, 155-6
Japan–US alliance *see* US–Japan relations
Jiang Zemin 103, 105, 107; American hegemony and 150-1; foreign policy and 121; leadership on military 106; Shanghai Cooperation Organization and 145-6; Taiwan issue and 132, 133; Three Representations 113
Johnson, Alastair Iain 122n.1
Jo Myong Rok 94
Juche *see* Chuch'e

Kang, David 82n.17
Kang Sok-Ju 47
Kang Xiaoguang 138
Kawaguchi Yoriko 156, 157
Kelly, James 47, 95
Keohane, Robert O. 12n.10
Khabarovsk 152-3

Khakamada, Irina 149
Khmer Rouge 128, 129
Khodorkovsky, Mikhail 148, 151, 152; *see also* Yukos Oil Company
Kim, Samuel S. 13n.17, 123n.15, 125
Kim Dae-Jung 5, 24, 30, 87, 88, 94, 193, 206; *see also* Sunshine Policy
Kim Il Sung 27–8, 89, 90
Kim Jong Il 28; Bush and 95; inter-Korean relations and 91, 94; Kim Il Sung and 89–90; Koizumi and 43; military-first politics 90; missile issue and 154
Kim Young-ho 41
Kim Young-sam 24, 87, 88, 92, 93, 94
Kitashiro Kakutaro 173
Kobayashi Yoshinori 52
Kobayashi Yotaro 173
Koizumi Junichiro: East Asian community and 49; economic partnership with Southeast Asia and 174; energy and territory issues and 157–9; Japan–North Korea summit 43; populism 177; view on China 169; Yasukuni Shrine visit 6, 23, 114, 173, 177–9, 207
Kokubun, Ryosei 181n.7
Kono Yohei 178
Kozyrev, Andrei 144, 146
Krause, Keith 202n.22
Kyoto Protocol 188
Kuomintang 25

Lampton, David M. 83n.31, 141n.33
Lapshin, Mikhail 146
Lavrov, Sergei 154, 155, 157
Leading Small Group (LSG), China 103–4, 109
Lee Teng-hui 26, 76, 130
Liberal Democratic Party (LDP) 21–2, 166, 171
light water reactors (LWRs) 70, 93
Lim Soo-Kyong 192
Lin Biao 108
Li Peng 103
Lippmann, Walter 82n.8
Li Zhaoxing 105
Lu, Ning 122n.3, 141n.18
Lukin, Alexander 150

MacCormick, James M. 81n.5
MacDonald, Gabrielle Kirk 190
MacDougall, Gay 191
Machimura Nobutaka 170

MacSweeney, Bill 202n.24
Mahathir bin Mohamad 9, 20
Mann, James 83n.28, 141n.23
Mann, Thomas 62
Mao Zedong 103, 131
McCain, John 71
Milner, Helen V. 12n.10
Minamata Declaration 186
Missile Technology Control Regime (MTCR): Chinese position 105, 111
Moravcsik, Andrew 86, 98n.2
Morishima Michio 42
Mori Yoshiro 156
Murayama Tomiichi 5, 170; apology and 50–1

Nakagawa Shoichi 170
Nakasone Yasuhiro 22, 46, 176
Nathan, Andrew J. 123n.11
National Defense Program Guideline *see* Japanese foreign policy
national identity *see* Chinese foreign policy
nationalism 208–9; China 26, 27, 117–18, 128, 130, 132, 134, 137, 138; China and Japan 52–3; China, Japan, South Korea, Russia 206–7; Japan 22, 171
neorealism 4
Network of East Asian Think Tanks (NEAT), China 45, 175–6
newly industrializing economies 165
Nixon, Richard 74; Nixon Doctrine 86
non-governmental organizations (NGOs): developmentalism 186–9, 199; environmental issue 188–9; humanitarian aid 193; human rights issue 199; Japanese NGOs in China 174; ODA for 189; peace initiative by 193–4; regional cooperation and 7–8; regionalization of 185–6; Roh Moo-hyun and 87; security issue 192–9, 200; US military base issue 197; war crimes issue 189–92
Non-Proliferation Treaty (NPT) 48, 70, 85, 92, 93, 105, 111
normal state *see* Japanese foreign policy
North Atlantic Treaty Organization (NATO) 126, 145, 146
Northeast Asia: anti-communist alliance in 40; community-building of 38, 44; domestic politics in 21–9; economic cooperation in 40–1; history of 38; nations belonging to 1, 8; security threats in 9

Northeast Asian community 38, 40–2, 53–4; *see also* Common House of Northeast Asia
Northern Territories 144, 155–9, 208
nuclear crisis (or weapons development), North Korea 9, 28, 47–9, 92–4, 95–7

Obuchi Keizo 155
official development assistance (ODA) 165, 189
Okada Katsuya 171
Opium War 132, 137, 140
Ostpolitik 135
Ozawa Ichiro 22

Park Chung Hee 23
Peace Boat, Japan 198
Peace Depot, Japan 7
peaceful rising (or peaceful evolution) *see* Chinese foreign policy
peace movement, South Korea 185, 195
Pempel, T. J. 5, 34n.19, 35n20
Peng Guangqian 135
Peng Zhen 108
People's Liberation Army (PLA) 103, 108; budget priority on 115–16, 130; foreign policy and 105–6; military modernization 26, 113; Taiwan issue 133–4
People's Plan 21 (PP21) 187–8
Perry, William 72, 94
Pew Global Attitudes Projects 203n.26
pipeline, Russia 151, 158–9; competition between China and Japan 10, 208; *see also* energy
political culture, Russia 143, 149
Pollack, Kenneth 135
Powell, Colin 72, 75
Primakov, Yevgennii 146
Putin, Vladimir 143; business oligarchs and 148–9; controlled pluralism 147; Duma and 147, 149; local oligarchs and 149; policy toward Asia Pacific 3–4, 150–9; territorial issue 208
Putnam, Robert D. 12n.9, 84n.43, 85, 98n.1

Qian Qichen 105
Qiao Shi 108
Qing dynasty 132, 137, 140

Raikov, Gennadii 147
Reagan, Ronald 74, 76
regional community 2

regional economic cooperation 2
regionalism 2, 167, 174–6, 179
regionalization 185, 199
Rogozin, Dmitrii 150, 157
Roh Moo-hyun: civilian sector and 87; lenient policy toward North Korea 96, 97; Northeast Asia Age and 44; peace and prosperity policy 24, 206; presidential election and 195; visit to Russia 155
Roh Tae-woo 24, 88
Rosenau, James N. 2, 12n.1, 82n.12
Rozman, Gilbert 12n.2, 160n.3
ruling coalition: Japan 21; regional cooperation and 7; Southeast Asian countries 19, 20
Rumsfeld, Donald 154
Russett, Bruce 12n.10
Russian foreign policy: Asia Pacific region 150–9; domestic politics and 143–4, 159; Korean peninsula issue 145, 153–5; multipolarity 150; pro-Western 144–6; Putin and 150–9; strategic partnership with China 145; Westernizers on 144–6, 148, 153, 159

Scalapino, Robert A. 181n.18
Self Defense Force, Japan 170
September 11 89
sexual slavery 189–92, 199; *see also* NGOs
Shanghai Cooperation Organization (SCO) 116, 126, 146, 150
Sharansky, Natan 141n.39
Shinoda, Tomohito 182n.26
silovik 146, 147; *see also* Putin
Six-Party Talks 6, 45, 48, 73, 95–6, 114, 117, 121; *see also* nuclear crisis, North Korea
Snyder, Jack 12n.10
Sobel, Richard 82n.9
Social Democratic Party of Japan (SDPJ) 170, 171
soft power 113
Solingen, Etel 12n.10
South China Sea 125, 129
Southeast Asia Nuclear Weapon-Free Zone Treaty 18
South-North Sharing Campaign 193
state consolidation, Russia 147–50; *see also* Putin
Strategic Arms Reduction Talks 146
Suettinger, Robert 141n.19
Sunshine Policy 88, 94, 193, 206; *see also* Kim Dae-jung

Sutter, Robert G. 81n.1, 122n.2
Suzuki Muneo: Northern Territories issue 155–6, 158

Taiwan Strait 25–7; China–Japan relations and 179; China's non-cooperation 129–34, 137–40; crisis of 119, 168; independence movement in Taiwan 26; regional security threat 9; Taiwan Relations Act (TRA) 74, 75, 76, 79, 80; Taiwan Security Enhancement Act 78
Tanaka Akihiko 32, 46, 180n.1
Tanaka Hitoshi 46
Tanaka Kakuei 170, 177
Tanaka Makiko 170
Tang Jiaxuan 105
Tarrow, Sidney 201n.4
territorial dispute 179, 208–9; *see also* East China Sea, Northern Territories, Dokdo/Takeshima
three-level game 86
Tiananmen incident 109, 115, 118, 130, 145, 168
Track Two 5
transnational (or transborder) cooperation 185, 187
Treaty of Amity and Cooperation in Southeast Asia 18
Tripartite Environmental Ministers Meeting 188
Tumen River Area Development Project 3
two-level game 4, 85, 86

United Nations (UN): Chinese foreign policy and 126; Commission on Human Rights 191; Conference on Environment and Development 188; Peacekeeping Operations (PKO) 127; Security Council 121, 128, 178
United Russia 147, 149; *see also* Putin
uranium enrichment program 72
US foreign policy: domestic politics and 62–4; North Korea issue and 64, 69–73, 78, 95–7; Nuclear Posture Review 95; partisan politics on 63–4, 69, 79, 80; role of public opinion on 63–9; Taiwan Strait issue and 66–9, 73–7; tension between president and Congress 61, 62–3, 76–7, 79–80

US–Japan relations 10, 22; alliance 9, 168, 169, Consultative Talks (2+2 Talks) 168; New Defense Guidelines 168
US–North Korea relations: axis of evil 47, 95; North Korea Threat Reduction Act 69, 72; nuclear crisis and 92–7; perceptions in 91–2; South Korean view on 193–4; *see also* US foreign policy
US–South Korea relations: alliance 79, 80, 96, 194, 195; military base issue 193, 195; North Korean nuclear crisis 193–4, 206; perceptions 89; 386 generation on 87, 89

Vietnam War 63, 64
Vogel, Ezra 180n.1

Waever, Ole 202n.22
Waltz, Kenneth N. 4, 12n.7
Wang, Jisi 181n.7
War Bereaved Family Association (Izokukai), Japan 171
Wen Jiabao 27, 152
Williams, Michael C. 202n.22
World Health Organization 129
World Trade Organization (WTO) 126, 152
Wu Xueqian 105

Yamamura, Kozo 180n.3
Yang Shangkun 103
Yasukuni Shrine 6, 23, 49, 114, 169, 170, 171, 173, 176–9, 207
Yeltsin, Boris: China and 110, 145; Japan and 155; pro-Western policy 3, 144–6, 149, 159
Yuan Ming 180n.1
Yukos Oil Company 120, 148, 151, 152; *see also* Mikhail Khodorkovsky

Zhao Ziyang 103
Zhirinovsky, Vladimir 146
Zhou Enlai 103, 104
Zhu Rongji 174
Zone of Peace, Freedom and Neutrality Declaration 18
Zyuganov, Gennadii 146

For Product Safety Concerns and Information please contact our EU
representative GPSR@taylorandfrancis.com
Taylor & Francis Verlag GmbH, Kaufingerstraße 24, 80331 München, Germany

www.ingramcontent.com/pod-product-compliance
Lightning Source LLC
Chambersburg PA
CBHW050428280326
41932CB00013BA/2028

9 780415 651400